Gita Sahgal is an independent filmmaker working in Britain and in India. She has made a number of current affairs programmes on gender issues for Channel 4 television, including *Struggle or Submission? Women under Islam*, on the impact of the Rushdie affair on Muslim women in Britain; and *The Provoked Wife*, on women who have killed their husbands after enduring years of domestic violence.

Nira Yuval-Davis is a Reader in Ethnic and Gender Studies at Thames Polytechnic. She has written extensively on theoretical and practical aspects of women, nationalism and racism in Israel and in Britain. She has recently co-edited *Woman – Nation – State* (Macmillan 1989) and *The Gulf War and the New World Order* (Zed Books 1991), and has co-authored, with F. Anthias, *Racialized Boundaries: Ethnic, Gender, Colour and Class Divisions and the Anti-Racist Struggle* (Routledge 1992).

Both editors live in London and are among the founding members of Women Against Fundamentalism.

D1236010

Refusing Holy Orders

WOMEN AND
FUNDAMENTALISM
IN BRITAIN

Edited by Gita Sahgal
and Nira Yuval-Davis

Published by VIRAGO PRESS Limited 1992
20–23 Mandela Street, Camden Town, London NW1 0HQ

*A CIP catalogue record for this title is available
from the British Library*

Typeset by Centracet, Cambridge

Printed in Great Britain by Cox & Wyman Ltd, Reading, Berks

Contents

Acknowledgements

....

This book could not have been written without the collective contemplations and actions of Women Against Fundamentalism (WAF), of which both editors and many of the contributors are members. We are therefore dedicating this book to WAF, and hope that it will promote its political agenda.

Introduction: Fundamentalism, Multiculturalism and Women in Britain

GITA SAHGAL AND NIRA YUVAL-DAVIS

*I*n Margaret Atwood's book on a futuristic fundamentalist society, *The Handmaid's Tale*, 'Aunt Lydia' explains that there is more than one form of freedom. There is 'freedom to' as well as 'freedom from'. She claims that fundamentalism can provide the 'freedom from'. This tension, between the 'freedom to' (to be autonomous, to be self-defined, which has characterized feminist politics) and freedom from (uncertainty and insecurity, which has characterized fundamentalist women's politics), runs through the various contributions to this book.

Women, their roles, and above all their control, are at the heart of the fundamentalist agenda. That they should conform to the strict confines of womanhood within the fundamentalist religious code is a precondition for maintaining and reproducing the fundamentalist version of society.

All the essays included here focus on women's relationship to different fundamentalist movements. They all share a feminist anti-fundamentalist perspective, although they might differ on the particular ways in which they define both feminism and fundamentalism.

Unlike the widely held British stereotype, fundamentalism is not peculiar to Islam. 1991 has signalled the beginning of the 'Decade of Evangelism'. During the Gulf War, the

1

American President, George Bush, after ordering the beginning of the war in which the explosives used during the first night alone were equivalent to the nuclear bomb dropped on Hiroshima, went to seek spiritual solace from his mentor, the evangelist Billy Graham. At the same time, Saddam Hussein, who spent eight years fighting the Iranian Muslim fundamentalists and invaded Kuwait in a desperate attempt to resolve Iraq's post-war economic and political crisis, called the war a 'jihad' – holy war – against the 'infidels'.

For many years, religion has been thought – definitely by the Left and those prophets of modernity, the social scientists – to be withering away. Nationalism, argued Louis Althusser (1969), Ben Anderson (1983) and others, has come to occupy the place religion has had in previous epochs.

Yet in the closing decades of the twentieth century, not only has religion achieved a new lease of life, but particular forms of religious movements, which can be grouped under the umbrella concept of 'fundamentalism', seem to be the most vital force for (and against) social change all over the world and within different religions. Moreover, these forms of religious movements have often been incorporated into and transformed nationalist movements.

Britain has been involved in this global process. Its subordinate and satellite status after World War II meant that it was increasingly affected by trends set in the USA; as an ex-colonial power, recruiting many colonial subjects to work and settle in metropolitan Britain, it acquired new citizens who brought their national and religious politics with them. So Britain's post-war position meant that it was the receiver, rather than the initiator, of many global fundamentalist movements – although, of course, the seeds of many contemporary fundamentalist movements were laid during the colonial period, sometimes as a direct result of colonial policies (see, for example, Ann Rossiter's chapter). However, particular social structures and social policies in Britain formed the specific social context in which these movements have crystallized.

2

It was the Salman Rushdie affair and Muslims' mass demonstrations in protest – not only against *The Satanic Verses* and its author, but also against the ways in which the British state privileges Christianity – which put the issue of fundamentalism at the centre of British politics. However, different fundamentalist movements – Christian, Jewish, Sikh and Hindu, as well as Muslim – have been growing in Britain during the last few years, even before the Rushdie affair.

What is Fundamentalism?

The term 'fundamentalism', especially in the way it has been used by the media around the Rushdie affair, has become so confused with abusive labelling of Muslims as 'the Barbaric Other' that it has been suggested that the term should be dispensed with altogether. It is clear from the title of this book that we do not support this point of view. While struggling against anti-Muslim racism, it is important to realize that fundamentalism is a much wider phenomenon which cuts across religions and cultures, and with which we must engage.

The *Concise Oxford Dictionary* defines fundamentalism as 'strict maintenance of traditional, orthodox, religious beliefs, such as the inerrancy of Scripture and literal acceptance of the creeds as fundamentals of Protestant Christianity'. And indeed, the first modern religious groupings to be called fundamentalist were American Protestant Churches which, in 1919, established the World Christian Fundamentalist Association after the publication of the 'Fundamentals' – based on a series of Bible conferences which took place between 1865 and 1910. However, just as we reject the application of the notion of 'fundamentalism' only to Islam, we also reject its limitation to Christianity.

We do not want to underestimate the specific historical and cultural constructions of different religions. However, we need to be aware, first, that heterogeneity exists not only among religions but also within them, and secondly, that there is no such thing as 'strict adherence to the text'. All great religious scriptures include internal contradictions, and even the most 'fundamentalist' forms of religion have exercised selectivity.

Beyond all these differences, there are two features which are common to all fundamentalist religious movements: one, that they claim their version of religion to be the only true one, and feel threatened by pluralist systems of thought; two, that they use political means to impose their version of the truth on all members of their religion. Fundamentalist militantism must be differentiated, therefore, from liberation theologies which, while deeply religious and political, co-operate with, rather than subjugate, non-religious political struggles.

Fundamentalism is not merely a traditional form of religious orthodoxy. It is significant, as well as typical, that the original fundamentalist movement arose in the USA as a response to the rise of liberalism in general and the 'Social Gospel' movement within the Church in particular, which liberalized religion and had strong progressive elements.

Fundamentalist movements, all over the world, are basically political movements which have a religious imperative and seek in various ways, in widely differing circumstances, to harness modern state and media powers to the service of their gospel. This gospel is presented as the only valid form of religion. It can rely heavily on sacred religious texts, but it can also be more experiential and linked to specific charismatic leadership. Fundamentalism can align itself with different political trends in different countries and manifest itself in many forms. It can appear as a form of orthodoxy – a maintenance of 'traditional values' – or as a revivalist radical phenomenon, dismissing impure and corrupt forms of religion to 'return to original sources'.

Jewish fundamentalism in Israel, for example, has appeared in basically two forms, for which the state has very different meanings. On the one hand as a form of right-wing Zionism, in which the establishment of the Israeli state is in itself a positive religious act; and, on the other hand, as a non-, – if not anti- – Zionist movement, which sees in the Israeli state a convenient source for gaining economic and political power to promote its own versions of Judaism. In Islam, fundamentalism has appeared as a return to the Qur'anic text (fundamentalism of the *madrassa*) and as a return to the religious law, the *sharia* (fundamentalism of the *ulama*). In the USA, the Protestant fundamentalist movements include both fundamentalists in the original sense – those who want to go back to the biblical texts – and those 'born-again Christians' who rely much more on emotional religious experiences (see Sara Maitland's chapter, where she uses the term neo-evangelical to describe these movements). Given our definition of fundamentalism, it is clear why we would disagree with people like Abrahamian (1991), who would define Khomeiniism as populism rather than fundamentalism. It is precisely those features of Khomeiniism which lead Abrahamian to reject 'fundamentalism' as a label – such as Khomeini's manipulation of the Muslim traditions and of modern state powers – that are crucial, in our perspective, to defining fundamentalism.

Another important difference is between movements of dominant majorities within states, which look for universal domination in society (such as the evangelical New Right in the USA and Khomeini's Iran) and fundamentalist movements of minorities, which aim to use state and media powers and resources to promote and impose their gospel, primarily within their specific constituencies, which are usually defined in ethnic terms (such as the Jewish fundamentalists of the Lubavitch Hassids, and Hindu and Sikh fundamentalists in Britain). Identifying various heterogeneous forms of fundamentalist movements, however, does not invalidate the use of the term 'fundamentalism' as identifying specific social phenomena. All major social movements – national, socialist and feminist movements – have been similarly heterogeneous.

The recent rise of fundamentalism is linked to the crisis of modernity – of social orders based on the belief in the principles of enlightenment, rationalism and progress. Both capitalism and communism have proved unable to fulfil people's material, emotional and spiritual needs. A general sense of despair and disorientation has opened people to religion as a source of solace. Religion provides a compass and an anchor; it gives people a sense of stability and meaning, as well as a coherent identity.

In the West, the most influential fundamentalist movement has been the neo-evangelical movement which is at the heart of the 'moral majority' in the USA. (Sara Maitland's chapter examines this movement and its particular politics in Britain.) In the Third World, and among Third World minorities in the West, the rise of fundamentalism is also intimately linked with the failure of nationalist and socialist movements to bring about successful liberation from oppression, exploitation and poverty. We have seen – most recently in the Gulf War – that religion has also been utilized by militants as an 'indigenous' ideology with which to mobilize the 'masses' and confront racism, imperialism and superpowers' interventions. Since the Iranian revolution, this powerful development has affected, in turn, not only Muslims in other countries but also Jews, Sikhs, Hindus and members of other religions in which fundamentalist movements have grown and given new intensity to links between nationalism and religion.

One of the unchallenged 'truths' of the Left has been the assumption of the inherently progressive nature of anti-imperialism. Khomeini's revolution, as well as other fundamentalist movements which are clearly anti-Western and anti-imperialist, have been hailed as progressive, at least initially, by large sections of the Left. However, just because a political movement has the 'right enemy', that does not automatically transform it into a 'goody'. Moreover, fundamentalist movements in the Third World have not always developed against the interests of imperialism or neo-colonialism. Often they are found to be convenient models of accommodation, using traditional values and social relations as a bulwark against revolutionary social change (as, for example, is the case with Saudi Arabia's alliance with the USA). Maryam Poya's chapter examines the contradictions faced by women who had fought against the Shah but then fell victim to Iranian Muslim fundamentalism.

Fundamentalist movements have attacked the notion of secularism. The idea of a public sphere not controlled by organized religion is deeply threatening to them. Secularists' attempts to separate the spheres of religion and the state are perceived to be inherently contradictory to fundamentalist aspirations.

Secularism

Secularism has been linked to the Enlightenment project. One formulation of secularist ideology has been to create a separation between a non-religious public sphere and a private sphere in which individuals, families and communities have the right to practise the religion of their choice. Another construction has been a rationalist atheist ideology, in which the validity of all transcendental ideologies and religions would be challenged.

Secularism has often been attacked as a Eurocentric ideology which developed in specific conditions in European history, and is therefore inherently culturally imperialist when applied to non-European societies or non-European minorities within the West. Secularists, for their part, argue that secularist ideologies have acted as guarantors of the religious and cultural rights of minorities.

This has created a paradox of universalism and particularism within the secular democratic model. On the one hand, it constructs all individuals as – at least potentially – inherently equal. On the other, it constructs all groupings of people, with different norms and cultures, as having – at least potentially – the same collective rights. On the concrete level it can create conflicts between individual rights and group rights, especially in relation to gender and ethnic divisions in societies.

The issue of fundamentalism, especially of fundamentalist movements adopted by minorities of Third World origin in the West, has been particularly confusing for secular democrats. In the name of pluralism, intolerant ideologies have been accepted, as long as they were perceived as applicable only to members of other specific groupings. This perspective, which might be called multiculturalist, sees members of different groupings as essentially different from the 'norm' as well as internally homogeneous (see Yasmin Ali and Gita Sahgal's chapters).

Fundamentalism and Women

Women have been particularly vulnerable to the effects of the multiculturalist perspective. Minority women's demands for freedom and equality were seen as being outside 'cultural traditions' (often themselves only half understood) and were therefore not regarded as legitimate. By contrast, the most conservative versions of traditional 'womanhood' were considered to be the most 'authentic'. Yasmin Ali and Gita Sahgal describe how appeals to culture and tradition have been used to attack women's autonomous organizing.

Women affect and are affected by ethnic and national processes in several major ways. Some of these are central to the project of fundamentalism, which attempts to impose its own unitary religious definition on the grouping and its symbolic order. The 'proper' behaviour of women is used to signify the difference between those who belong and those who do not; women are also seen as the 'cultural carriers' of the grouping, who transmit group culture to the future generation; and proper control in terms of marriage and divorce ensures that children who are born to those women are within the boundaries of the collectivity, not only biologically but also symbolically (Yuval-Davis and Anthias, 1989).

It is therefore no coincidence that the control of women and the patriarchal family are central to fundamentalism, and are often seen as the panacea for all social ills:

A widespread evangelical conviction is that stability in the home is the key to the resolution of other social problems.

Once wanderers came 'home' and the poor acquired the sense of responsibility found in strong Christian familiality, poverty would cease. (Marsden, 1980, p. 37)

And women's desertion of their proper social role might mean a social disaster:

Woman has such a degree of biological disability and such huge family responsibilities, as to preclude her leaving purdah in a well ordered society. (Pundah Mandrudi, quoted in Hyman, 1985, p. 24)

One of the paradoxes discussed in this book is the fact that women collude, seek comfort, and even at times gain a sense of empowerment within the spaces allocated to them by fundamentalist movements (see especially the chapters by Yasmin Ali, Elaine Foster, Sara Maitland and Nira Yuval-Davis). Being active in a religious movement allows women a legitimate place in a public sphere which otherwise might be blocked to them, and which in certain circumstances they might be able to subvert for their purposes – for example, the relationship between young girls and their parents. It can also, at the same time, be less threatening but still a challenge and a space for personal accomplishment to which unskilled working-class women and frustrated middle-class women might be attracted. For women of racial and ethnic minorities, it can also provide the means by which to defend themselves as well as to defy the hegemonic racist culture.

However, the overall effect of fundamentalist movements has been very detrimental to women, limiting and defining their roles and activities and actively oppressing them when they step out of the preordained limits of their designated roles. This link between fundamentalism and women's oppression has been recognized by women in many countries where they have established organizations to fight against fundamentalism.

Women Against Fundamentalism was established in London

in spring 1989. The main groups involved are reflected in the case studies in this book. It is interesting to note, however (see, for example, the chapters by Ann Rossiter and Yasmin Ali), that many women who are engaged in this fight find themselves caught 'between the devil and the deep blue sea' – having to confront the fundamentalism within their own communities or countries of origin at the same time as having to confront the racism not only of society in general, but also of the Left and the feminist movements. This is probably why it is so difficult to find Afro-Caribbean women in Britain who fight against the fundamentalism of the Black Churches (in contrast to Africa, for example, where there is an active struggle against religious fundamentalism, both Christian and Muslim, largely imported from the USA (*Religion and Politics*, a special issue of *Review of African Political Economy*, 1991). In spite of women's inferior position within these churches (see Elaine Foster's chapter), they have been seen as a major source of women's empowerment. Those who have come out against these churches, with critiques which usually concentrated on a cultural/racist element, pointing out that the Black Churches, although reformed, originate from the cultural influence of those who enslaved the blacks. To articulate their critique they have often needed to use another religious discourse (such as that of Rastafarianism or Islam) to counter the influence of the Church.

For women who are political exiles (see Maryam Poya's chapter) the traditional solution for dealing with their sense of exclusion and estrangement from the society has been to remain distant from the local political 'scene' and to dedicate their attention and energy almost wholly to the struggles which happen in their countries of origin. Geographical and psychological/ideological boundaries need not necessarily overlap. The establishment of Women Against Fundamentalism, however, has supplied a rare opportunity for women who are engaged in the struggle against fundamentalism in different religious, political and social contexts to co-operate. The variety of their experiences and analysis has enriched the narrow ethnocentrist British politics in which they are situated and supplied them with some insights in their political struggle. Of particular importance have been the experiences of women who have come from countries in which fundamentalist movements have come to control the state (see Maryam Poya and Ann Rossiter's chapters).

Before we turn to look more specifically at the political agendas of the women associated with WAF, however, we would like to explore the British context within which they operate.

Religion and the State in Britain

Full separation between religion and the state has never taken place in Britain. This is all too often ignored in the analysis both of the Left and of sociologists of religion, who have assumed that religion has either disappeared in secularized society or withdrawn into the private arena. So the enquiry into religion in Britain has predominantly focused on attitudes, beliefs and membership of religious organizations.

According to the latest statistics (*Social Trends*, 1989), less than 20 per cent of the population are members of religious organizations (only 15 per cent are members of 'Trinitarian Churches', such as the Established and the Catholic Churches). However, 75 per cent of the population have a religious affiliation, the majority associated with the Established Churches. In a survey carried out by the Independent Television Authority (ITA) in 1970, eight out of every ten Britons felt that the Christian identity of Britain was very important or important to them. This is the context in which Enoch Powell's notion of Englishness expressed in the 'Rivers of Blood' speech has to be perceived. And indeed, when David Jenkins (1975) wrote about *The British, Their Identity and Their Religion*, he remarked:

> The more I considered what it means in specific terms to be distinctively English, Scottish or Welsh, the more important became the place of religious inheritance in the process of definition. (p. vii)

11

The Christianity of Britain, however, is not just a question of religious affiliation or even just a part of British nationalist ideology. It is anchored in law, and extended beyond the symbolism of the Queen being the titular head of the Churches of England and of Scotland. First, the church hierarchy participates in the British legislative process. The two archbishops and twenty-four bishops are members of the upper house in the British Parliament, the House of Lords ('the Lords Spiritual'). It is the Prime Minister's duty to appoint the Archbishop of Canterbury, and as debates in the media before the appointment of the last archbishop pointed out, the Prime Minister's religious affiliation and attitudes have to be accommodated in appropriate manner. Moreover, in the *Jewish Yearbook*, in the section on British laws which specifically concern the Jews, it is claimed that legally it is unclear whether a Jew (or any other non-Christian, for that matter) can become a British Prime Minister, as it is illegal for a non-Christian to appoint the Head of the Church – this might apply only to British royalty, but it probably applies also to the Prime Minister. The case has never been tested in British history (Disraeli converted to Christianity . . .).

Another major way in which the relationship between Church and state in Britain affects British public life is in the existence of the blasphemy law, which protects the Church of England from attacks which are legal against other religions. Attempts in court by Muslim leaders to expand the application of the law to Islam, prompted by the Rushdie affair, have failed. The blasphemy law might not be invoked often by Christian, but it is available for use. Mary Whitehouse brought a private prosecution against *Gay News* for printing a poem which implied that Jesus had homosexual fantasies, so it is of more than mere symbolic importance.

Another facet of the incomplete separation between religion and the state – probably the most important one in contemporary political debates in Britain – is the fact that under the 1988 Education Reform Act all state schools are required to have a daily act of worship. (Not coincidentally, this amendment in the law originated in the House of Lords.) Christianity, therefore, is given an affirmed legal status as the ideological cement of national culture. As such, it also provides legitimation for eminent church personalities to express opinions on social and political matters such as poverty and homelessness which cause great discomfort to the government. Nevertheless, this construction assumes a correspondence between national and religious identity, which means that members of non-Established Churches, and especially non-Christians, can be only partial members of the British national collectivity. They are defined, to a lesser or greater extent, as outsiders. Christianity, therefore, is one of the most important bases for inherent racism in the hegemonic notion of Englishness. Significantly, the recently passed Broadcasting Act, which lays down codes of practice for broadcasters, exempts only religious programmes from censorship for expressing partisan opinions. Sara Maitland points out that it is a powerful Christian evangelical lobby in Parliament that has achieved recent gains in asserting the importance of the Christian character of the British state.

While membership in the Established Churches has tended to fall continuously, at least until recently (*Social Trends*, 1989 mentions a figure of 14 per cent in the previous three years, but since then the figure seems to have stabilized) membership of minority churches (like Spiritualists and Jehovah's Witnesses) has risen by 26 per cent during the same period. Non-Christian religious groups, especially Muslims and Sikhs, have almost doubled their membership. Religious affiliation has therefore come, in different ways, to signify collective identity and a central mode of inclusion and exclusion among ethnic minorities in Britain, as well as its majority.

The reinforcement of religious affiliation as a central principle of identity politics is partly due to global developments and to the rise of religious fundamentalist movements in the countries of origin of non-Christians living in Britain, such as the revolution in Iran or the rise of Hindu fundamentalism in India (as Gita Sahgal's chapter notes, British Hindus have raised funds to send blessed bricks to build a temple on the site of a mosque, claiming that it is the birthplace of the god Rama, in India). However, part of the phenomenon is also a result of the multiculturalist policies prevalent in the English education system and in what is known as 'the Race Relations Industry'. Paradoxically, these policies, which were intended to legitimize heterogeneity in British national culture, have ended up by creating the space for the development of what Yasmin Ali terms, in her chapter, ethnicist (and Islamist) movements. Nevertheless, one should not underestimate the importance of the two-way flow of information, social contact and material resources between the groupings in Britain and abroad. (For example, leaders of the movement against Rushdie said that they first heard about *The Satanic Verses* from their contacts in the Indian subcontinent, although the book was actually published in Britain; for international links in the context of Jewish fundamentalism, see Nira Yuval-Davis's chapter.)

Multiculturalism and Racism

There have been many attempts in Britain to deal with the related problems of racism and the absorption by mainstream British society of people drawn from the old Empire who settled in Britain after the war. The policy of multiculturalism, despite some misgivings by both Left and Right, has been widely adopted as a more tolerant way towards integration of the minorities, rather than full assimilation into a 'British way of life'. It has been accepted as a tool of social policy and in education, where it was first articulated. In 1977, an Inner London Education Authority document stated:

> The authority serves the city where the presence of people of diverse cultures with different patterns of belief, behaviour, and language, is of great importance . . . Recognizing this, we have reaffirmed our determination to sustain a policy which will ensure that, within a society which is cohesive, though not

uniform, cultures are respected, differences recognized and
individual identities are ensured. (Connolly, 1990)

Under the terms of the multiculturalist consensus, fighting
against racism is reduced to preserving the 'traditions and
cultures' of the different ethnic minorities. Cultural differences between various groups in society become of paramount
importance, rather than tackling the central problem of racism
itself: unequal power relations which bring about 'modes of
exclusion' inferiorisation, subordination and exploitation'
(Anthias and Yuval-Davis, 1992, p. 3) and which prevent certain segments of the British population from full participation
as citizens. However, even 'anti-racism', which has attempted
to correct some of the glaring omissions of the multiculturalist
approach in the later 1970s, has shared with multiculturalism a
lack of awareness of the contradictions, inconsistencies and
ambivalences which are inherent to racist ideologies and
practices and – most vital to our concerns here – to collectivity
boundaries (Rattansi, 1992; Anthias and Yuval-Davis, 1992).

In the multiculturalist discourse, minority communities are
defined by a stereotypical notion of their 'culture', which is
increasingly being collapsed into matters of religious identity.
This could be seen in the ways children in multicultural schools
were taught about various religious holidays as one of the
main means of acquainting them with other cultures. Even
more seriously, it could be seen in the way the British 'Race
Relations Industry' (mostly Community Relations boards and
local councils) have been financing mosques and temples (but
not usually churches, even Black churches) as a major part of
their work. The racialization of religion, especially Islam,
reached a new peak after the Rushdie affair. Communities
which were previously known by national or regional origin –
Pakistani, Mirpuri, Bengali, Punjabi, etc. – are now all seen
as part of a single Muslim community. This construction was
brought about both by external agencies, like the press, and
by self-definition.

With the decline of secular nationalism, identities based on nationality have acquired less resonance. In addition, the contradiction in the country of origin between nationalism and religion is not necessarily apparent in Britain. Bangladesh, for instance, is a country which gained its independence from Pakistan in 1971, after a bloody war. Memories of the liberation are still strong in Bangladesh, as is the bitterness of the memory of the collaboration of many religious groups with the Pakistani army; the Bangladeshi struggle for nationhood was a secular struggle. In Britain, however, young Bengalis' sense of themselves, honed under constant racist attack which intensified during the Gulf War, is one of being attacked for being Muslims. With the rise of strong evangelical Islam, often fuelled by converts, an available and more aggressive Muslim identity is being offered to these young people.

Fundamentalist leaderships have been the main beneficiaries of the adoption of multiculturalist norms. In pressing their demands upon the British state, they have sometimes been portrayed as 'medievalists' who have rejected British values. In fact, their campaigns have been fought within the framework of multiculturalism – it has provided their chief ideological weapon. They argued to extend the blasphemy law to Islam under the banner of 'Equal Rights for Muslims'. They presented themselves as the most 'authentic' representatives of the different communities and prevented 'outsiders' from taking sides in power struggles within those communities, on the grounds that such intervention was racist. On the other hand, Christianity as a signifier of 'Western civilization', or 'civilization' in general, has become one of the major ways in which white racism has come to be expressed.

Women Against Fundamentalism (WAF): The Political Agenda

Although the direct impulse to establish WAF stemmed from public debate around the Rushdie affair, the organization encompasses a broad range of women's groups and individuals from different ethnic and religious backgrounds – English, Asian, Iranian, Irish, Jewish, and many others. The various campaigns in which the organization has been involved during its short history can delineate the wide and complex ways in which fundamentalist politics affect women's lives in Britain.

The Rushdie affair

The meeting which lead to the founding of WAF was called by Southall Black Sisters (SBS) and the women's section of the Ealing Labour Party in 1989 on International Women's Day to discuss the rise of fundamentalism across the world and analyse its effects on women. At the end of the meeting, Southall Black Sisters issued a statement which defended Salman Rushdie's right to free speech, without falling into the traps to which a divided and confused Left fell prey:

> As a group of women of many religions and none, we would like to express our solidarity with Salman Rushdie. Women's voices have been largely silent in the debate where battle lines have been drawn between liberalism and fundamentalism. Often, it has been assumed that the views of vocal community leaders are our views, and their demands are our demands. We reject this absolutely.

On 27 May 1989, shortly after WAF was founded, a huge Muslim march took place in London to demand the banning of *The Satanic Verses*, and the extension of the blasphemy law. WAF decided to picket the march to defend their right to dissent.

There were about forty women on this small picket. They argued that the blasphemy law should be abolished as a more equitable way forward, but they were criticized for lending themselves to a racist backlash by sections of the Left who would not recognize the legitimacy of their position. At the march the Anti-Fascist League demonstrated alongside the main Muslim march, emphasizing the Muslims' right to resist racism, and to counter fascists who had threatened to attack the march. Another fascist organization supported the march, seeing it as Muslims expressing their inherently different cultural and nationalist essence. The picket of Women Against Fundamentalism ended up being attacked by fascists who stood shoulder to shoulder with young Muslim men who also shouted abuse and assaulted women pickets.

The specificity of women's experience of the fundamentalist threat has not often been adequately recognized. Women from within black communities in Britain have to uphold the honour of the anti-racist tradition, not to protest publicly against internal discrimination. For some, it has become the same as concealing your oppression to uphold the honour, or *izzat*, of the family as well.

The Education Debate
One of the first focuses of WAF campaigning was counteracting the growing support (particularly within the Labour Party) for separate religious schools, especially Muslim, which has been demanded under the banner of equal rights. Instead, they called for the phasing out of state subsidies for all schools in the voluntary sector and the development of a strong anti-racist education policy which would grant rights of private worship, diet and dress for any religious group in a state school (see Saeeda Khanum's chapter).

The issue of separate religious schools is one of the major demands of fundamentalist leaders. At the first session of the 'Muslim Parliament' organized by Kalim Siddiqui of the pro-Iranian Muslim Institute in January 1992, state funding for Muslim voluntary-aided schools was a primary demand. In Britain today, up to a third of British schools are part of the voluntary-aided or religious sector. Voluntary-aiding is a system by which the government partly funds schools run by religious establishments, on condition that their curriculum and general standards conform to state requirements. (This is in contrast to completely privately run schools, in which no such supervision is imposed.) Most of the voluntary-aided schools in Britain are Church of England or Roman Catholic, with a few Jewish schools, but until now no Muslim, Hindu or Sikh school has been granted such a status by the Department of Education. A major part of the public debate on the provision of separate education has revolved around the question whether educational standards, cultural difference or pure racism have been at the root of this refusal. However, the 1988 Education Reform Act and the provision for individual schools to opt out of local-authority supervision might make it easier for the transformation of former state schools into schools controlled by religious fundamentalists in neighbourhoods in which specific religious minorities constitute a large majority – though in some areas, notably Glasgow and Southall, parents have voted against opting out (see Gita Sahgal's chapter).

These demands for separate schooling are likely to be fuelled by the education crisis, which has caused severe teacher shortages in many schools:

> In Tower Hamlets, in London's East End, some four hundred to five hundred Bangladeshi children languish without education because there are not enough school places for them. Yet the Roman Catholic state-aided schools in the borough have dozens of empty spaces, because they would only offer ten percent of them to non-Catholic children. (Melanie Phillips, *The Guardian*, 1 June 1990, Connolly, 1991).

Sexual segregation of the children has been seen as a central issue in the question of separate schooling. Some feminists also consider that single-sex schooling for girls is good for their academic achievement. Without boys in the classroom they would be less affected by traditional sexual divisions of academic interests, and free from sexual intimidation. However, this feminist thinking assumes a structure and curriculum similar to those of a mixed school.

This is not the case where religious education is concerned. It is no coincidence that most of the private Muslim schools which have been established in Britain, with the exception of a couple of seminaries, are for girls only, as Saeeda Khanum's chapter on a Muslim girls' school indicates. Their purpose is very clearly to bring up girls to be dutiful wives and mothers. They teach Creation theories in science (like Christian fundamentalists) and offer poor facilities for the achievement of any qualifications. Although most Asian parents would probably prefer single-sex education, they would not necessarily prefer to send their daughters to religious schools; even fewer would risk their sons' futures. However, few parents would dare publicly to oppose religious demands. By making separate education for girls a central plank of their national campaign (along with banning *The Satanic Verses* and extending the blasphemy law) Muslim fundamentalists have shown a keen awareness of their constituents' fears. Their discourse ties the control of girls to the dangers of growing up in a secular society in the 'morally degenerate West'.

Though Muslim fundamentalists are the most vocal, they are by no means the only group. Ultra-Orthodox Jews and Seventh-Day Adventists have asked for voluntary-aided status for private schools. In Southall, Southall Black Sisters has been part of a campaign to prevent two local high schools from opting out and becoming Sikh schools (see Gita Sahgal's chapter).

'Community' Control

Conflict over the control of women in fundamentalist communities has not been confined to the question of separate schools. It has spread also to women's refuges, which were initially established by the feminist movement to provide women with a private space away from their husbands' violent attempts to control them. The debate about refuges shows how the contradictory influences of feminist and multiculturalist policies adopted by local authorities (mainly in Labour-led councils) affect the rights of minority women.

In the early 1980s black women who had set up autonomous women's groups took up the issue of domestic violence and began to argue for local council funding for refuges. They were bitterly opposed by conservative community leaders who argued that domestic violence did not exist, or that it was a problem which could be solved by traditional mechanisms within the community. Some white feminists also felt that separate refuges were in contradiction to the central idea of the women's movement: the notion of sisterhood. Black women countered, from the perspective of the anti-racist movement, that there was a need for Asian (and sometimes Afro-Caribbean) women to have separate spaces to live with women who understood the pressures they felt, including dealing with racism. But the essential aim of all the refuges was the same – to provide an alternative space for women who have suffered from domestic violence.

Anxious to implement equal-opportunity policies, some councils did fund these refuges (although, as befitted the multiculturalist approach, they were open to arguments about the needs for separate space due to cultural and linguistic differences, much more than to arguments concerning racism). While initially the Asian refuges provoked a community backlash, the situation changed with the years. Today the problem of domestic violence is so well recognized that a claim from community organizations for funds to provide advice or other services dealing with it is a significant factor. This has created a sharp turnabout. Community leaders who had earlier opposed the provision of refuges are now applying for funding themselves, but their purpose is to reintegrate women back into the family. The notion of 'cultural difference' has turned the idea of a refuge on its head.

New refuges are being funded solely on the basis of religious allegiance. Fundamentalist leaderships are venturing into areas from which the old guard shied away. Some councils have tried to impose religious leaders on the management committees of refuges as a form of 'community control'. Feminist women, by definition, were deemed outsiders.

Women from WAF have been involved in several of these conflicts. Those who are concerned with refuges and advice centres have also been involved in conflicts with various social services authorities who prefer to send teenage girls to families of the same 'cultural background', sometimes interpreted as an orthodox religious background, ignoring regional, even linguistic differences – even when the girls in question have escaped from their homes as a result of conflicts which stemmed directly from their unwillingness to continue to be constructed by these specific 'cultural' norms.

Reproductive Rights

The abortion debate and the wider issues of women's reproductive rights have always been at the heart of the feminist agenda, as well as that of the pro-life movement. In the last few years abortion clinics in Britain have been picketed by anti-abortionists, inspired and coached by Operation Rescue, a North American organization which is part of the evangelical 'Moral Right'. This is just one instance of the growing influence of this movement on the British scene (see Sara Maitland's chapter).

WAF women have been mainly involved in a campaign which relates to another branch of the pro-life movement (as discussed by Ann Rossiter in her chapter on the struggles of Irish women in Britain and Ireland). In Britain there has always been a tradition of women coming from Ireland – both South and North – to have an abortion, which is illegal in the Republic of Ireland. Women from WAF have been part of the support movement for these Irish women, which helps them before and after this traumatic experience. As a result of a decision by the Irish High Court, it has also become illegal for women in Ireland to give information and advice to women who seek abortion.

In February 1992, the Irish government imposed an injunction against a fourteen-year-old rape victim who travelled to Britain for an abortion, a decision which was reversed by the Supreme Court amid much embarrassment. The Irish state had attempted to impose Irish law outside its own jurisdiction and infringe the right of free travel outside the EC. The case has reopened the debate on abortion in Ireland and that of the relationship of member states of the EC to its directives and policies.

Along with other organisations, WAF has held pickets outside the Irish Embassy in London, to support Irish activists and draw out the fundamentalist ideological challenge to abortion information and the civil rights of women in the EC.

The Rabia Campaign

The contradictions and constraints on migrant women's lives from their countries of origin, as well as from the British state, have been highlighted in the 'Rabia Janjua must stay' campaign which was started by Southall Black Sisters and sponsored by WAF. Rabia, who has since been granted 'exceptional leave' to remain by the Home Office was under threat of removal to Pakistan, where she faced a charge of *zina* (unlawful sex or adultery). The charge carries a possible sentence of ten years' imprisonment and public flogging. Rabia escaped to Britain with her husband, who then subjected her to severe violence. She left him with her two young children but immediately faced the prospect of removal to Pakistan, as her husband, who is a British citizen, brought her here not as his wife but on a tourist visa (without her knowledge).

In their campaign, SBS and WAF highlighted several issues. First, they drew attention to the degrading *zina* laws of Pakistan. Secondly, they campaigned against the generally unjust and discriminatory nature of immigration legislation in Britain, especially in relation to refugees. In particular, the Rabia campaign pointed out women's extreme vulnerability to the whims of their husbands as a result of the immigration rules, which stipulate that if the marriage breaks down within a year of entry to this country, wives are liable to be deported.

Last but not least, the campaign highlighted the gender-specific character of the definition of refugees. A political refugee is defined as someone who is suffering from state persecution as a result of political, ethnic or religious conflict. There is no space for persecution based on the politics of sexuality. This is true not only in British law but also in campaigning bodies like Amnesty International (although as a result of the Rabia campaign and similar mobilizations – discussed in Maryam Poya's chapter – there seems to be a change on this front).

WAF as an organization has tried to combine the different yet related concerns of women in Britain, both those born here and those who have come as migrants or as refugees. In this way it is virtually unique in British feminism, and has been sensitized to some of the complexities of 'sisterhood politics'.

As we have seen, in many of WAF's political campaigns, the boundaries of concern go beyond British shores. The politics of exile and migration are not mere temporary visitors – they affect the stuff of British politics itself, and are in turn transformed. One of the issues that surfaces repeatedly is how women from minority groups can struggle against fundamentalist and other reactionary politics within their own communities and countries of origin, while they face racist stereotyping by the majority (see especially Ann Rossiter and Gita Sahgal's chapters). Yet these struggles of minority and exile women could enable the majority to combat fundamentalism, without colluding with racist and sexist assumptions and being caught in multiculturalist guilt-tripping (see the chapter by Maryam Poya).

Britain is still far from being a fundamentalist country. Its 'Moral Right' is smaller and not as overtly political as in the USA; its black and non-Christian fundamentalists come from oppressed racialized minorities. Yet the continued close ties between the state and Christianity on the one hand, and the collapse of anti-racism into multiculturalism and the equation of culture with religion on the other, are fertile ground for the growing influence of fundamentalist militants.

The various campaigns in which WAF has become involved in its short history demonstrate the complexity and variety of issues in which the connections between anti-racist and anti-sexist struggles, international and intranational developments, and the rising threat of fundamentalists' control of women have to be made.

Issues of racism and sexism are intricately interwoven. However, this is no reason always to prioritize one struggle in favour of the other. The task ahead is to find effective ways to confront the contradictions and conflicts within minority communities as well as oppression and racism in the state and society at large. To find ways to resolve the tension between autonomy and tolerance, diversity and equality. To have the right to dissent and oppose both racism and sexism – and, of course, fundamentalism.

Biblicism:
A Radical Rhetoric?

....

SARA MAITLAND

> When people say politics and religion don't mix
> I wonder which bible they're using.
>
> (Desmond Tutu)

*T*here is currently a profound cultural confusion in Britain. The statistics show that Britain is a secular country, with a low level of religious practice (under 15 per cent, compared with approximately 40 per cent in the USA and 36 per cent in Italy). Yet the Church of England – and the Church of Scotland – remain Established, with the Queen as their leader and Parliament as the final arbiter of their doctrine and practice. There has been no formal separation of Church and state, and repeatedly, in different ways, the state continues to act as though Christianity was – and should be – central to the lives of its citizens: the refusal to withdraw the discriminatory blasphemy law, the religious education provisions of the Education Reform Act 1988, the criticism of the staff of St Paul's Cathedral after the conflict in the Malvinas (Falkland) Islands. At the same time, a religious revival appears to be under way (in 1988 the attendance figures for the Church of England showed their first rise in twenty years), which is exciting an immense amount of media coverage of a pretty scathing and derogatory kind. There seems to be a great deal of muddled thinking and misunderstanding about the phenomenon, which is not helpful.

It is now a commonplace that 'Christian fundamentalism' is an emergent force in Britain, nourished by a powerful parent movement in the USA. Endless feature columns in the 'responsible' Sunday papers, in line with the screaming news headlines in the tabloids, have rushed to introduce us to the weirder fringes of Christian cultic practice. Since the *cause célèbre* of Rushdie's *The Satanic Verses*, the word 'fundamentalist' has been both popularized and distorted – 'Muslim fundamentalist' has become pseudo-polite-speak for 'mad mullah' and, by extension, the same word, when applied to Christians, now carries 'loony extremist' connotations.

Accompanying this commonplace is a package of inter-twined ideas about 'fundamentalism': that it is *necessarily* reactionary, misogynistic, homophobic, censorious (in both moral and legal understandings), lower-middle-class, hysteri-cal and both silly and in bad taste. Alternatively (and often from exactly the same sources), Christian fundamentalism is a bulwark of respectability, the hope of the nation against the dangerous heresies of liberalism and modernism. I would like to suggest, in this chapter, that the very real dangers – particularly to women – of the current enthusiast revival are neither exposed nor challenged by these easy assumptions.

We are not seeing, in Britain, a revival of Christian *funda-mentalism*. This is partly because there is nothing to revive: the very concept of fundamentalism is – and this should not be surprising – a comparatively new one. There cannot be a 'return to fundamental principles of biblical inerrancy' until these principles are themselves questioned. Such a challenge did not occur until the nineteenth century, when evolutionary theory, especially Darwinism, undermined the biblical accounts of the Creation and the new biblical scholarship exposed the intellectual problems of 'direct inspiration' and literal inerrancy.

The *Oxford English Dictionary* does not even have a re-corded use of the words 'fundamentalism' or 'fundamentalist' before the 1933 supplement. Throughout the 1920s these words were being used only in inverted commas to indicate that they were neologisms, and pretty odd ones at that. At a more serious level, too, we are not seeing a revival of a Christian fundamentalist tradition. The leaders of the current revivalist movement would not call themselves fundamentalists, and they would be right. That genuinely fundamentalist movements towards biblical purity and literalism have existed is not in doubt – one thinks particularly of the Shaker communities – but they have been movements of withdrawal, of conservatism as formally understood: a move away from the modern world and into exclusive communities of the faithful who have endeavoured to make their experiences match, as nearly as possible, those of the ideal Israelite communities as described in the Old or New Testament. This tradition tends to be agrarian and private – 'rendering unto Caesar the things which are Caesar's' and wishing mainly to live peaceful lives 'outside' the contemporary world. The current revivalist movement's engagements with the forces of this world – in the political lobby and the stadium, or on the television – are light years away from this tradition.

This movement could more correctly be called 'evangelical'. Evangelicalism has a long history within British Christianity: it exists both within and beyond the Established Churches. Within the Church of England itself, evangelicals are one of three main parties (the other two being broadly a liberal-establishment alliance and the Catholics), and at the moment they are in the ascendant. One of Margaret Thatcher's last appointments, the new Archbishop of Canterbury, George Carey, for example, is from the evangelical tradition. At present more than 50 per cent of the students in training for ordination are evangelicals (this compares with 10 per cent in 1956 and 31 per cent in 1969). Outside the Established frameworks there is also a growth of independent churches. *The UK Christian Handbook* has a projected estimate of half a million members by the end of this decade: the housechurch movement, for example, claims about 145,000 members, which – given that it has existed for only twenty years – is impressive. What these widely differing groups have in common – and in common with the history of evangelicalism – is a shared theology based on a belief in salvation by faith alone, on personal conversion, and 'metanoia' – a form of repentance involving a 'restart', a 'new life in Christ', being 'born again'. Along with this core go other beliefs, including the Second Coming of Christ (as we approach the year 2000 this is likely to prove important), the authority of the Bible, and the direct manifestations of the Holy Spirit in 'charisms' – gifts of grace, including talking in tongues, prophecy and miracle-working. From this theology have emerged certain other factors: an authoritarian style of leadership, which at the same time can give enormous responsibility and power to very young people; an imaginatively gripping vision of the Kingdom of God here on earth; an emotionally exciting style of worship; a freedom from bureaucratic procedures; and a justification for savage intolerance of anyone who does not agree with you.

This neo-evangelical movement, however, also has elements which are not found in the older tradition. These include the view that the mass media, far from being iniquitous, are an instrument for God's work; a conviction that matters of personal morality are – or should be – the concern of the state; a very direct belief in the power of the Devil; a willingness to accept – indeed, embrace – leadership from the USA; an organizational network which it is hard not to admire; and a political climate which encourages the belief that personal success is a sign of moral superiority.

I would like to suggest that what we are seeing is something new, and rather frightening. It is not revival of fundamentalism but, rather, a committed attempt – which is at present apparently proving alarmingly successful – by the 'New Right' to wrest the tradition of radical biblicism from the Left. It is part of a wider political movement, visible both in the USA and in Britain, towards the creation of a 'radical conservatism'.

Historically, within the Christian West, biblicism – holding up the authority of the biblical text against the authority of the Church's hierarchical structures – has provided an important moral and imaginative impetus for radical movements. It is a claim to 'own' the text, to have the right to interpret and use it. This was clearly understood by both 'sides' in medieval England. The demands of the Peasants' Revolt were closely tied into and fuelled by the demand for a vernacular Bible. At that time the Bible was officially available only in Latin. It was against both canon (church) and secular law to translate it. The political sensitivity of the text continued after the Reformation: there were strict political controls on the translation even of the Authorized Version under James I, and alternative versions remained criminal. The Revolt demanded a biblical text that would be directly accessible to the peasant classes, unmediated, unowned by the educated and priestly castes, who were seen (correctly) as being in allegiance with feudal powers. The famous slogan of the Peasants' Revolt:

> When Adam delved and Eve span,
> Who was then the gentleman?

shows the force of the argument. (And, incidentally, the concept that these ancient liberties included women should not be overlooked, despite the obvious division of labour.)

This pattern continued: the basis of the Protestant Reformation was the reclamation not just of biblical life patterns, but of far more of the biblical text itself. In a more extreme form, the Levellers, the radical wing of the Cromwellian army, used their right to their own reading of the Bible not merely to claim individual religious freedom (as opposed to the presbyterial and puritanical model of the Cromwellites) but also to challenge all systems and laws based on class or status. (The Levellers' demands for universal suffrage include the first English petition for women's suffrage on record.) Methodism presented itself as freedom from the restrictive worship of the state, in the power of an 'unfettered gospel of biblical salvation'. As George Eliot explores in *Adam Bede*, early Methodism gave new and dynamic authority to women – *despite* the Pauline injunctions against women preaching.

The role of biblicism in South American liberation movements is well known; and biblical rhetoric has played an important part in some African Nationalist movements. In 1829 David Walker issued his *Appeal to the Coloured Citizens of the World*, which:

> is steeped in Biblical language and prophecy. It is certainly one of the most remarkable religious documents of the Protestant era, rivalling in its righteous indignation and Christian radicalism Luther's *Open Letter to the Christian nobility of the German nation*, published in Wittenberg in 1520. (Wilmor, 1973)

Biblicism became part of the motivating force for emancipation and black liberation. The point was not lost on white slaveowners: 'black Christians who were ardent in their devotions had to be watched carefully'.

Thus there has been a historical pattern whereby biblicist Christianity has been radical, while less biblical modes – either ecclesial (those that stress the Church's authority to own and interpret the tradition) or pietistic (those that stress the mystical and moral condition of the individual, with rewards in heaven as the ultimate objective) – have favoured the status quo and have therefore met with the approval of the Establishment and been, in that sense, reactionary.

There have always, of course, been limitations to this radicalism: in the first place, the biblical text itself was never the direct word of the God of Freedom, but was the text, developed by a priestly (that is to say, ecclesial) caste in their own interest and for their own ends. Although parts of the text do indeed speak of the freedom in God that God's people have a right to enjoy, those sections are usually directed at the enemy 'out there' – the Egyptians, the Medes and Persians, the persecutors of the early Church, and so on.

Paul, for example, can rhapsodize about the freedom from the Law to be enjoyed by the baptized: but he is also quite convinced that slaves should be subject to their masters and women should keep silent in church and not presume to teach, and they can be safely 'saved through childbearing' and through obedience to their husbands.

Claiming authority from the Bible must also mean subjecting oneself to its authority. Radical biblicism is in constant danger of slipping over into legalistic and conservative fundamentalism. Three groups come to mind as finding ways out of this potential trap: the first were the Montanists, a second-century heretical group who maintained very strongly that the Bible was not a closed book – that revelation continued through the work of contemporary ecstatic prophecy, and that the Bible was therefore not necessarily the ultimate court of appeal. The Society of Friends argued for the autonomy and freedom of the individual by making what their founder, Charles Fox, called 'the light within' – the individual spark of holiness integral to the fullness of personhood – the ultimate authority: the Bible was no more than an (important) guide. Certain Black Pentecostalist Churches also seem to have escaped the double bind – partly by the radical step of claiming 'the black Christ' over against the ecclesial ownership of Jesus. Since Jesus was not in fact 'black', this claim alters the relationship of the community to the biblical text. It prioritizes solidarity and need over a static, authoritative, immutable text.

It is in this sense, then, that it is necessary to see the current 'moral majority' evangelicalism both here and in the USA as a completely new phenomenon – one which, in a complex way, uses many of the discourses of 'old' Christian radicalism to new and conservative ends. Simply calling it 'fundamentalism', with the current load that word carries, is not useful. While the rhetoric of the Left in Britain is still so profoundly informed by nineteenth-century radical Nonconformist (and hence biblicist) discourses, simply dismissing the whole movement as reactionary is nearly impossible. It is more useful, perhaps, to consider why it has developed now – and, in the context of this chapter, what sort of impact it has, or might have, on the lives of women, both those involved first hand, as members of the movement, and the rest of us whose autonomy is directly challenged by neo-evangelicalism and its claims on the state.

I do not want here to attempt an analysis, or even a history, of the growth from the US South of neo-evangelicalism, nor of the radical conservatism which forms the larger social context in which it is flourishing. I do, however, want to suggest some reasons why this ideology is apparently so attractive to women, and where its particular dangers to the development of women's autonomy lie.

It is extremely difficult to find any hard statistics about the membership of neo-evangelical churches – either here or in the USA. However, it is impossible to escape the observation that here, as in other segments of the Christian churches, numerically women are well represented and are probably even in the majority; although the public leadership is predominantly male. More importantly, the social platform (as opposed to the purely 'spiritual' aspects) of the movement is dominated by issues which the Women's Liberation Movement has claimed over the last twenty years as women's issues: pornography, abortion, sexuality, the family, and also 'law and order' which – as Beatrix Campbell makes clear in *Iron Ladies* (1988) – is a 'women's issue' relating closely to feminist questions about safety and freedom. Indeed, the superficially strange alliances, and shared political demands for legislative censorship, that we are currently seeing between moral-majority evangelicals and radical feminist groups, both opposed to pornography, underlines the complexity of the relationship.

I am suggesting that although many women in neo-evangelical sects see themselves as bitterly opposed to feminism, which is contrary to biblical teachings on the role of women and has also criticized the family and (in popular belief) advocated sexual anarchy, in fact they have been profoundly

33

influenced by it. Moreover, the women's movement and neo-evangelicalism share certain styles: both value emotion and the expression of emotion in ways that are alien to the dominant culture. Both stress the solidarity and affirmation of the group; and a direct physical involvement. Both use drama and symbolism to express their criticism of dominant culture; and both take the restructuring of the 'self' as their ethical starting point.

In particular, neo-evangelicalism has taken up the feminist slogan that 'the personal is the political', and in that sense it agrees with the women's movement that nothing falls into an entirely private sphere. Furthermore, neo-evangelicalism has demonstrated an impressive corporate, anti-individualistic and public stance, which is so far from the pietistic churchiness or passivity in the face of the status quo that feminism has been used to confronting that it has been very hard to contest. In certain areas the commitment to direct action and the corporate unity within neo-evangelicalism have actually forced feminist retreats.

The history of Rescue is perhaps a good example. Rescue is a direct-action anti-abortionist organization. Founded and well established in the USA, in the last three years it has developed branches in this country, not merely inspired by but actively supported (and probably funded) from the USA. Its principal activity – indeed, its whole *modus operandi* – is to mass-picket places in which abortions are actually performed and endeavour to prevent both the clinic's personnel and women seeking abortions from entering the premises. Rescue members use tactics gleaned from the peace movement – no violence, passive resistance to arrest, the sit-in/lie-down techniques. They also engage very directly with individual women, offering them both alternative means of support if they continue with the pregnancy and highly emotive material emphasizing the 'humanity' of the foetal child.

The success of Rescue is hotly disputed: its claims to have 'saved lives' and to have persuaded individuals have been questioned both by pro-choice organizations and by the press.

The distress caused, however, is not: Rescue members do not dispute it. On the contrary, they insist that an emotional response to abortion is a proper one, that women persuaded by their presence are women who had not previously been given an opportunity to face up to the emotional implications of their choice, and that their choice was not, therefore, a free or complete one. To some extent Rescue has already wrested the direct, street-action, politicized approach to abortion away from the women's movement, which is increasingly forced to defend abortion from a bourgeois individualist, or 'civil rights' position: to use the rhetoric of 'privacy', to repudiate the politics of feeling and experience, and to work more within the traditionally middle-class liberal parliamentary and lobby tradition, thus distancing the movement still further from a mass constituency and from working-class women. Feminist and pro-choice writers have increasingly acknowledged ambivalence around specific choices to abort in a way that would have been unacceptable ten years ago; the tone of much feminist writing is now apologetic and exploratory.

In a different form, the same thing is happening within the campaigns around representation and, particularly, pornography. In the late 1960s and 1970s Mary Whitehouse and the National Viewers' and Listeners' Association – in a campaign that was overtly puritanical – saw themselves as defending already existing standards, as the humble but loyal members of an existing Establishment under threat from wild youth and dangerous commies. The NVLA explicitly distanced itself from feminism, and from the style of feminist politics – indeed, it saw and presented feminism as the enemy: as anti-morality and 'family values'. (This was made easier, of course, by the far less establishment and respectable image that 'Women's Lib.' then carried, and by the odd combination of socialist alignment and sexual libertarianism within the early Women's Liberation Movement.)

The newer evangelical-based coalitions, however, do not present themselves as the supporters of an existing

Establishment, as the allies of present governments, but, on the contrary, as *the* radical movement for change, and as the providers of protection for those whom the Establishment has neglected or abused. The effectiveness of their demands for censorship of sexually explicit material has deeply divided the women's movement – between those who are reluctant to be associated in any way with either the language and imagery of the radical Right, or with the use of state apparatus to control and direct appropriate representations of sexuality; and those who, in order to protect women from the assault of pornography, are prepared to use the power and effectiveness of the Right to bring about necessary preventive legislation. The lobbying skills and emotional pressure from the neo-evangelical Right have forced into the public arena differences and antagonisms between feminists which had previously been contained; and has further weakened the capacity of the women's movement to develop a united front, or an effective voice, on this extremely difficult issue.

The reader may note in all this a kind of sneaking admiration for the techniques and power of the neo-evangelical movements – or, at the very least, a real respect for a worthy enemy! There may be some truth in this, but both as a socialist feminist and as a Christian myself I am profoundly convinced of the dangers of these neo-evangelical movements and very much aware of how deftly they exploit and utilize the socially constructed inferiority of women.

First, despite the rhetoric of 'freedom in Christ', neo-evangelical movements are highly authoritarian. Moreover, because the source of the leadership's authority is initially 'charismatic' – that is, it resides in the personal (supposedly God-given) gifts of the individual leader and is not conferred by the community through any sort of process – it is extremely hard to challenge. The freedom from bureaucracy can also be seen as a version of the tyranny of individualism. This individual charismatic leadership can easily be turned into a cult; and it is undeniable that a major evangelist with a substantial following is exposed to certain marked temptations to abuse his power (including – and not only in the USA – the chance to get most unbiblically rich). But although these charismatic leaders draw their initial authority from their own skills and dynamism *as preachers*, they are able to use the authority of the biblical text to strengthen their personal authority. They are the ones who choose what sections of that text their followers will hear, and they have the power to interpret them. This ability to dictate the content and the interpretation of the preached text is necessarily increased by tele-evangelism, where the 'congregation' necessarily becomes completely passive; and by the mass rally, where the control and emotional manipulation of events lies so powerfully in the hands of the organizers.

In this sense the authority within neo-evangelicalism does not really lie with the Bible but with those who claim and have the authority to interpret it. This authority is, of course, identical to the most oppressive articulations of the Roman Catholic magisterium, and the claims of Papal Infallibility, but is not in any way contained either by a long and carefully developed tradition, or by 'constitutional' or formal limits. While the authority of a non-answerable leadership presses heavily on the freedoms of all the members, in this context it especially limits women, because the biblical authority which the individual leaders claim is usually very directly based on both the Old Testament and the Pauline writings: that is, it prefers (along with most other sections of Christendom) those elements of the biblical text which are most strongly opposed to any significant leadership role for women.[1]

This brings me to a *second* serious danger for women within these sections of Christian practice. Like all fundamentalisms, the neo-evangelical biblical readings are highly selective, not to say peculiar. I, no doubt, like everyone else, bring my own critical interpretations to the biblical text, but it is hard to find a reading of the Bible which does not strongly suggest that the Old Testament condones polygamy and the New Testament is highly critical of – if not actually 'anti-' – the concept of the family.

Taken as a whole, the most serious moral offences – those most consistently condemned – in the biblical texts are (a) ritual pollution, including breaches of the complex dietary laws; (b) usury (lending money on interest); (c) allowing state institutions too much power; and (d) standing in judgement on one's neighbour. None of these figures in the popular discourses of neo-fundamentalism. Or – to put it another way – the biblical text is absolutely clear that the consumption of prawn cocktails is totally contrary to the Law of God, while homosexuality is barely mentioned and the few references to it are contradictory and uncertain: this is not what one would glean from the public pronouncements of neo-evangelicalism.

The bulk of the biblical texts are not, in fact, a series of moral injunctions; they constitute a large and complex but highly artful body of different writings – narratives, poetry, and curious genres not easily decoded today. However, ambivalence, sophistication, artistry are not very amenable to an authoritarian teaching ministry whose principal medium is the extended sermon. It is easier to break the text into small manageable chunks, and to focus especially on those that provide direct ethical directives. A great many of these, as it happens, are strong expressions of patriarchal domination. Thus it is much easier, in the context of a charismatic harangue, to claim Pauline authority for the self-confirming directive that women should not preach, or lead, than it is to present the complicated delicate stories in which women are both commanded to teach and obey that instruction. Or the narratives that, while not directly mentioning women, make it clear that the power of the spirit is free to fall on anyone it chooses.

For example, the Creation mythologies represented in the first chapters of Genesis are actually rather complicated. In none of them do women exactly emerge shining with divine glory compared to men. However, a full reading makes it clear that the simplifiable statement that Adam shall have dominion over Eve because she has been so wicked is not the only moral to come out of the story. Nevertheless, it is about the only one that can be reduced to a direct and usable authorized quotation about how people 'ought' to behave. Even if one accepted in the first place that these Creation narratives are an adequate scientific account of the beginnings of the universe supplied direct by God for the moral edification of humanity, one would still not have to make this the central reading. Neo-fundamentalism, however, does make that claim, for reasons that are not inevitably dictated by the texts.

To summarize: in the first place, the biblical texts are undeniably patriarchal texts; in the second place, reduced to such a reading, they allow even less space for women's autonomy and authority than they might be persuaded to in a different context and within a different exegetical framework or impulse of interpretation. (A feminist exegesis, for example, produces entirely different readings of the same biblical texts. See, for example, Elizabeth Schustler Fiorenza's *In Memory of Her* [1986].) If women are persuaded to accept evangelical types of biblical interpretation as the only route to salvation, their integrity and self-valuation are inevitably going to be seriously damaged. Moreover, their capacity to make common ground with other women, to see a shared interest, is going to be undercut.

Thirdly, the emotion that is released within neo-evangelical Christianity is emotion for its own sake. Although it is highly valued, it is valued not as material for analysis but simply as 'proof' of the presence of God. In this sense it is not even 'owned' emotion. The strong sense of identity and desire for change that women have gained through the recognition of the strength of their own emotion and the power of its expression is short-circuited; it cannot be used to any practical or even psychological end. Members of these sects would deny this latter statement, of course; the emotion, they would argue, does indeed lead to self-recognition and a desire for change (repentance and conversion); but since the recognition is of one's self as an individual 'sinner' and the change is to be 'born again' – an experience which is both infantilizing and separates one from the community of other women – this seems unreassuring. Within the linguistic imagery of a male God and a correct feminine response, ideas of letting God take control, giving one's life to Jesus, submission and obedience, such validation of the emotions seems suspect.

But most seriously, this combination of dependence, submission to authority and transcendent certainty, which seem to be the principal factors in the success of these religions, leads to an almost desperate avoidance of difference. This is particularly dangerous when so much of the agenda is personal. Neo-fundamentalism's twin obsessions with Satan and Sex (neither of them, it should be stressed, remotely central to biblical teaching) lead very easily to a frightening level of self-righteousness and judgement. Difference is too quickly labelled deviance: the rabid homophobia of neo-evangelical groups is a frightening demonstration of this; and the 'divine authority' with which it is propagated allows space for seriously aggressive anti-gay activity. Responses to AIDS as God's judgement, Jews as 'Christ-killers', people of different ethnic origins as pagans (hence demonic) and feminists as unnatural (where 'natural' is given the added weight of being *also* simultaneously supernatural) all show the difficulties in handling difference either of choice or of personal identity with any tolerance or breadth whatsoever. It is from these perspectives that neo-fundamentalism enters the political arena, in direct competition with both Left and liberal progressives; and it is here that it becomes dangerous not just to women who find themselves involved in such cults, but to women more generally.

The radical Right challenges the liberal position of individual freedom and the right to difference on the grounds that our lives do not properly belong to ourselves, but to God; and if we will not admit this and hand ourselves over into God's power, as interpreted by the authorized cult leaders, then we are damned anyway, so there is no particular need, or even point, in treating deviants or their ideas with respect. The challenge to classic socialism, however, works on exactly the opposite premiss: it is only the individual who sins, not the structures which are outside the business of the divine. For as long as they have not acknowledged the Kingship of Christ they are sinning; therefore their claims to collectivity are part of sin. Their corporateness is therefore satanic and calls not for tolerance, understanding or negotiation, but for confrontation.

Because of the authoritarian structures of leadership, the very real feelings of power and personal security generated by the sense of being 'saved' can be exercised only as power over others. And this power is entirely justified as being for the others' 'real' good – or, at least, for the good of their innocent children, who will otherwise be murdered in the womb, sexually depraved or (at best) left godless and damned. Last year at the Wembley Praise Day, Noel Stanton, an American charismatic leader, addressed a 25,000-strong crowd with the words: 'You are not meant to sin; you are not meant to be a moral cripple . . . you are meant to rule!'

There is a sense in which neo-fundamentalism brings back into the political arena precisely those elements that the feminization of religious experience, under earlier capitalism, attempted to remove. By privatizing – or domesticizing – ethics and spirituality, and by maximizing gender difference (the whole argument of separate spheres, the moral and spiritual superiority of women which needed protection from contamination in the 'real world', and so forth), Victorian society succeeded to a considerable extent in eliminating awkward Christian social principles from the capitalist workplace and international power-broking. The utopian Left's and feminism's insistence that these so-called private issues of morality, and particularly of sexuality, belonged in the political – or public – sphere set an agenda which has allowed the radical Right access to that sphere too. The fact that the political agenda of moral-majority Christians seems so determinedly set by feminism's concerns emphasizes these points.

The problem is that all this might be seen as a rather amusing American aberration were it not for the ideological strength that the radical Right in general can draw from the

discourse of neo-evangelicalism: entrepreneurial capitalism –
'each man for himself and the devil take the hindmost' – is
somewhat lacking in emotive force unless you can actually
believe in a devil only too eager to take the hindmost; if you
can link individual endeavour to eternal salvation, even at the
most subliminal level, there is a much stronger chance of
putting your message across.

It is too easy to assume that neo-evangelicalism is a cranky
movement, a fairly insignificant articulation of the frustrations
and self-righteousnesses of the right-wing segment of the
lower middle classes. Although the style and approach of
British evangelicalism are not the same as those in the USA,
there is clear evidence that the British version is learning fast,
its lobbying power is increasing and its influence is growing.
Some of Margaret Thatcher's closest advisers were evangelicals – including Brian Griffiths, former head of the Number
10 policy unit. Under her leadership the Conservative Family
Campaign, a pressure group of thirty-one backbench Conservative MPs, achieved some notable successes: they wrote the
clauses on collective acts of worship and 'predominantly
Christian' religious education (both of which must be seen as
dangerous to multicultural education) for the 1988 Education
Reform Act. They also claim to have been responsible for the
clauses removing the powers over sex education from the
Local Educational Authorities and handing them over to
parents and governors in 1986; and instrumental in getting
Clause 28 of the Local Government Act 1988 through the
House of Lords.

The Evangelical Alliance, along with Christian Broadcasting Council, Care Campaigns and other neo-evangelical
groups, co-ordinated a highly skilful lobbying campaign which
has led to the government changing its mind (and its Bill)
over the right of religious groups to own television and radio
stations. Although the Green Paper proposed not to permit
such ownership, the Act not only does allow but also increases
the freedoms of religious programmes, particularly in the
crucial area of appeals and advertisements. One company,

Vision Broadcasting International, has already been granted a licence for transmitting on cable television; and one, United Christian Broadcasters, has a radio licence.

More overtly political is a new group called the Movement for Christian Democracy, launched at the end of 1990 by Ken Hargreaves MP (Conservative) and David Alton (the Liberal Democrat responsible for one of the Private Members' Bills aimed at curtailing the 1968 Abortion Act). The MCD, which already has over 2,000 members, aims for 15,000 within the next two years. Its programme is clear: it intends to 'deliver the Christian vote' at elections to individual candidates who will endorse and support its objectives. It is a known fact that a very small, committed block vote can have a major effect in marginal constituencies. Although in theory the group could support members of any party, in effect it will be an anti-Labour organization for as long as the Labour Party continues to support women's right of choice over abortion. The potential power of such organized voting cannot long escape the attention of aspiring politicians or political parties.

Thus no sneaking admiration for tactical skills, based on placing apparent political and personal power in the hands of those more used to the experience of powerlessness; nor any understanding of the frustrations and powerlessness which lead individuals into right-wing neo-biblicist movements, can blind us to the real threat they present. A newly powerful radical right wing, drawing its strength from individualist populism, will support and encourage such an ideology. Ultimately, a right-wing government will find it in its interest to buy the support of such groups with titbits of sexual and other repressions, because these are not its ultimate concern. None the less the Left, and feminism in particular, must not ignore the high prestige that such cults can confer on their members, nor the potential and actual rhetorical force of the biblical texts.

A feminism which empowers (however relatively) liberal, educated bourgeois women, economically and socially, without similarly engaging with the structural disempowerments of less privileged women, will not be able to contest the threat to our freedoms which neo-evangelicalism imposes. There is an urgent political need to understand the hold that such movements exercise rhetorically and literally, and to think more creatively about ways of challenging them.

Note

1. Within the Church of England it is interesting to see the new alliance between the traditionally polarized Catholic and evangelical parties in opposition to the ordination of women to the priesthood. While one group has a fundamentalist approach to scripture, the other has a similar approach to the historic tradition of the Church. Both have a more authoritarian understanding of Christian leadership than the liberals. It is also interesting that although the independent black-led Pentecostalist Churches have many superficial points of style in common with the neo-evangelical groups, one of the conspicuous differences is their openness to female leadership; this springs, in part, from their very different – and much less static – understanding of the Bible and its authority. Nothing in this chapter is meant to be applied directly to black Pentecostalism, which is a completely separate phenomenon.

Women and the Inverted Pyramid of the Black Churches in Britain

ELAINE FOSTER

*H*istorically, there has been a dramatic rise, both quantitatively and qualitatively, in the participation of women in the Black-led Churches in Britain. There has not, however, been a corresponding rise in women's access to the positions of power within the church hierarchy. This chapter traces the historical background and the present state of inequality between women and men within the British Black-led church structures, and uses material from interviews with women church activists to assess the conflict.

Beginnings

There is a clear correspondence between the number of women present in the initial stages of Black-led Churches and the general pattern of migration from the Caribbean to Britain. It is generally believed that men were the first to migrate, followed by spouses, and then later, children. For example, in 1955, 62 per cent of those migrating from Jamaica, and 85 per cent of those from Dominica, were men. By 1960 this had dropped to 57 per cent and 59 per cent respectively. The number of children arriving from Jamaica rose from 331 in 1955 to 2,430 in 1960 (Davidson, 1962).

By the early 1960s, the sexual levels of migration began to even out – a result of several factors. Not only did spouses and female dependants increasingly arrive to join male relatives, but more independent women came, for example, to study nursing. There was also the combination of a high birth rate amongst West Indian women, most of whom were of childbearing age, and a relatively low death rate amongst this population.

Church membership mirrored these developments. Between the early 1960s and the end of the 1970s there was at first a steady and then a rapid increase in the number of converts and members added to many Black-led Churches. A number of sources discuss the gender breakdown of church membership. Malcolm Calley, in his study of the male/female composition of Black-led Churches in the 1960s (1965), stated: 'It is only since 1961 that they [the churches] have started to acquire the preponderance of female members characteristic of them in the West Indies.' Photographs of that period show both that women were gradually outnumbering men, and that they were active members.

Finally, in my interviews with the women themselves, several were able to recall the large number of women in their church groups and to point to their significant involvement in the prayer band, the choir and the growing Ladies' Auxiliaries – aptly called, in one organization, the Ladies' Willing Workers Band, and in another the Ladies' Missionary Band.

All the women I interviewed had been church attenders and often active members in the Caribbean before they came to Britain. One woman claimed that in the Caribbean, 'Everybody went to church.' Although this is not entirely accurate, it is true that religious activities, whether they were church- or sect-related, were part and parcel of the communities' *modus vivendi* and *modus operandi*.

Many women had been taught that Great Britain was the locus of all Christian activity, so the desire to continue to attend church in such a Christian country was natural.

The Inverted Pyramid

I would like to offer the following, based on the extent to which women have made the Black-led Churches their own, as a model of the relationship that exists between male and female church members. The model consists of two pyramids: one is upright, the other is inverted. They are superimposed on one another. The first pyramid is inverted and represents the 'female' Church. In this pyramid lies the spirituality, the life-giving and life-sustaining nature of the Church. The second is the upright pyramid. It represents the Church in all its patriarchal and hierarchical glory, and contains all leadership, juridical and priestly roles.

The first pyramid is inverted to represent the vast number of women actively involved in the spiritual life and upkeep of the churches. Regardless of how the men consider their own positions in the organizations, there is a sense in which they hold those positions only on the approval of the women. There is a silent collusion regarding this, one which is accepted by both sides. This mutual collusion results in a sense of agreement and avoids conflict.

There are many ways in which the women, if they wished, could defy, 'usurp', paralyse or neutralize the men within these organizations, 'but for the grace of God!'. When asked: 'What do you as women do in the Church today?', many of the women listed a large number of activities, but above all, as one woman said, 'Oh my Lord! We run the Church.' Others expanded on this:

> 'I'm local director for my church [Youth and Christian Education]. I'm assistant District Ladies' President, I'm on the District Youth Board, I'm in the catering department, sing in the choir, prayer band leader . . . Take, for example, the prayer band – how many men would you find in it? Two, and maybe about twelve, sixteen women.'

'They make the major contribution to the upkeep of the church, if it OK [sic] for them to be prominent in their finance [sic] and their presence, why can't they make major decisions?'

'If you take away the women from the church you wouldn't have anything left.'

The following list of activities spans the pastoral work of one woman pastor. It is unlikely that any of her male counterparts would be involved in such a comprehensive way with his congregation:

'When I'm not preaching, I'm cooking. When I'm not cooking, I'm sewing. When I'm not sewing, I'm visiting. When I'm not visiting, I'm praying, and my whole life is a life of work wrapped up in God. And socially, because you know I like to do a bit of community work. I go visiting the old people, say a word of comfort to them. It makes my life worthwhile living. And without that I don't think I am a Christian.'

The concept of women running the church, but men leading it, seems common in Caribbean women's understanding of the dynamics of their relationship with their men. The Jamaican poet Louise Bennett calls it the 'cunning' of the Jamaican oman. As she notes in her poem 'Jamaica Oman':

Jamaica oman cunny, sah!
Is how dem jinnal so?
Look how long dem liberated
An de man dem never know!

Look how long Jamaica oman
– Modder, sister, wife, sweetheart –
Outa road an eena yard deh pon
A dominate her part!

Jamaica oman know she strong,
She know she tallawah
But she no want her pickney-dem
Fi start call her 'Puppa'

So the cunny Jamma oman
Gwan like pants suit is a style,
An Jamaica man no know she wear
De trousiz all de while!

In a critique of Bennett's poem, Dr Carolyn Cooper comments on the relationship between males and females in Caribbean societies, where 'Cunning rather than overt male/female confrontation is the preferred strategy for maintaining equanimity' (ed. Kwesi Owusu, 1988).

In these terms, it appears that the women are more concerned about the survival of the community than about who leads or manages the organization. Dissent and instability must, therefore, be avoided. But there is a benign conspiratorial knowing among the women that without them the churches 'would not exist'!

Implicit in the voices of these women is a modest selflessness. They saw their involvement in terms of what they were 'called' to give, as a God-given responsibility. Therefore, these responsibilities were to be executed with grace and humility:

I'm not my own, I'm not my own, Saviour I belong to thee,
All I am and all I hope for, Saviour let me walk with thee.

Women's Influence in Black-led Churches

A Black-led church community in Britain is made up predominantly of Black women. The estimated percentage of women in Black-led Churches given to me by different church leaders varies between 65 per cent and 95 per cent. These women sustain the churches. Some of the departments – the Sunday schools, the Youth and Christian Education Departments, the choirs (which are commonly known as auxiliaries in the churches) – should rightly be defined as the foundations of the organizations. Historically, these 'auxiliaries' were the places where the women's labour and influence were most obvious.

From very early on, the women were the inspiration and the workforce behind the Sunday schools. Many of the young people who were recruited to the Sunday school were the children not of church members but of people who, while themselves not church attenders, thought that it was necessary at least for their children to attend Sunday school. Out of this band of children and young people, many converts were made to the developing churches.

The other youth and Christian education activities in which the women led the way included contacting the families with new-born babies to be blessed, the Youth Camps, Youth Weekends, Training Workshops, Youth Conventions and Youth Clubs, to name but a few. The women were not only teaching the youth the fundamentals of the faith, but also defining their moral values and standards. Many aspects of culture and tradition, language and folklore were transmitted by the women through these activities. Since such activities were for both members and non-members of the churches, they touched on the entire community.

Through their involvement in the choir, and therefore as lay ministers, women ministered through songs and choruses in all the main services. The choir and the women in it were often presented as the epitome of the holy.

Black-led Churches were, in their very early years, largely self-financing. At a local level they often defined their rules and directed themselves. It is widely believed that these churches are possibly the only Black organizations in Britain today that did not, in their initial stages of development, depend upon or seek revenue funding from government or from charitable organizations. What has not been recognized, however, is the tremendous amount of financial support which the women gave, and continue to give.

On the basis of the jobs women did and the wage or salaries they were getting, and consequently what they probably tithed to the church, it is just to assume that women gave proportionately more to their church than men did. As well as their own personal giving, the women found ways to generate funds from within their local situations and to fund-raise successfully from outside their organizations.

The burden of the financial upkeep of the church fell so heavily upon the women's shoulders that it is probable that without them the Afro-Caribbean communities would never have had their own churches. One of the sisters I interviewed told me:

> 'The church wouldn't survive without the women . . . I mean, the women contribute in all different ways, financially, spiritually, because you find that the women are always praying and travelling more so than the men. When it comes to finance, you can't stop a woman fe raise funds. If you have a survey . . . to see how much the men contribute, how much they bring in and compare to the women . . . the women knock them out . . . Seventy-five per cent more than the men . . . The women are more dedicated and whatever a woman intends to do, nothing stops her.'

Another sister intervened with a pertinent biblical reminder:

'Mark you, originally it was the women, even in the Bible, it was women who went with the first message of Christ's resurrection.'

Given that the women believe that they run the churches, is there anything about the churches that is uniquely womanist? Let us examine the worship services.

Worship in Black-led Churches is communal. From the singing, extempore praying, dancing, testifying and affirmation of the sermon, we see the participation – or the opportunity for participation – by the whole congregation. There is a vibrancy and a liveliness which reflect the style of the women. There is no place for isolation in Black-led church worship. Worship provides for fellowship, comfort, edification and exhortation. It draws heavily upon oral and other traditions associated with the members' African past. For example, members are often asked to 'claim the victory' by giving a handclap offering to the Lord. Singing and 'dancing in the Lord or in the Spirit' are common features of many worship services.

However, the dominant factor in worship is the guidance and 'moving' of the Holy Spirit, and women are expected to be attuned to this. In many ways the women act as keepers and purveyors of socio-religious traditions in Black-led Churches. There was a time when most worship services began with what was then known as a 'song service'. Although it is no longer popularly known by that name, worship services still begin with a session of songs and choruses, usually led by a team of women. The task of this team is to 'get everyone in the right attitude for worship', or to 'warm up' the worshippers. Their duties extend to choosing the appropriate songs and choruses for worship, and setting the mood and pace in which worship will continue to take place. Perhaps the women also choose songs and choruses which specifically reflect their concerns, as well as the perceived needs of the congregation.

Extempore prayer, by its nature, includes both those who can and cannot command the written form. Because such prayer is dynamic, it is a useful tool with which the believer can respond to his or her changing daily spiritual and material needs, as well as those of other sisters and brothers.

Testimonies essentially depend upon openness and a sharing of experiences, in the knowledge that what is said will not be used to ridicule the testifier, or become a source of idle gossip. No one testimony is ever deemed better than another, so there is no hierarchy of testators based on sex, age or leadership status. Since women are the predominant group of people testifying, to some extent they define and standardize testimonies. They provide both the idiom – that is, the language which is shared by all the congregation – and the formula – that is, the structure of the testimony. The subtleties and the interplay between text and subtext in testimonies are also, in the main, defined by women.

Leontine T. C. Kelly, in her article 'Preaching in the Black Tradition' (1981), gives a vivid portrayal of a woman's testimony and the responses of the congregation:

> WOMAN: I know how Daniel felt in the Lion's Den!
> RESPONSE: (Men, children and the other women): Yes!
> WOMAN: I know how the Hebrew children felt in the fiery furnace!
> RESPONSE: (crescendos): YES!

(The 'I knows' would continue in an ascending tonal excitement with companion response until a climatic affirmation was spoken.)

> WOMAN: But, like Job, I know my Redeemer lives!
> I know that he goes to prepare a place for me!
> I know that this old world is not my home!

(In the midst of the emotion-packed affirmation some personal experience of the week would be shared, and the testimony would come to a close on a peaceful plea.)

> WOMAN: Brothers and Sisters, just pray for me that I may press on! That I don't grow no ways weary [the ascending tone begins again, and the entire group is lifted with it], no ways tired. I just want to press on to see what the end will be!

(The 'Amens' and the 'Thank you, Jesus' betrayed not only the emotion of the moment, but the experiential sharing of a common harshness of life. The emotional response testified to faith in a God who would, in the end, bring victory to the believer.)

In Black-led Churches it is the practice of the word of God which counts. By their fruit you shall know them. The real 'work' of the Church – whether defined in terms of the praying, the fasting, the laying on of hands, or the cooking, the counselling or the cleaning – are activities almost solely undertaken by women. Women also see to the physical environment in which worship takes place by making it comfortable and welcoming.

Women have created the context in which the social, spiritual and emotional needs of the congregation – and, at times, the wider Black community – are taken care of. Black women in the churches are often the ones who share the pain and hurt of division in the family and the community. The women's ministry is well described by Letty Russell (1974) as 'curative diakonia, in the healing of wounds of those who have become victims of life; providing help to the sick, the hungry, the homeless'.

From their experiences as mothers, some women bring children into the 'fold', as in the highly symbolic naming ceremony performed by the Church of the Cherubim and Seraphim, an independent Church with origins in Nigeria. Here the prophetesses of the church march up with the child and the mother to the altar, where they are presented to the priest, who performs the ceremony. The women cry with other mothers whose sons have been criminalized or involved in deviant activities. It is the women in the churches who, in the end, embrace the young unmarried mother and her child, even though the evidence of her 'sins' is there for all to see.

Sexism in Black-led Churches

Black women in the churches are part of a collective Black history steeped in colonialism and imperialism. Race, class and sex oppression have always underpinned their existence. In *Ain't I a Woman*, bell hooks makes the connections in the following way:

> In a retrospective examination of the black female slave experience, sexism looms as large as racism as an oppressive force in the lives of black women. Institutionalized sexism –

that is, patriarchy – formed the base of the American social structure along with racial imperialism. Sexism was an integral part of the social and political order which colonizers brought with them.

Racist oppression in Britain has been perpetuated by the policies of successive governments, the activities of various institutions and agencies (in some cases supported by legislation which is racist in outcome, if not intent) and the actions of white individuals and communities. Institutionalized and personal sexism is perpetuated by white and Black men. Taken together, these are powerful forces of oppression in the lives of Black women. And although the sisters in Black-led Churches have found their local fellowships life-affirming, a source of strength and void of racism, they cannot say that the churches are free from sexism. Black men have not begun to address the question of their sexism, and Black women appear to be far too protective to force the issue.

It seems that what needs to happen is for women and men to 'unpack' the term sin, and name sexism as one of the sins which perpetuates inequality and oppression. How can we all be one in Christ Jesus when women are held back from fulfilling their potential in the life and work of the Church? How can Black men be helped to rid themselves of the guilt and burden of sexism, and to be whole persons?

In Praise of Women and of Sisters in the Lord

Part of this process of liberating the community from all that binds it is the uplifting and celebration of the history and contributions of the sisters. It almost goes without saying that Black Pentecostal Churches in Britain do not generally have any icons of Black females. Only in the African Methodist Episcopal Church did I hear reference made in the liturgy to Harriet Tubman and Sojourner Truth of the anti-slavery movement. They were remembered for their work in the struggle for freedom, and presented as examples for women to follow.

Even so, other possibilities for change already exist in the language and meanings in women's talks, through creative interpretation of the Bible around the theme of liberation from persecution, fear and captivity: liberation from sexism. For example, the majority of church women are from working-class backgrounds. They 'know' that the Gospel speaks consistently to their needs, and have developed ways of interpreting the scriptures in relation to their daily lives and experiences.

> 'We have persecution, we don't know how we are going to overcome it. Sometimes the mountain is so high, how we are going to get over it? Brother Paul said, "What can separate me from the love of God?". . . We can see many things that would separate us, but because we know in whom we believe – "Nay in all these things we are more than conquerors." You know sometimes the battle is really hard, we can hardly make it . . . He is our mighty rock. He is our everything.'

Persecution, the mountain, sorrow, heartache and trial are themes commonly repeated in the prayers, exhortations and testimonies of women, referring to the wide range of problems in their lives.

There is a strong tradition in songs and choruses which embody images of the Christian woman. The central messages of these songs are based upon an evangelical/Pentecostal interpretation of scripture, and could be categorized thus:

Wholeness and forgiveness from sin for women who are seen as particularly prone to adultery, as embodied in the image of the woman of Samaria in this song:

The woman of Samaria, the woman, she left her water pot and gone.
The woman of Samaria, the woman, she left her water pot and gone.

Jesus asked her for her husband and she said she had none, she said
she had none, she said she had none . . .

and

> Jesus gave her water that was not from the well,
> Jesus gave her water that was not from the well,
> She came there sinning and she went away singing,
> For Jesus gave her water that was not from the well.

Spiritual and physical cleansing for any woman, as seen in the
story of the woman of faith who had a haemorrhage, touched
Jesus, and was healed of her physical illness as well as of sin:

> Oh it is Jesus
> Yes, it is Jesus,
> It is Jesus in my soul,
> For I have touched the hem of his garment and his blood has
> made me whole.

The mother image is depicted as essential to the protection
and sustaining of the Christian family, so it is the mothers
who are remembered as bringing children to Jesus to be
blessed in another popular song:

> When mothers of Salem their children brought to Jesus,
> The stern disciples drove them back and bid them to depart,
> But Jesus saw them ere they went, and sweetly smiled and kindly
> said,
> 'Suffer the little children unto me.'

Woman as mother also teaches her children and prays for
their protection:

> My mother prayed for me, she taught me right from wrong,
> Of her I have sweet memories and now from me she's gone.

This subversion of the message of the scriptures also appears in the songs and choruses which seem to celebrate qualities of Christ which would be regarded as female. Christ is portrayed as a loving saviour, gentle, caring, forgiving and full of grace:

> In all the world around me I see his loving care . . . None other is so loving so good and kind . . .

Io Smith, a pastor in the New Testament Assembly, uses the image of mother as pastor:

> Women do succour the Church. When a woman is pastoring an assembly she is as close to the flock as to the child on her breast. They have a tender feeling towards someone in their struggle, and will give out to them as if they are breast-feeding a child. They watch their growth closely. Sometimes I have only to sit and listen to someone crying to know exactly what is coming behind that feeling. (1989)

Single Women in Black-led Churches

Despite their intimate involvement with the churches and the development of their own theological and ethical systems within them, women have not begun to confront certain other issues. In 1988 four of the leading Black-led Churches estimated that 60 per cent of the women in their congregations between the ages of eighteen and thirty-five were single. Also, there is a notice-able drop-out rate in this age range. In the past, women mainly left the Church either because they were having a relationship with an 'unsaved' man, or because they were pregnant. More recently, however, they have been leaving because of their disappointment with some of the church rules and regulations.

In my own congregation, about 50 per cent of the women in the thirty-six-to-sixty-five age group are married to men who are saved members of the Church, and the other 50 per cent to men who never became saved. In the latter case, most of the marriages would have taken place before the woman became a Christian, but there are a few exceptions. It follows that a Black-led Church can accurately be characterized as 'the Church of the single women'.

In recent years, the singleness factor has been high on the list of concerns of many churches, for the Church holds marriage between believers and the raising of children as a God-given privilege and as the foundation for the Church's growth and prosperity.

With hindsight, the churches can recognize the factors which have contributed to the disproportionate representation of women: evangelisation strategies which were geared more to women than men, support groups for women within the Church, and a strong commitment to ethical standards. Many churches are not sure what to do about this. Many church leaders, including the women, are fierce defenders of marriage, but will accept celibacy if God wills it. A number of older women who were victims of unplanned and early pregnancies, and of children born out of wedlock, fear any emulation by their daughters.

At the moment the churches' response to single women is at best insensitive. They often forget that these women have needs that are particular to them, and that they are not failures. As Elaine Storkey puts it:

> 'Single women often find churches unsympathetic and alienating with their contemporary focus on the family and their adulation of motherhood. If to be a truly successful Christian woman is to be a wife and mother, then surely they have failed on all accounts?'

The question of singleness can best be understood in the context of Caribbean societies. In the Caribbean, Pentecostal and evangelical Black-led Churches held strong beliefs about the high moral standards which would mark them out as different from the 'sexually permissive' societies around them and what was sometimes allowed in some of the 'nominal' churches. The late 1960s and 1970s were seen as years of radical permissiveness and lax sexual behaviour and, here in Britain, Black preachers preached hell and damnation on this sort of behaviour.

Rastafari was a strong influence amongst young Black people. Although they would deny that they were preaching loose morals, Rastafari rejected Christian marriage and taught that African people could not afford to commit genocide by using contraceptives. This was viewed by Black-led Churches as a potentially dangerous doctrine. Some churches, to counter such teachings, laid down stringent rules about how young women and men were to relate to each other. Courting young couples were chaperoned and people were encouraged to marry as soon as possible after the decision was made. A period of engagement was often seen as dangerous because it gave the couple the right to be together alone for periods of time in which they could easily 'commit fornication'. Even in church, young men and women had to sit in separate pews or on different sides.

Questions of courtship, sex and contraception were almost never raised publicly, as they were seen as matters for prayer rather than healthy debate. When questions about sex, contraception and abortion were raised at meetings, they were treated as if the very thought of these topics was sinful.

Today there is a range of responses to the question of singleness in Black-led churches. These are indicative of both the spiritualization of an eminently practical and material matter, and the lack of an appropriate and sensitive organizational response. Older women recalled – and agreed with – the oldest responses to singleness: pray that the Lord will find you a partner; wait upon the Lord; and 'Thou shall not be unequally yoked with unbelievers'. Those with faith in prayer felt that God would grant their prayers in accordance with His plan for their life.

Some women are resigned to the single life, but not without regrets. One of the women I interviewed said:

> 'The sad thing is that some of us Black females will have to realize that our lives are going to be lived without any men and that it is just going to be a relationship between us and God, and that's the way it is going to be . . . Because there are just not enough males in the church to go around and we have got to be realistic and not try to go against God's will.'

Another woman talked of her wish to have children, and of her impatience with a God who seemed to take for ever to answer her plea:

> 'I can remember praying and repeating the verse of scripture: "They that wait upon the Lord shall renew their strength". I believed that if only I waited on the Lord and was patient the Lord would find me a partner. In the end I could wait no longer.'

This young woman was one of many who decided that her childbearing years were fast decreasing, and she wanted to find someone to love and share her life with. In the end she discontinued her membership of the Church and went after her own happiness.

In Pentecostal and evangelical circles, one often hears that believers 'should not be unequally yoked with unbelievers'. This is taken to mean that a Christian sister should not be married to a non-Christian/unsaved man, or vice versa. It is a strongly held belief that persons so unequally joined have chosen a path which will eventually lead to their spiritual downfall. One elderly church mother's comment on the subject sheds some light on this dilemma:

> 'Christian girls marrying unsaved men . . . in my whole life as a Christian, it has never worked out, . . . yes, some people's life is the means of bringing another, but then we still have to

61

> go back to scripture, which says we should not be unequally yoked.'

Despite the tinge of hopelessness in that view, it is also held by some younger women:

> 'We can't court unsaved men, can we? We can't go out with a man who smokes and drinks . . . imagine fifty years of that . . . and here's me going to my church . . . in the end he's going to have to leave me . . . because we are incompatible. It is sad to say God wants this for two-thirds of His people . . . then why does He not bring in a whirlwind of men? . . . Bring in the two-thirds that matches us . . . there is just nothing that can be done.'

In the increasingly open conversations with women around the issue of the unmarried single woman, one could detect a growing ambivalence. Perhaps the fact that a number of young women had made the choice to leave the Church in order to find partners rather than accept a life of singleness was too important a factor to overlook. The churches would, after all, prefer to keep their sisters than lose them.

Perhaps unintentionally, Black-led Churches have created an 'order of single women devotees'. Many of the women I spoke to on this issue agreed with marriage and would choose to be married. However, the question of choice concerning marriage is taken away from women and replaced by a choice made for them by God. Is there not a need for the churches to find ways of positively including the single women's issue as something worthy of serious concern? It is no coincidence that so many young women (and men, for that matter) are voting with their feet – choosing to leave the churches rather than be considered lesser humans.

The question of the single woman's sexuality and sexual feelings is the one most shrouded in secrecy and silence. Single women are human beings, and no amount of 'cleansing in the Blood of the Lamb' is going to deny those feelings.

These women need the space to talk about and affirm their feelings as natural. Too many women have suffered untold guilt over their thoughts, feelings and physical intimacy with a partner, but instead of finding support in the churches, they find only the labels 'weak' and 'backslider'.

Furthermore, although I have heard homosexuality and lesbianism harangued from the pulpit, I have yet to come across anyone who has countenanced the thought that there might be single women who are both passive lesbians and members of the Church. Only with the recognition of lesbians as human and part of the body of Christ can the Church proclaim the full extent of the body of Christ.

Perhaps now is the time for the Black Churches to begin to apply their understanding of spiritual liberation to their everyday experiences and the structures they operate in, and to understand the role of the individual as a tool in the system. The churches should also recognise that liberation is also about being set free from the oppressions of race, sex and class.

The Upright Pyramid: Man in the Organizational Structures of Black-led Churches

Given the fact that men still control the hierarchies of the various Black-led Churches, it is doubtful that the issues around singleness and female sexuality will be dealt with openly and honestly. It is with problems such as these that the two pyramids I referred to above clash. To understand the nature of resistance to change within the Black-led Churches, we must understand the roles played by men within their structures and how those structures operate to exclude the genuine spirit of liberation.

The Church I know best is the New Testament Church of God. Its leadership structure basically reflects that of the predominantly white American headquarters to which it belongs organizationally, but adapted to suit its British situation. At a national level the Church's structure has a top tier which consists of the National Overseer. A second tier, the

Executive Council, is made up of prominent ordained and District Overseers. The third tier is comprised of District Overseers who have oversight of a fourth tier of local ministers or pastors. There are no women to be found in the top three tiers of the organization. The Church's auxiliaries – by which I mean the Youth and Christian Education Department, the Ladies' Ministries, the Men's Fellowship, the National Evangelism Project, and others – are, with only one exception, led by men. The exception is, of course, the Ladies' Ministries.

A similar imbalance exists within the varied structures of the First United Church of Jesus Christ, the Wesleyan Holiness Church, and the Church of God of Prophecy.

How has this happened? Some may argue that it is simply men operating religious institutions to suit themselves, as they do other areas of society. As far as the churches themselves are concerned, however, they clearly believe that their governing structures are built upon – in the main – the teachings of New Testament scripture. Consequently, the question is raised as to whether it is the men who interpret the Bible in a sexist manner, or the Bible itself which is sexist.

Women are excluded from ordination on the basis that Jesus did not have any female disciples. So not only are men to be found in the decision-making and leadership stratum of the churches, they also have the monopoly over the priestly functions.

There are a number of other ways in which the position of male leaders in the churches are further strengthened. All the Black-led Churches have a plethora of national, regional and local events, loosely called conventions. In the main these are worship and teaching meetings, often serving to reward members for their work on behalf of the organizations. The meetings are often used to signal the programmatic, financial or administrative plans of the organization.

A small sample of convention programmes reveals that at major national conventions, male ministers preached approximately 99 per cent of the time. At the same time, however, the supportive duties were almost exclusively undertaken by women. These included the catering, secretarial, choir, first-aid, children's church and altar workers. Nevertheless, only the men held visible leadership roles.

There is a complete absence of critical examination regarding the assumption that men have inherent leadership and management abilities. As long as neither brother nor sister questions the male monopoly of power within the Church, women will never be able to play their full part in the church community. The only deviation from this norm can be found in those churches which have the post of Church Mother for aged, loyal women. The Church Mother wields enormous influence over matters such as the maintenance of moral codes of dress and behaviour. She upholds the spiritual disciplines of prayer, fasting and spirit-filled worship. Church Mothers are well respected, often having the last word in official church business as well as in the personal matters of people they counsel.

In most churches women participate in an active way in the members'/business meetings. But at least one Church – the Church of God of Prophecy – does not allow them to speak at meetings. Anything they wish to say must be said outside the meeting or by proxy through a male member. If a woman should speak in such a meeting, any decisions taken are declared void and the meeting itself is declared 'shallow'.

Women's Responses to Men in Leadership and Management Roles in the Churches

Some responses suggest that women have not reflected upon or developed a critique of their position in the churches. My interviews appeared to have given them the first opportunity to talk about the part they were playing in their churches. Their church work was generally invisible. While churches might report various quantifiable achievements (number of sermons or of new members, or size of bank balance), they never reported the number of the sick visited and fed, or the length of time spent in fasting and praying. Although these are the activities which make the Church what it is, women's achievements are rarely celebrated.

Some women expressed the feeling that only men could make correct decisions despite the fact that many women are, for example, competent heads of households:

> 'Personally I think right decisions, and good decisions which will help to promote the work of the Lord . . . should be made by men . . . and the women can endorse it [sic] but I think the men – men of God . . . because Peter said you should select men filled with the Holy Ghost – should make the decisions.'

The man is seen as possessing something which is essentially different from that which is possessed by women:

> 'The only things women can't do in our church . . . is baptize, dedicate babies, marriages and burial . . . They do every other thing . . . Maybe I am from the old school. I don't think they should . . . men and women are different. The man has something we have not got in their inner strength . . . and I would not like a woman to baptize me . . . the only thing I think she could do is to dedicate a baby because she is a mother.'

Another declared herself to be totally against women in priestly roles. Her explanation is couched in her understanding of scriptures, and informed by traditional views about men and women:

> 'Well, I think that's one thing they might throw me out of the Church for . . . I am not in agreement with it [females in the ministry]. A woman should never be a pastor, because according to the word of God – if we are going by the word of God – it says man is the head. So I don't understand how a woman could be the head.'

To reiterate: many of the women I interviewed not only saw men as exclusively capable of making the right decisions, they also appeared to view themselves as justifiably subservient in the hierarchy of the churches – all of which, they suggested, was verified by the scriptures.

As the popular chorus attests:

> Give me that old-time religion . . . It's good enough for me.
> It was good for Paul and Silas . . . It's good enough for me.

Despite the worrying features relating to gender in the organizational structure of the churches, it is a fact that the churches have given many Black men self-worth, dignity and a positive identity, in contrast to the ways in which white British society has alienated, devalued and effectively excluded them from many forms of legitimate involvement in the wider society. Given the pressure on Black men to 'prove their worth', it is difficult to see how those who have achieved some status and power in, and through the churches, are going to relinquish it.

In addition, many of our church leaders who emigrated from the Caribbean were not equipped to function in 'the belly of the beast' of white British society. Many came from countries suffering neo-colonial rule, mainly from peasant and working-class backgrounds within those societies, and lacked 'acceptable' paper qualifications. Perhaps it was within the context of white historical churches that the position of potential Black church leaders became amplified. The historical churches emphasized academic qualification and training as the route through to priesthood or the clergy. The episcopal hegemony and speculative approach to theology of the historical Christian Churches were sure ways to deter any who did not fit the bill. Black-led Churches were a better alternative, with their emphasis on biblical fundamentalism, the infallibility of the Bible, and the power and leading role of the Holy Ghost in and through believers regardless of social class, status, academic qualifications or Bible school training.

It is difficult to envisage a time when Black-led Churches in

Britain will allow women the freedom to define themselves, particularly since both males and females continue to believe in the patriarchal organizational structures.

The message of equality and partnership implicit in the following chorus probably sums up the churches' current thinking on the issues:

> We are heirs of the father, we are joint heirs with the son.
> We are children of the kingdom, we are family, we are one.

Conclusion

Without disparaging the obvious power, position, responsibilities, tremendous burden and task of leadership vested in the hands of the males in Black-led Churches in Britain, it is clear that in a very real sense the churches are the women, and the women are the churches. When we examine the role and responsibilities which the women have assumed, the way in which they have defined the churches and the spirituality of the churches, the men's positions pale into insignificance. One wonders if these functions could be dispensed with in a Black-led female-run Church. The fact that men 'run' things appears to be based upon scripture, and is therefore sanctified and constant. To change this model, they claim, would be to change scripture, and since scripture never changes, the model defies change. In my opinion, the churches need to revisit scripture, listen to what women are saying in the theological debates about the priestly and pastoral functions of males and females in the body of Christ, and seek to learn, from their challenges, of the present iniquitous patriarchal structures.

'Between the Devil and the Deep Blue Sea': Irish Women, Catholicism and Colonialism

ANN ROSSITER

'We take cheerful bets on it, here in Ireland', says Nell McCafferty, the Irish feminist and journalist, writing in the magazine *Everywoman*:

> How long will we be in attendance at a meeting before the familiar dreary whine erupts? Five minutes? Ten minutes? Not at all. Chances are that the instant litany of our perceived oppressions will fall like clichés from the lips of a British feminist in the opening words of her speech. Abortion, divorce, gay rights, she will intone. Contraception is scarcely available either, she will throw in for good measure. Listening to a British feminist on Ireland, one gets the impression that we spend our lives barefoot, pregnant and tied to the kitchen sink – with a Catholic male pig in the parlour to add to our woes. As it happens, contraception is legal though not nearly available enough (just as in Britain); in the wake of Mary Robinson's presidential victory, the government [of the Republic] has announced that homosexuality will be legalised and signalled that divorce will soon be introduced. That leaves abortion . . . when it does come, it will be introduced by the will of the people, as were all the other measures. (p. 4).

While it must be said that not all Irish feminists share Nell McCafferty's belief that the coming of Mary Robinson necessarily heralds a sea-change in the affairs of women, gay men and lesbians in the Irish Republic – a point discussed later in this chapter – her irreverent description of the British feminist reaction to things Irish, especially to religious influence in the area of reproductive rights and sexuality, finds resonance amongst those of us who live in Britain.

The troubled relationship between Ireland and Britain has spawned a host of contradictions and distortions, of which religion is only one, and the impact of these has been keenly felt by the Irish immigrant community. Irish women, and particularly Irish feminists, in Britain have had to face the central paradox of confronting, on the one hand, a highly orthodox – if not fundamentalist – Catholicism, and to a lesser degree a fundamentalist Protestantism, which form the central core of Irish identity, and, on the other, a psychological hang-up of massive proportions in British culture which sees religion in its Irish context in pathological terms and as the singular cause of the great Irish 'predicament'.

Confronting the obscurantism that surrounds the religious question, and the interconnected Irish national question, however, is only one part of the struggle. The proximity of Ireland itself, the close contact with home maintained by most immigrants, the constant renewal of Irish emigration and, most importantly, the latest Anglo–Irish war, which has ebbed and flowed over more than two decades, all ensure that a struggle has to be maintained on many different fronts: an Irish immigrant feminist politics and infrastructure have had to be built up, an input into the political debate in Britain and in Ireland itself has had to be maintained, and repression of the Irish community in Britain by the state, part of the fallout of the war, has demanded unremitting political activism.

Very little has been published about Irish feminism in Britain, a result of the complexities of the politics involved and the distortion and censorship which surround the Irish Question generally. This means that the experiences of women from what is the largest ethnic community in Britain, both historically and in the contemporary period, are ignored.

While this chapter cannot redress the balance, it focuses on Catholicism, the religion of the majority on the island, in an attempt to dispel the notion that it is a metaphysical phenomenon rather than a construct of a particular historical process in which the British imperial enterprise played a pivotal part. To this end, there is a concentration on the evolution of the Catholic nation and state in the South (the Irish Republic) and its function in women's oppression. A further aim is to highlight the struggle of progressive forces in Ireland, of which feminism is one, to rectify the distortions wrought by centuries of colonialism. Finally, given the important role being played by the Catholic Church worldwide in reversing the gains made by women and the small, but significant number of rights achieved by gay men and lesbians, the import of the Irish situation inevitably extends far beyond its Anglo–Irish context.

British and Irish Feminist Solidarity: A Casualty of War

In this society, the widespread association of the Irish with backwardness, stupidity and irrationality, in large measure seen as stemming from a religious atavism, has a history dating back to the twelfth-century colonial military intervention, and the renewal of conflict in Northern Ireland has resulted in a major resurgence of these sentiments. The rationale for the latest wave of anti-Irish prejudice – and, indeed, anti-Irish racism – is not difficult to decipher. Since 1969, when British troops went into Northern Ireland in what the politicians termed a 'peacekeeping mission' aimed at keeping two warring Irish factions apart, the British authorities have consistently presented themselves as honest brokers in a local intercommunal problem. With the connivance of the media it has been relatively easy to obscure the realities of the sectarian Northern Ireland statelet (see L. Curtis, 1984a; Rolston, ed., 1991) and the fact that since 1970 the 'impartial' British army has launched all-out attacks on the nationalist population, thus ensuring the maintenance of the status quo. In her historical study of British perceptions of the Irish, *Nothing but the Same Old Story: The Roots of Anti-Irish Racism* (1984b), Liz Curtis observes:

> Over succeeding years [since 1969], the British authorities, aided by the media, presented a topsy-turvy picture of events in order to sustain the image of British impartiality. They played down the atrocities committed by the British forces, minimised loyalist responsibility for violence, and depicted the situation as one long succession of violent acts committed by republicans. They portrayed the IRA as the cause – rather than the product – of the conflict . . . they refused to acknowledge that partition and the continuing British presence were the root of the problem . . . it was the same old story. (p. 77)

Against this background, the Irish in Britain have found themselves caught up in a modern witch-hunt stemming from the determination of the security apparatus to muffle public protest at British military activity in Northern Ireland, and the desperate drive for scapegoats in the aftermath of each IRA bombing. Between 1974 and the end of 1989, 6,763 people, most of them Irish, were officially listed as having been arrested in England, Scotland and Wales under the Prevention of Terrorism Act (PTA) for offences in connection with Northern Ireland. Of these, only 569 were charged and 411 subsequently convicted (Irish Information Partnership, 1987) – a conviction rate which has led many to question whether the whole purpose of the Act is to terrorize rather than to facilitate the detection of crime. Added to this, 409,422 people were subjected to police security checks at British air and sea ports between 1977 and 1985 (Irish Information Partnership, 1990, pp. 43, 56). Large numbers of Irish people are also stopped at railway and bus stations, or in the street, or visited at their homes, where they are frequently interrogated. Provided the detention is for less than twelve hours, the police may question anyone on British territory or passing through British ports without any grounds for suspicion. Lord Colville, who has carried out reviews of the PTA annually on behalf of the government, has estimated that a million people a year may be questioned under this power, if only for a few minutes (Jessel, 1990).

Repressive state measures such as these have had serious effects on women, as Maire O'Shea emphasizes in her essay, 'Policing Irish Women in Britain' (1989). Referring in particular to the aftermath of the IRA bombing of a Birmingham pub in 1974, she says:

> The whole Irish community in Britain was being punished, and women bore much of the brunt. They would be dragged out of bed during raids, wearing only nightwear, to face degrading sexist jibes. They would have to comfort their children who might be locked in a room with them, terrorized by the police dogs. In the days that followed, they would fear for their menfolk and suffer abuse and attacks from British neighbours. But they had to carry on with their lives and cope with their children in the ruins of their homes. Some blamed their husbands, believing that they might have become politically involved. The effect on the community was devastating. Families and friends turned against one another. Marriages broke up. At best, there was a climate of constant uncertainty and fear. When wives and families of the six men framed for the Birmingham bombings in 1974 were attacked in their homes or burned out by British people seeking revenge, they were refused protection. Some who had been settled in Birmingham for many years were forced to leave.

Of course, women have also been arrested and imprisoned, and the list includes Maire O'Shea herself, who conducted a political defence at her trial in 1986 and brought about the collapse of the Crown's case against her. Others were not so lucky. The sisters Aine and Eibhlin Nic Giolla Easpaig, Martina Shanahan of 'The Winchester Three', Annie Maguire, and Carole Richardson of 'The Guildford Four', served long prison sentences while vigorously protesting their innocence. Judith Ward, convicted on faulty evidence, is still in prison, but her case is currently under review.

A significant number of Irish activists and writers have insisted that the prolongation of the war in Ireland and the intense policing and repression of the Irish in Britain have been facilitated by racist attitudes widely prevalent in all sections of British society – Right, Left and, indeed, feminist. Maire O'Shea argues (1989) that such attitudes have been deliberately inculcated during eight hundred years of British rule in Ireland, during which stereotypical views of the Irish as 'thick', dirty, lazy, wild, treacherous, violent, ungovernable, and possessing an irrational attachment to religion were fostered.

Liz Curtis (1984b), also arguing from this position, draws attention to the inclusion of the Irish in pseudo-scientific theories of race propounded by Victorian anthropologists and ethnologists which gained common currency through popular literature. In this scheme of things, 'races' were said to have inherited differences not only of physique but also of character, and were placed in a hierarchical scale of measurement where Anglo-Saxons were to be found at the top, black people at the bottom, and Celts and Jews somewhere in between. The object of the exercise was not only to prove English superiority but, inevitably, the unsuitability of the 'inferior' races for self-government. A study by the American writer L. Perry Curtis (1971) highlights the efforts made throughout the Victorian era to prove that the English and the Irish were separated by clear-cut racial as well as religious and cultural barriers.

Physiognomical differentiation was central to this endeavour, and men of letters invested considerable energy in measuring the cranium, facial angles, thickness of lips, size of jaw and levels of pigmentation to provide a scientific basis for their claim. The 'bulging forward of the lower part of face', the 'chin more or less retreating', the 'large mouth and thick lips', they deduced, indicated a 'quickness in perception', but a 'deficiency in reasoning power' (L. P. Curtis, p. 18).

Liz Curtis and several others have attempted to show that

although anti-Irish racism has ebbed and flowed according to the state of Anglo–Irish relations, it was always present in British society and erupted once again when British troops returned to Irish streets in 1969. In a recently published oral history work (Lennon, McAdam and O'Brien, eds, 1988), Anne Higgins recalls being 'under a kind of siege' in the Irish Catholic community in Manchester in the 1930s and 1940s. Jews and Irish, she says, were in the same ghetto in the north of the city and were 'very much sympathetic to each other as minorities'. Other testimonies in this work vividly recall the 'No Irish, No Coloureds' signs which so many immigrants of the 1950s and early 1960s encountered in their search for accommodation. Establishing that the Irish experience constitutes a form of racism has proved a difficult exercise, even when in British racial discourse the majority of theoreticians concede that the category 'race' is not a biological but, rather, a social construct, and that 'racism' refers to a whole cluster of cultural ideas, beliefs and arguments which transmit mistaken notions about the attributes and capabilities of 'racial' groups. Rex, probably one of the most frequently quoted of the theoreticians, states (1970) that racism is present whenever any 'deterministic belief system' regards group characteristics as narrowly 'fixed' and therefore leading inevitably to rather rigid and exclusive barriers between one group and another.

The claim by many Irish feminists in Britain that a 'deterministic belief system' prevents their British counterparts from comprehending the Irish situation is widely heard, with the twin issues of nationalism and religion cited as driving a wedge between the two sides. Given this scenario, it is hardly surprising that solidarity between Irish and British feminists should have been one of the casualties of the latest Anglo–Irish war, although at the beginning of the crisis, when Northern Ireland was the focus of political and media attention worldwide, matters looked as if they might take a different turn.

In that period, the early 1970s, often described as the heady days of 'universal sisterhood', women from many different backgrounds – Irish, British, American, Australian and continental European – came together in Women and Ireland groups to highlight the role of the British state in Northern Ireland, military occupation, and the implications for women there, and here. Understandably, the British Women's Liberation Movement was regarded as the natural constituency of such groups, and meetings, conferences and gatherings of the movement were addressed. But fatigue with what were regarded as the complexities and 'alien' nature of the Irish situation set in very quickly, and although Women and Ireland and other groups were springing up in towns and cities from Bristol to Dundee, by the end of the 1970s it was becoming increasingly apparent to activists that Ireland was quite marginal, if not irrelevant, to the concerns of most British feminists. Even a cursory glance at histories of the British Women's Liberation Movement, such as *Sweet Freedom* (Coote and Campbell, 1982), or a more recent work, *Hyenas in Petticoats* (Neustatter, 1989), confirms this. Feminist perspectives on the state, apart from its welfare aspects, are conspicuously absent from such histories, as are other issues thrown up by the Northern Ireland situation, such as nationalism, unionism, religion and, of course, political violence. Significantly, the existence of Women and Ireland groups and activities concerned with the Irish National Question do not even get a mention.

This marginalization and even obliteration of Irish issues resulted in a gradual shift towards Irish women-only groups and activities from 1980 onwards, although certain campaigns, notably those against strip-searching and the treatment of women political prisoners have retained a mixed membership. Even an area of seemingly universal concern, such as reproductive rights, has been permeated by the tensions of war. In the 1970s, British and Irish feminists jointly supported campaigns in Ireland for contraceptive rights, but the Irish Women's Abortion Support Group, formed in London in 1981 to provide information and practical help to Irish women seeking abortions in Britain, has restricted its membership to Irish women (1988, p. 68). A separatist politics has clearly had positive outcomes, not least a strong commitment to developing a feminist analysis and agenda which is not only Irish in character but relative to the needs and aspirations of immigrant women. The problem of marginalization remains, however, compounded by the lack of an Irish feminist journal or magazine in Britain and the reluctance of activists to write for, let alone speak, to the media, partly for fear of distortion, but mainly because serious and informed debate has, more often than not, proved impossible.

The formation of Women Against Fundamentalism in 1989, with the involvement of women from countries with a long history of colonization, has opened up one forum, at least, for the discussion of religion in a political context which takes account of historical and economic processes. A positive development from this was the picket of the Irish Embassy in London called by WAF on 15 May 1990 to highlight the appearance in the European Court of Human Rights at Strasbourg of two Dublin organizations, the Dublin Well Woman Centre and Open Line Counselling, to argue against their prosecution in the Irish courts by the British organization the Society for the Protection of the Unborn Child (SPUC) for providing information on abortion clinics in Britain. The presence on the picket line of British, Irish, Indian, Israeli, Iranian and Pakistani women, and women from some of the Catholic countries of Europe, was a testimony to the urgent need for an understanding of the gathering momentum of religious fundamentalism worldwide, and the specific conditions for its existence in the West and elsewhere.

The Rise of an Irish Catholic State

When the Republic of Ireland put a foetal civil rights amendment into its Constitution in 1983 to copper-fasten its absolute ban on abortion dating back to the time of Victoria's rule, this was widely perceived in Britain as a backward step by a backward nation on the periphery of Europe, traditionally at odds with Western social thinking and therefore all too easily dismissed. However, since the US Supreme Court's decision in 1989 opened the way for individual States of the Union to restrict abortion rights, it becomes apparent that Ireland was the cutting edge of a gathering movement headed by Christian fundamentalists – not only to curtail or outlaw abortion worldwide, but to grant civil status to the foetus, which involves, as Ruth Riddick graphically puts it:

> the legal idea of personhood of the foetus, the inhabiter and potential product of the womb. This new 'person', the foetus, qualifies for constitutional guarantees not necessarily extended to adult women and may constitute a litigant against women in matters of pre-natal care and birthing procedures. (1990, p. 12)

And if further proof of an international pro-life movement with a common agenda were needed, the recent legal ruling in Guam, the US Pacific island state where abortion was already banned, to prohibit the propagation of information on abortion available outside its jurisdiction, and similar moves by the Catholic Church in Poland, appear to be carbon copies of the prohibition imposed by the Irish courts.

The choice of the Republic of Ireland as a launching pad for foetal civil rights and a worldwide campaign to prevent the proliferation of information on abortion is not too difficult to understand. Its reputation as a highly religious country was borne out by a survey of Irish values and attitudes in 1984 (Fogarty, Ryan and Lee, 1984) which found that only 1 per cent of those surveyed described themselves as 'convinced atheist' and 1 per cent as having 'no religion'; 95 per cent believed in God, 81 per cent prayed regularly and 82 per cent attended church weekly. Interestingly, 79 per cent expressed considerable confidence in the Catholic Church, which means that in the minds of the majority of respondents there was no dichotomy between religion as a system of belief and the Church as an institution.

One explanation of how the Church maintains its power and influence over the population is to be found in the education system. In the Republic, primary and secondary schools are privately owned, although they are funded by the state. With the exception of a small number of Protestant, Jewish, Muslim and non-denominational schools, the majority are owned by the Catholic Church. Policy matters, such as teachers' conditions of employment, and ethical issues, such as sex education, are to a large extent decided by the private owners of these schools. The state has attempted to intervene in the latter in recent times, with only limited success. The universities are formally undenominational, but the National University of Ireland, with colleges in Dublin, Cork, Galway and Limerick, experiences the heavy hand of the Catholic hierarchy, who have traditionally been part of its governing body since its establishment in 1908. That the Catholic Church in the Republic of Ireland performs the role of the state in education is only part of the story, for its control also extends to hospitals and many areas within the social services.

Apart from the affinities forged through the education system, the relationship between the Irish people and Catholicism which, uniquely in Western Europe, has survived in such strength until the late twentieth century, stretches back many centuries and must be understood in large measure as a form of resistance to imperialism. It was the British imperial enterprise which first opened up the Pandora's Box of religion, after the implementation of what came to be known as the Penal Laws by British colonial rulers in the late seventeenth century. The idea was to reduce Catholics to a servile caste by debarring them from the vote, public office and many of the professions. Catholics were forbidden to open schools or teach in them, to manufacture or sell newspapers and books. Churches were closed down, church property was confiscated and the clergy were ordered to leave the country. Anglicanism became the Established religion, but could never claim more than one-sixth of the population as adherents.

While in principle the people were not compelled to attend Protestant religious services, all had to pay tithes to the Established Church. In the banning of 'popery' in Ireland under the Penal Code, the aim was the total elimination of the Catholic Church and its clergy. Instead, the Code had the effect of turning the Catholic Church into an immensely popular institution, and those priests who succeeded in remaining in Ireland became folk heroes. In time, the impact of some of these laws was reduced, either by violation or by circumvention, but those aspects of the Penal Code concerned with property were successful.

Catholics had been subjected to special taxes and restraints if they were landowners. For instance, no Catholic farm could be inherited intact: it had to be divided between all the male children (Lee, 1978, p. 39). Catholic ownership of land was in the region of 90 per cent in 1600; by 1703 it had fallen to 14 per cent, and by 1770 it was only 5 per cent (Corish, 1981, p. 74). Although by the mid 1800s Catholic emancipation had been achieved, which meant that many of the civil rights withdrawn by the Penal Code were now restored the use of religion to distinguish colonist from colonized had already been firmly established.

In this respect, Ireland differs from other Catholic European countries such as France, Italy and Spain, where the Catholic Church as an institution was closely associated with the feudal order, and with absolutism. When the Church in Ireland made its big comeback after centuries of persecution, it had relatively few aristocratic allies and relatively little of an anti-democratic past to live down. In fact it was intimately connected with the drive for civil rights and democracy, especially in its support between 1823 and 1840 for Daniel O'Connell's Catholic Association, which aimed to remove all disabilities Catholics suffered under the Penal Codes. These aims included the abolition of tithes to the Anglican Church, the achievement of municipal reform to grant more representation to Catholics, and, crucially, the repeal of the 1800 Act of Union, by which the island became an integral part of Britain.

The mass movement of those years, involving all sections of the people – peasants, farmers and the middle class – and with the clergy providing a ready-made political apparatus, ensured that Catholicism and nationalism were firmly intertwined thereafter. This relationship was further compounded by the Church's role in rebuilding a shattered Ireland after the Great Famine of 1845–9, known to the Irish peasantry as the 'Great Starvation', when perhaps a million people died and one and a half million emigrated as a result of the British administration's mismanagement of, and frequent refusal to distribute, the ample food stocks held in the country. The trauma of those events led to what has been termed 'a devotional revolution' and major organizational changes occurred, not least a dramatic increase in the numbers of clergy and religious Orders (Hynes, 1978). In 1840 there had been one priest to every 3,500 members of the laity; by 1900 that figure was one to every 900. The Church came to play a major socioeconomic role in the Irish peasantry's drive to reduce population growth. The custom of subdivision of land in pre-famine years was ended, and single inheritance became the norm. Late marriage for those lucky enough to inherit or receive a dowry was universal, and the remaining siblings either remained celibate or emigrated. The Church's role in the policing of sexuality and the creation of a strict puritanical climate was essential in this enterprise.

The partitioning of Ireland by Britain in 1921 enforced the influence of the Catholic Church, primarily because the population of the Southern state was mainly Catholic, and this homogeneity meant that few concessions had to be made to any form of pluralism in the institutions of state, in the education system, or in the culture generally. Equally, the first Prime Minister of the Northern state, James Craig, set about creating 'a Protestant state for a Protestant people', despite the large Catholic minority in the territory. Before his execution for his part in the nationalist rising of 1916, the socialist leader, James Connolly, had predicted that the partitioning of Ireland would lead to 'a carnival of reaction' as both sides conducted the business of state from their respective *laagers*. He was to be proved right, and to this day religion has retained its status as the cornerstone of Irish identity.

Almost as an act of rebellion or declaration of ideological separation from Britain, the rulers of the new Southern state set about constructing a Catholic social order and reversing centuries of British and Protestant domination. A moral purification campaign was set in motion, resulting in a series of laws being passed in quick succession: in 1923, the Censorship of Films Act; in 1929, the Censorship of Publications Act; and in 1935, the Criminal Law (Amendment) Act, which in effect outlawed the practice of contraception. The Public Dance Halls Act of 1935 was officially aimed at prosecuting those responsible for unlicensed and unsupervised dance halls, but in reality was concerned to curb 'occasions of sin'. In 1925, a test case petitioning for divorce was brought to the Dáil; it was unsuccessful. The 1861 Offences Against the Person Act, outlawing abortion and homosexuality, passed into the laws of the post-colonial state. Taken together, this body of legal imperatives hermetically sealed off the society from outside influences and ensured that an extremely orthodox Catholicism remained unassailed until recent times. For almost thirty years the Censorship Board issued lists of banned books every month – to the extent that by the mid 1950s Southern Irish readers had been prevented from reading the works of nine international Nobel Prizewinners and those of virtually every serious contemporary Irish writer as well. It was not until 1967 that a major reform of the censorship laws occurred (Brown, 1981).

In 1935 the Irish government passed the Conditions of Employment Act which imposed a maximum proportion of women workers in industry, with the discretion to prohibit them entirely if necessary. A marriage bar was introduced in the Civil Service and other occupations, forcing women to give up their jobs on marriage. This bar was not removed until 1973 (O'Dowd, 1987, p. 15). The nature of the new state was firmly established when, in 1937, a constitution was promulgated which accorded 'a special position' to the Catholic Church. Although Church and state were intended to be separate and the clergy were to be supported entirely by the donations of their congregation, there was no genuine separation between the two. Some commentators have rightly suggested that while a marriage between Church and state did not in fact occur, a state-within-a-state was created by the 1937 Constitution, which banned divorce, established the family (not the individual) as the basic unit of society, and enshrined the position of women within the home in the following Article:

> In particular the State recognises that by her life within the home, woman gives to the State a support without which the common good cannot be achieved.
>
> The State shall, therefore, endeavour to ensure that mothers shall not be obliged by economic necessity to engage in labour to the neglect of their duties in the home. (Constitution of Ireland, 1937, pp. 136, 138)

Challenges to the Catholic State

It is often suggested that the progressive nature of the Catholic Church in the long struggle for an independent Ireland is clearly discernible, but its central role as the most powerful institution in the post-colonial state is not so easily explained. In fact there are several reasons for the Church's continuing dominant position, and the field of education has already been mentioned. Very importantly, also, the Church acted as a social glue when the coalition of class interests that comprised the nationalist movement fell apart with the signing of the Treaty with Britain in 1922. The substantial commercial and trading elements, the larger farmers and the Catholic Church supported the Treaty; the petty bourgeoisie, the small farmers, the poor and the dispossessed were opposed. A bitter civil war ensued, and there was serious unrest amongst the urban working class due to drastically reduced living standards following the years of upheaval in the country and growing worldwide depression.

In an attempt to redeem the situation from chaos, the Irish government enlisted the support of the Catholic Church to denounce workers' strikes, and the clergy duly dragged out the red herring of communism, 'the Antichrist', which, they insisted, 'was devouring all before it' as it advanced westwards through Europe. It was abundantly clear that both communism and socialism had very fragile roots in the country. There were outbreaks of clerically inspired mob violence, and for a while an Irish brand of fascism emerged. The government of the time was successful in restoring a form of stability, but a heavy price was exacted. A kind of quietism reigned which depended on invoking 'the will of God' in the face of all adversity, and the perpetuation of this ideology was the function of the priests and the religious Orders (Milotte, 1984). The merely discontented and the troublemakers alike quickly became part of the vast and continuing haemmorhage of emigrants, making the words of Heinrich Mann, 'emigration is the voice of a nation that has fallen silent', particularly apt.

The drastic underdevelopment of Ireland wrought by centuries of colonialism was hardly challenged in any significant way as the decades of independence progressed. Agriculture, the principal industry, continued as under British rule to be geared almost entirely to supplying the British market with cheap food. The industry continued to have low productivity levels and produce low incomes, and, in turn, incurred low taxation, which meant that surplus for investment was miniscule. No serious efforts were made to develop an industrial infrastructure (the industrial heartland of Ireland being cut off by Partition) and while post-war Europe may have experienced an economic boom, national income in the Republic of Ireland rose by a mere 8½ per cent between 1949 and 1956. The numbers at work actually declined and emigration averaged 40,000 a year, a serious annual exodus from a country where the population stood at fewer than three million (Daly,

1981, p. 163). Underdevelopment continued to retard the progress of civil society, and social relations remained fossilized. Naturally, the Catholic Church, as the only developed institution, continued to maintain its hold, although there was a famous, albeit unsuccessful, attempt to introduce state control in the field of health in the 1950s.

A radical mother-and-child health scheme which aimed to provide full free medical care before, during and after childbirth and free GP and hospital care for all children up to the age of sixteen was devised by Noel Browne, Minister of Health from 1949 to 1951. It also aimed to provide free gynaecological care for women. The 'Mother and Child Scheme' immediately became a *cause célèbre* and was attacked by the medical profession, who feared for their economic interests, a position endorsed by the Church, and very surprisingly so, given the dire poverty, malnutrition, and extremely poor state of health of very large sections of the population. The hierarchy's principal concern, however, was that the service was in direct opposition to the rights of the family established in the Constitution. 'The right to provide for the health of children belongs to parents, not to the State. The State has the right to intervene only in a subsidiary capacity, to supplement, not supplant', it was stated; and, furthermore:

> Education in regard to motherhood includes instruction in regard to sex relations, chastity and marriage. The State has no competence to give instruction in such matters. We regard with the greatest apprehension the proposal to give to local medical officers the right to tell Catholic girls and women how they should behave in regard to this sphere of conduct at once so delicate and sacred. (Browne, 1986, p. 25)

Dr Browne was abandoned by all his colleagues in government, including Labour members and trade unionists, and he resigned as Minister of Health. Shortly afterwards the government fell.

Not until the late 1960s and early 1970s was a second challenge to the Catholic state issued. This time it came from a number of sources, but the most important factor was the changing nature of Irish society itself. After a body of Keynesian solutions was devised in the late 1950s and 1960s, the state became directly involved in economic expansion and the country opened up to multinational capital, with attractive financial inducements in the form of capital grants and tax-free holidays. Never mind that the multinationals imported the bulk of their input and exported the bulk of their output, and that their large profits were quickly repatriated to countries of origin. It seemed to matter little that no organic ties with the domestic economy were being created, and that from the point of view of changing social relations in Ireland, the multinationals merely tended to form 'modern' enclaves in a traditional society. The drive was to reduce unemployment and stem the tide of emigration. Notwithstanding, Irish society began to assume different demographic patterns for the first time in over a hundred years: an increase in the rate of marriage; a drop in the average age at marriage; an increasing birth rate. A 13 per cent increase in the birth rate was recorded between 1971 and 1979 (Ranelagh, 1983, p. 243) and, most importantly, emigration was no longer regarded as an automatic option or a safety valve.

These demographic realities in themselves posed a challenge to official church teaching. Increasingly, young couples wished to improve their standard of living and quality of life by reducing family size. They were unwilling to accept Christian doctrine virtually unaltered since the pronouncements of Augustine (354–430 AD). Augustine had ordained that the sexual act had but one purpose, procreation, following from the biblical imperative to Adam and Eve to 'Go forth and multiply'. In his *De Conjugiis Adulterinis*, he stated: '. . . it is unlawful and shameful to have intercourse even with one's own wife if the conception of children is avoided. Onan the Son of Judah did this and God slew him for it.' Any other use of coitus, therefore, was contrary to God's law. Augustine not only condemned any use of contraception, but insisted that to seek intercourse for pleasure was sinful, but if it took place within marriage it was protected by the sacrament and therefore a pardonable sin (Enger, 1966, pp. 117, 145).

Throughout the centuries the Augustinian doctrine on sexuality and marriage remained virtually unaltered. When Thomas Aquinas (1224–74) wrote his *Summa Theologica* eight hundred years later, his views on marriage and sexuality were firmly Augustinian, and he was as unambiguous as Augustine in his condemnation of the sexual act being used for any purpose other than procreation. Aquinas, like Augustine, set limitations on the kind of relationship which can develop between a man and a woman: '. . . she is, after all, a defective man, conceived because of weakness in the seed, or because a damp south wind was blowing at the time . . .' (Enger, p. 141).

The traditional theological view of coitus as a purely genital act became less convincing as the nineteenth century progressed and a debate on the purpose of intercourse recommenced. When the papal encyclical on marriage, *Casti Connubii* (Christian Marriage), was issued by Pius XI in 1930, it was neither fully accepted nor fully rejected. The encyclical declared that love in Christian marriage held 'a kind of primacy of excellence', thus affording love a position it had never before held; in this it represented a break with Augustinian theory (Noonan, 1966, p. 495). However, the encyclical restated the Church's fundamentalist position and insisted that all true Christians must view the sexual act as primarily intended for procreation, and fertility could be limited only by abstinence or use of the 'safe period'.

This pronouncement differed sharply from the Protestant viewpoint. The Anglican Church in Britain, for instance, cautiously approved of contraception in 1930. However, it must be emphasized that it was not until 1958 that the ruling body of the Anglican Church, the Lambeth Conference, could declare:

The responsibility for the number and frequency of children has been laid down by God upon the conscience of parents everywhere . . . The means of family planning are in large measure matters of clinical and aesthetic choice. (*Encyclopaedia Britannica*, 'Birth Control', 1984, p. 1071)

Humanae Vitae: *A Break with Catholic Fundamentalism?*

The determination of Catholic women and men to practise birth control despite religious prohibition became evident following the introduction to Ireland of the birth-control Pill in 1962. The Pill itself could not be prescribed as a contraceptive in view of the legal prohibition, so doctors prescribed it as a 'menstrual regulator'. At the end of 1967 it was estimated that 12,000 Irish women were using the Pill (R. S. Rose, 1976, p. 31), and this figure continued to rise to 38,000 by 1973, despite the huge disappointment in Ireland at the papal encyclical *Humanae Vitae* (On Human Life), published in July 1968. Pressures from the world Catholic community had led Pope John XXIII, the reformist Pope, to establish an international commission in 1963, consisting of theologians, gynaecologists, psychologists, demographers and married couples, to study the issue of contraception. The majority report of the commission condoned so-called 'unnatural methods' of contraception, but Pope Paul VI, who took office following the death of John XXIII, rejected 'any action, which either before, at the moment of, or after sexual intercourse is specifically intended to prevent procreation – whether as an end or as a means', and specified that 'married people may take advantage of the natural cycles immanent in the reproductive system . . . at precisely those times that are infertile, and in this way control birth.' (R. S. Rose, 1976, pp. 33, 34)

The imperatives issued in *Humanae Vitae* prompted a heated discussion in the Irish media and gave rise to some interesting initiatives, the most spectacular being a highly publicized stunt by members of the Irish Women's Liberation

Movement who imported contraceptives from Belfast and declared them to Customs officials at the railway station in Dublin. The 'contraceptive train' event was to send shock waves throughout Irish society and was aided by the fact that the re-emergent feminist movement included a number of journalists who quickly disseminated the movement's message to the media. A manifesto, 'Chains or Change', was delivered to the people of Ireland on a popular chat show, the 'Late Late Show', on 6 March 1971. It contained five demands: equal pay, equality before the law, equal education, contraception, and justice for deserted wives, unmarried mothers and widows (Levine, 1982, p. 155). A report by the Commission on the Status of Women appeared in December 1972. The commission was formed in 1970, partly as a result of Ireland's preparations for joining the European Economic Community.

Legislative change was finally achieved by Mary McGee, a twenty-nine-year-old working-class woman, the wife of a fisherman and the mother of four children, with serious health problems. With financial support from the Irish Family Planning Association, and Mary Robinson as her Senior Counsel, she took her case to court and won. The action of one brave woman would eventually lead to the enactment of the 1979 Health (Family Planning) Act, which legalized the distribution and sale of contraceptives, but to married couples only. It would take another six years for the Irish government to legalize contraception for all those over the age of eighteen, married or single.

Superficially, it could be said that this response from the Catholic Church was very different from its response to the 'Mother and Child Scheme' two decades earlier. Maintaining its fundamental teaching on artificial birth control, the hierarchy, stated:

> The question at issue is not whether artificial contraception is morally right or wrong. The clear teaching of the Catholic Church is that it is morally wrong. No change in State law can

make the use of contraceptives morally right since what is wrong in itself remains wrong, regardless of what State law says. It does not follow, of course, that the State is bound to prohibit the importation and sale of contraceptives. There are many things that the Catholic Church holds to be morally wrong and no one has ever suggested, least of all the Church herself, that they should be prohibited by the State. (Irish Press, 1973)

For the first time, the Church was publicly recognizing the rights of the state in an area which traditionally it has seen as its personal fief, and this battle was lost, it is suggested, because through the confessional the Irish clergy were acutely aware of the strength of feeling amongst women – and men – about the need to regulate family size for economic reasons, and of the desire to improve maternal health and well-being. It appeared that the Catholic Church was being forced to concede to the modernization of Irish society or risk losing large numbers of its adherents. As if to reinforce this view, a constitutional referendum in 1972 which removed the 'special position' of the Catholic Church did not suffer from the opposition of the hierarchy; on the contrary, it received their support. From the clergy's point of view, however, the war to retain and institute fundamental Catholic doctrine in the area of sexual morals and human reproduction was far from being lost.

The significance of *Humanae Vitae* and Vatican II, says Dick Spicer of the Campaign to Separate Church and State in Ireland, is:

difficult for anyone outside the Irish Republic (and indeed for many within it) to comprehend . . . it is from the time of Vatican II, or more precisely the run-up to that event, that the mould of the Irish Catholic nation was broken and the diversification of Irish culture became possible . . . the effect of all this on Ireland was shattering. Here we had a culture and a church that was blissfully unaware previously that you could mention such things as contraception and sex. Here we were

> busy establishing the model Catholic culture, enshrining canon
> law in our civil laws, and now suddenly the whole moral
> certainty of what we were doing was undermined by the very
> institution to which we looked for guidance. Here was the
> Church debating publicly its view of the world, the Pope it
> seemed veering towards a liberal position and our sainted
> society forced to discuss and consider things the very mention
> or thought of which was alien to our whole outlook . . .
> Ireland, like Humpty Dumpty, could never be put together
> again. (Spicer, 1991)

Or could it? While the clergy were forced to concede on the
sovereignty of the state, they had not shifted on their
fundamentalist position regarding contraception. Those elements within the Irish population who believed we were on
course for a progressive social revolution had a very rude
awakening when the right-wing backlash actually occurred. In
1981, just three years after the enactment of the Family
Planning Act, lay elements, with the strong backing of the
Catholic Church, secured a promise from both the Taoiseach
(Prime Minister) and the Leader of the Opposition that an
amendment granting civil rights to the foetus would be
inserted in the Irish Constitution. An umbrella body, the Pro-
Life Amendment Campaign (PLAC), was formed, encom-
passing groups such as Family Solidarity, the Responsible
Society, Opus Dei, the Catholic Nurses' Guild, the Knights of
Columbanus and the British-based Society for the Protection
of the Unborn Child. Alliances were made with anti-abortion
organizations worldwide, especially in the United States, and
aggressive American campaigning-style techniques were
adopted wholesale.

Although abortion had already been outlawed in Ireland
since 1881, and much of Ireland claimed to be anti-abortion,
PLAC's campaign was to prove the most divisive issue in Irish
society since the Civil War in the 1920s. For nearly two years,
between 1981 and 1983, a battle raged between PLAC and
opposing forces united under the banner of the Anti-

Amendment Campaign. A referendum was held in 1983 which produced a 2–1 vote in favour of granting equal rights to mother and foetus from the moment of conception. The extent of public disquiet was evident in the fact that only half the electorate voted, despite the clergy's best efforts to persuade them otherwise (Jackson, 1986).

Not satisfied with its achievement in the referendum, the Catholic Right has remained highly active. In 1985, SPUC took legal action against the Dublin Well Woman Centre and Open Line Counselling on the grounds that they were in breach of the newly amended Constitution by referring women to British abortion clinics. Following a court case the Well Woman Centre was prevented from carrying out referrals, and Open Line was closed down. An appeal by both organizations in 1988 was lost, and legal costs amount to a total of £80,000. Both organizations had their case referred to the European Court of Human Rights at Strasbourg by their Senior Counsel, Mary Robinson, and a decision is being awaited at the time of writing (see Rossiter, 1990; Burtenshaw, 1991).

In 1988, SPUC turned its attention to the student unions, which had been openly distributing information on abortion. Student unions have no legal status in Ireland, and as such cannot be prosecuted, but this detail did not deter SPUC. An injunction prohibiting their activities was served on fourteen named student officers. Refusing to obey, the students were taken in October 1989 to the High Court, where SPUC sought to have them jailed for contempt. However, SPUC lost their round, since the woman Justice, Mella Carroll, conceded that Defence Counsel Mary Robinson had raised a valid point of EC law, namely, that information on a legally available service in one member state should be accessible in another. Consequently, the case was referred to the EC Court, the European Court of Justice in Luxembourg, whose decisions, unlike those of the European Court of Human Rights, are legally binding. Meanwhile the saga continued, this time with SPUC applying to the Irish Supreme Court for a further injunction, which they were duly granted. Despite this, and under investigation by the Irish Special Branch (police intelligence unit), the students continued to distribute information publicly until June 1990, by which time their term of office had come to an end.

In March 1991, the European Court gave its first decision. It held that medical termination of pregnancy constitutes a service under the meaning of Article 60 of the Treaty of Rome. However, the Court ruled that the Irish state was entitled to prohibit the distribution of information by the defendants, as they had no economic links with abortion agencies in other member states. The ambit of the European Court had been primarily in economic and commercial matters, owing to the nature of EC relations to date. Nevertheless, the Court went further and ruled that member states have the right to derogate from European law where moral issues are concerned. Because the unborn's right to life is enshrined in the Irish Constitution, it was said, the Irish people have made it clear that they want to rule for themselves on the moral issue of abortion; therefore, European law cannot intervene in this matter. In May, the Advocate General of the Court gave a similar opinion, and in October thirteen judges, drawn from different member states, concurred with the original decision. The verdict has now to be applied in the Irish High Court.

Although the judgement seemed decisive, a nebulous area of EC law remained unresolved. For instance, there could be no guarantee that organizations commercially linked to abortion clinics in Britain, or elsewhere, would not test Article 60 of the Treaty of Rome at a future date. At this stage SPUC and the other elements of the anti-abortion lobby, as well as the Irish government, were quickly rescued from a tight corner. In November 1991, as the Maastricht Summit approached and the process of European political and social integration was being set in motion, there were rumblings that the signing of the Social Charter could open up the possibility for Irish sovereignty to be clawed away in a number of important areas. Disquiet was expressed, in the Dáil debate preceding Maastricht, that EC law had the potential to strike right at the heart of Irish culture and traditions. Senator Des Hanafin argued that 'we should not surrender to a body whose values are quite different to our own in matters of human life, human rights, and family rights'. Further, he stated that 'we are different from any of the nations of Europe in our ethos'. Mindful of this criticism and the damage the anti-abortion lobby could wreak at a future date, when full European union would have to be put to a national referendum, the Taoiseach put forward the following 'protocol' to the Treaty on European Union:

> Nothing in the Treaty on the European Union, or in the Treaties establishing the European Communities, or in the Treaties or Acts modifying or supplementing those Treaties, shall affect the application in Ireland of Article 40.3.3 of the Constitution of Ireland. (Irish Times, 1991 [Article 40.3.3 established foetal civil rights]).

As we all know, the Maastricht Summit ended in chaos, primarily due to the British government's intransigence, but despite the chaos, the inclusion of the Irish protocol on abortion was agreed by the member states. By acceding to this protocol they have ensured that any future testing of Article 60 of the Treaty of Rome is unlikely to succeed, and they have also thrown into question the whole nature of the EC legal system generally, and specifically the situation with regard to abortion throughout the twelve member states. It is also important to note that the protocol refers not only to the forthcoming European Union Treaty but to all previous EC treaties (Rossiter, 1992).

Hardly was the ink dry on the Maastricht protocol than the horrendous but inevitable outcome of the EC's collusion with the Irish government became apparent. The Attorney General, on learning that a 14-year-old rape victim had travelled to Britain for an abortion on 6 February 1992, imposed an injunction preventing her from having the termination. The girl's family had contacted the police in Ireland to enquire if foetal tissue could be used in building up a DNA profile of the rapist and found that such evidence was inadmissable in Irish law. They also found that daughter and family would be prosecuted and probably exposed to the full glare of publicity on their return to Ireland if the abortion went ahead. Consequently, the family returned home and in the ensuing two weeks Irish society experienced a collective trauma which may lead to the removal of the 1983 Amendment to the Irish Constitution in the long term. Large, angry demonstrations and scuffles between protesters and the police occurred almost daily outside government buildings. Parliamentary opposition parties called for the resignation of the Attorney General and an *Irish Times* editorial pointedly asked, 'With what are we now to compare ourselves? Ceausescu's Romania? The Ayatollahs' Iran? Algeria? There are similarities . . .' Many people queried how the EC could have sanctioned such a violation of British jurisdiction, a question echoed by the British and international press. Following intense political activity Irish society breathed a sigh of relief when an emergency hearing of the case in the Supreme Court in Dublin lifted the injunction and permitted the 14-year-old girl to travel to Britain. A Repeal the Constitutional Amendment Campaign has been formed, but already the Catholic Church and the anti-abortion organisations, such as SPUC, are on the defensive.

Despite the best efforts of SPUC, the Irish government, the Irish courts, and latterly the EC Court, the number of women crossing the Irish Sea seeking abortions in Britain has not abated; in fact, they are increasing annually. Official statistics show that 261 women resident in the Republic obtained legal abortions in England and Wales in 1970; by 1990 the figure was in excess of 5,000. In reality, the number of terminations is much higher – estimates suggest up to 10,000 per year – as Irish women frequently give false British addresses to abortion clinics for fear of detection. British women's magazines, which circulate widely in the Republic, were one of the last sources of abortion information, but in October 1989 *Cosmopolitan* was given six months' notice to remove abortion advertisements or face being banned by the Irish Censorship of Publications Board. The magazine now circulates in the Irish Republic with blank spaces where abortion clinic advertisements should appear, and other magazines have had to follow suit. Information is still getting out through some of the student unions, the Women's Information Network operates underground from the Dublin area, and the Irish Women's Abortion Support Group operates a telephone line, counselling and support services from London.

The Election of Mary Robinson and the Modernization of Irish Society

Mary Robinson, feminist, member of the Upper House of the Irish Dáil and constitutional lawyer who had been the prime mover in the legislative change in the area of reproductive rights and sexuality, was elected President of the Republic in November 1990, after a presidential campaign in which the depths of misogyny had frequently been plumbed (Finlay, 1990). Some of the most powerful forces in the land, including Fianna Fáil, the largest political party, were ranged against the winner. Can we say, therefore, in the words of Yeats, that yes, 'All's changed changed utterly'? Most commentators acknowledge that Robinson's election was part of the fallout over the abortion and divorce referenda results and the subsequent opening up of a public debate on the role of the Catholic Church in Irish society. That social change on these issues is occurring is indisputable, and especially since the recent rape case, but the extent of it is still very much an open question, as is the length of time the whole process is going to take. A recent survey by the Reverend Michael McGreil, a sociologist at Maynooth, the ecclesiastical college, shows that 82 per cent of the population attend Sunday Mass compared to 87 per cent in 1984 and 91 per cent in 1974. Formal religious practice is shown to be much lower in the Dublin area, where a figure of 64 per cent was recorded. Despite the decline, however, the survey underlines the fact that Ireland is still the most religious society in Europe, and while the strength of the Catholic Church has been dented somewhat, it is still triumphant (Pollack, 1991).

Nell McCafferty's claim – with which this chapter opened – that it would be only a matter of time before divorce, homosexuality and even abortion would be legalized fails to take account, much as does Rostow's economic 'stages' theory in relation to Third World societies, that the structural underdevelopment of the Irish economy produces serious impediments in the way of a measured progress in the social as well as the economic life of Ireland. The serious crisis in which the Irish economy found itself in the mid 1980s, with large-scale unemployment and massive emigration, was in part a product of world recession, but the depth of the crisis was due to the fact that scarce local financial resources had been diverted into foreign multinationals attracted to Ireland in the late 1960s and 1970s. Local industry, starved of capital, was severely damaged, as 64 per cent of all available Irish grants went to foreign firms based in Ireland between 1979 and 1983 alone. In 1983, for example, £500 million in multinational profits were taken out of the Irish economy, and Irish foreign debt per head is about twice as high as that of Argentina, Mexico and Brazil, countries whose debt crises have been making world headlines (Jennings, 1985, p. 138).

In order to place the exigencies of the economy aside, and to extract his government and party from the political crisis which the presidential election represented, one of the Taoiseach's first acts was to promise the liberalization of a number of areas, including divorce and contraception. Following from this, a legal process was begun whereby the current age limit for access to condoms would be reduced from eighteen to sixteen. The Republic of Ireland has a very serious drugs problem, the highest rate of heterosexual AIDS cases and the highest rate of babies infected with the virus in the EC, but as a result of a clerical onslaught led by Dr Cahal Daly, the ultra-conservative Catholic primate, Charles Haughey and his government backed down, muttering loudly that they weren't 'really all that keen on this condoms for sixteen-year-olds business' and that the proposal for the introduction of contraceptive-dispensing machines in public places was being ruled out.

Clearly, in Ireland as in many debt-torn countries through-out the world, capitulation to right-wing conservatives and religious fundamentalists is a common phenomenon. Even the introduction of divorce has posed serious contradictions, as the failure of the 1986 referendum clearly showed. At the time, it was estimated that 72,000 adults were directly involved in marital breakdown, and there seemed to be a widespread consensus on the need for a legal resolution of their situation. However, a Church-backed Anti-Divorce Campaign was suc-cessful in touching a raw nerve in Irish society by issuing warnings that the introduction of divorce could lead to the break-up of the family farm, leaving men to bear the intoler-able burden of two families; and that women would find themselves impoverished, given the paucity of employment oppportunities for them (Prenderville, 1988).

Economic and political contradictions apart, feminists and women generally in Ireland were euphoric at Mary Robinson's election, regarding it as a major event in the annals of feminist history worldwide, despite criticisms of the President's position on Northern Ireland, which would seem to favour the maintenance of the Union with Britain. Some might read this as a manifestation of support for the shelving of the Irish National Question, the acceptance of the reality of Partition and the inference that the political project should henceforth be an exclusive concentration on the 'modernization' of the Southern state. While it must be said that elements within the Republic's feminist movement insist that Irish women have, as Edna Longley puts it, 'been starved and repressed by patriarchies like Unionism, Catholicism, Protestantism, Nationalism', and that 'Catholic Nationalism has often been as great an oppressor of Irish people, Irish women, as British imperialism or Ulster Unionism' (Longley, 1990), there are still substantial sections of the movement which recognize that religion, nationalism (whether of the Southern Catholic or the Northern Protestant variety) and women's oppression are caught in a dialectical relationship, and that Partition will for ever cast a long shadow on the Irish body politic, feminist and otherwise, until a just settlement is achieved in the North. Whatever their political persuasion, most feminists have shown that they are unwilling to wait for any form of geopolitical settlement and are participating in the debate which Mary Robinson's election has opened up, as well as engaging in the brave new language the President speaks – that Ireland should adopt 'a European model' of a socially progressive country which is inclusive rather than exclusive.

And in Britain . . .

The response in Britain, especially from feminists, has been instructive. Irish women are probably somewhat more chary of accepting that a dramatic reversal of the past is possible – in the short term, at least. Their 'insiders" knowledge of the continuing flow of emigration, the sure barometer of recurring economic failure, and their experience in dealing first hand with Ireland's social rejects, especially the women seeking abortions in Britain, inevitably temper their response. Amongst British feminists the coming of Mary Robinson was welcomed, one manifestation of this being her election as '*Guardian* Woman of the Year' in 1991. Beyond this show of interest there has been no serious analysis of the phenomenon this woman represents in a country which has been Britain's backyard for so long, nor for the three million women-plus of Irish descent living in Britain. In fact the only analysis by a British feminist published at the time of writing is Melanie Phillips's *Guardian* article of 27 February 1991.

Unfortunately, this article is frequently marred by the 'deterministic belief system' described earlier in this chapter, one example being:

> When the people elected her, it was as if they had looked into a mirror and admired the reflection. In some ways the image wasn't their own at all, but no matter; it was how they wanted to see themselves. For this is a landscape of distorting mirrors, where nothing is straightforward, where every message is ambiguous.

To some this may be an explanation of the dilemma facing Southern Irish society today: whether to move forward in step with Western Europe or retain the old values which set it apart. To many of us it represents a classical 'mind-set' in relation to things Irish, all too often found in British feminism, which ignores the historical contradictions and fails to emphasize the long and hard struggle of so many women in Ireland – and outside it – to rectify a situation which has meant being caught 'between the devil and the deep blue sea' in relation to nation, race and religion.

Muslim Women and the
Politics of Ethnicity and
Culture in Northern England

YASMIN ALI

W omen are the hidden factor in the politics of
ethnicity in the Muslim communities of Northern
England. The broader context to the apparent silence of
women lies in a matrix of patriarchy and imperial experience,
as well as the impact of Orientalism on contemporary European culture. In other words, there is a culturally embedded
assumption that women should know their place, colonial
peoples should know their place, and oriental women are too
ethereal to have a place at all. The regional context of
Northern social conservatism has also had its impact upon
how women in all communities, including Muslim communities, are constructed. Last but not least, the particular ways in
which a male community 'leadership' has sought to ossify
culture and ethnicity have suppressed and denied women's
difference, making invisibility a safe but ambivalent position
for South Asian women. These different – but mutually
reinforcing – stereotypes of women render the problem of
Muslim women conspicuous, even whilst their presence is
hidden.

In this chapter I want to examine the factors which have
thrown such a shadow across the experience of women from
South Asian communities in the North of England, and have
so distorted the dynamic of community development in general. That women are largely invisible needs little argument.

The spotlight thrown on to Muslim communities in the North of England by *The Satanic Verses* affair illuminated few female faces, and women's voices were little sought by cultural commentators eager to understand what they saw as an anti-Enlightenment spasm in the Pennines. Women, it was variously assumed on several sides, were either passive supporters or victims of the *mullahs*.

The truth is more complex, and its origins lie as much in what minority communities experienced after coming to Britain as in the particular features of the 'cultures' they are alleged to inhabit. Uprooting and crossing continents to start life again has an impact, and continuing reverberations, upon groups as well as individuals. As communities have experienced the trauma of their creation in the process of migration, so forms of politics have developed within them which have looked – inevitably, considering their marginalization – for more powerful allies or patrons (real or imagined) in the country of origin, or in Britain, or in both. I want to examine the ways in which two different – at some levels antagonistic but ultimately complementary – forms of politics have had an impact upon women in Muslim communities. One of these forms of politics is multiculturalism; the other is ethnicism. An apparent 'third way', anti-racism, will be considered briefly because of the role it played, inadvertently, in facilitating the triumph of ethnicism. Finally, I will suggest that a real alternative, arising out of resistance to the conservatism of both state and the current construction of community, is, in however fragile a way, beginning to emerge, particularly through the experience and struggles of women. In order to explore these possibilities, however, the communities must be looked at in historical and political context.

The Impact of Multiculturalism

Multiculturalism grew from the state's response to growing New Commonwealth communities in Britain in the 1960s. It is based on an assumption – not always explicit – that minorities can be given limited autonomy over internal 'community' affairs, such as religious observance, dress, food, and other supposedly 'non-political' matters, including the social control of women, without their presence offering any major challenge to the basic framework of social, economic and political relations in society. Multiculturalism has provided the ideological justification of – and coherence for – a range of policies designed to contain communities and isolate them from – or mediate their limited entry to – the local political arena. It has also had the purpose, as far as governments of both the Labour and Conservative parties have been concerned, of depoliticizing 'race' as an unpredictable populist factor in British politics.

Whilst it has clearly been less successful in the latter mission to subdue popular racism, multiculturalism has had astonishing success in the former task of viewing local communities primarily as targets of social policy, rather than as actors in the democratic system. Multiculturalism has also taken on a certain life of its own as it has become rooted as the dominant ideology of 'race' in a range of key professions, notably education and the social services, perhaps because of the ease with which it can be incorporated into existing assumptions about the proper functioning of the welfare state. Multiculturalism has been able to endure since the 1960s, when it was named (perhaps one should say 'christened') by Roy Jenkins as Home Secretary in the context of the first Race Relations Act (1965), the Local Government Act (1966), and the consolidation of highly restrictive immigration controls, because in its slippery pragmatism it typifies British political bipartisanship on questions of 'race'.

Pragmatism, of course, is, the preferred British term for a policy lacking any defensible basis in principle. In the 1960s the Home Office had looked at the kinds of policies then being developed by the Johnson administration in response to the demands of the Black Civil Rights Movement in the United States of America. The Civil Rights approach (itself not unproblematic in relation to questions of class) was rejected as unsuitable in British circumstances. Multicultural-ism was preferred because it draws much less upon assumptions about citizenship in a democratic state than upon the experience of colonial administration in the age of decolonization. The multiculturalist state could, for example, liaise directly with an unelected community leadership rather than face the uncertainties of democratic coalition-building.

Multiculturalism's impact upon communities has been one of delimiting and delineating the extent of autonomy to be exercised by an elite self-selected or confirmed by patronage, in exchange for a more general social and political quiescence. In other words, through multiculturalism the state sought to find a means whereby the 'integration' of South Asian communities could be achieved by constructing a stratum of mediators who could represent the community to the state (usually the local state), and interpret the state to the community, without recourse to the ballot box or the slower processes of political socialization which accountability would have required.

From the beginning, women were not wholly excluded from the ranks of appointed community representatives; early membership lists of 'race relations' bodies reveal the presence of women's names. However, because of the pattern of mass migration – in which men came to Britain alone, to be joined much later by women and children – few working-class women would have been in Britain in the 1960s and so eligible for such co-option, even had it been likely. Thus, as with many routine duties associated with *noblesse oblige*, it was not unusual for the wives of doctors and academics in the 'migrant aristocracy' to be the ones who made early contributions to the policy of 'race relations' by community leadership. Recognizing their role as 'interpreters' of their own working class to white authority, such women could collude in stereotyping working-class women, whilst retaining – the exception proving the rule – their own relative autonomy. It is now difficult to find documentary evidence to illustrate this process as it occurred in the 1960s and 1970s, but I certainly winced through meetings in Lancashire in the 1980s in which middle-class women misrepresented working-class women to white audiences eager to feed upon stereotypes.

Such an inherent class bias in the initial construction of the community leadership also points to an ethnic bias, in that the urban educated middle class from the subcontinent did not necessarily share the same ethnic profile as the mass of working-class migrants they were called upon to represent. At the very least there was often an urban/rural divide between the middle class and the working class of the same national origin, sometimes exacerbated by linguistic differences. The subsequent growth of communities in the 1970s in particular did lead to the emergence of what might be seen as more authentic or organic community leaders, often with a commercial rather than a professional background of achievement. This shift to a petty-bourgeois leadership was clearly not in itself unproblematic (some of the problems will be explored below), but in any case the legacy of the earlier 'leaders' remained evident in traces in community politics, particularly where three factors obtained: where the professional middle class were marginalized within their professions (this was particularly true in the medical profession); where they shared ethnic or religious affiliations with the local working-class communities; and where the local political culture was inherently conservative, even if not in a party political sense.

These three factors are found in many non-metropolitan areas in the North of England, particularly parts of West Yorkshire and East Lancashire. Socially conservative, pious, and lacking in glamour or significant career opportunity in some of the professions, majority and minority communities have mutually reinforced their latent hostility towards further change or upheaval. The particular social matrix obtaining in parts of Northern England had other effects in the context of the rise of multiculturalism – effects of particular significance for women.

For the present, it is sufficient to say that the greater

diversity of social and political contests and conflicts in large cities makes even conservatism a conscious political choice. Where that is the case, conservatism becomes a position with which it is legitimate to engage in argument because it is self-evidently not monolithic within the community. Relative isolation from diverse social and political currents renders such engagements nearly impossible in the non-metropolitan regions; there, conservatism is the dominant force. This point is important, because the forms that an alternative politics must take in such a conservative environment are different from 'mainstream' or overt opposition, and must be camouflaged in ways that appear to deny any political content or intent. This is particularly true in relation to oppositional stances taken by women, who are subject to a more limited political arena, as well as a greater degree of social censure, in comparison with their male peers in these communities.

Northern Conservatism

It is worth illustrating the operation of Northern conservatism. Its unattractive features – insularity, parochialism, and an apparent obsession with the social control of women and girls – can be contrasted with the more positive benefits of community cohesion in the face of racism and external hostility. This can help to explain the strong ties that bind women – of their own volition, in large part – to communities which in other ways frustrate their aspirations. It is also important in this context to contrast metropolitan media images of Northern communities with the more complex reality.

The North of small-town East Lancashire and West Yorkshire is in many respects materially poorer than other regions of Britain which experienced substantial settlement of minorities from the Indian subcontinent. The industries into which people were recruited, such as textiles, were already in decline in the period when primary immigration was taking place. There is evidence that the settlement of women and children occurred more slowly in the North than in other areas of

Britain, principally the West Midlands and London (Vaughan, 1988, p. 9), so rendering the process of creating genuine communities (in gender and age structure) much slower. Apart from the migrants from the New Commonwealth, such regions had, for some time, experienced net population outflow, so depriving them of the political, social and cultural fertility associated with the continuous movements of people characteristic of cities. Such an environment, its difficulties exacerbated by the economic recessions of the 1970s and 1980s, was inherently socially conservative.

Migrants, in response to the shock of their audacity in moving across the globe, can become defensive when the promise of their move is not fulfilled in reality. When such migrants face real, material difficulties, the tendency towards conservatism is understandably reinforced. When the communities into which they have come are also – sometimes for similar reasons – rather defensive, suspicious and conservative, the environment for progressive rather than defensive radicalism is poor. Thus the construction of Northern Muslim communities as a strange 'Other' – an 'enemy within' – is in part reflective of an endemic lack of knowledge or understanding shown by politicians, the media, and other (particularly metropolitan) 'opinion-formers' about the white working class in 'closed communities'.

The point can be illustrated by looking at the comparative treatment of the 1984–5 coal dispute and *The Satanic Verses* affair. Coverage of both events in the media traded upon stereotypes of wrong-headed but cohesive and single-minded communities. Yet stereotypes of the white working class are more ambivalent than those of working people of minority ethnic origin. Romanticized or heroic evocations of white labour have an echo in British political culture – and not solely on the Left – so that stereotypes can have a positive as well as a negative emotional charge. The result at the time of the coal dispute was to leave some space open for sympathy and political contestation of a subtle kind, as in Lord Stockton's tribute, as a former Conservative Prime Minister, to miners as the 'best kind of Britons'. Such understanding and respect did not attend the characterization of Bradford's 'book-burning barbarians', because this was an 'unknown' community.

So the obvious connections have never been made between the characteristics of the white Northern working class and South Asian working-class communities who live in such close geographical proximity. The social conservatism of both groups, and some of the social roots of their intermittent disaffection, are in many respects a regional British factor. To lose sight of that whilst evoking the spectre of 'religious fundamentalism' is to misunderstand and to misrepresent the dynamic of Northern Muslim communities.

There is, then, a North/South divide affecting South Asian experience in England which has been obscured by most media explanations of *The Satanic Verses* affair. A Harris Research Centre public opinion poll conducted among South Asians in Britain for the BBC television programme 'East' in May 1990 demonstrated this clearly. With the exception of answers to questions about the *Satanic Verses* issue, the most significant division to emerge from the national picture given by the poll was not between Muslims and other religious groups but between Lancashire, Yorkshire and the East Midlands, and the large South Asian communities of the West Midlands, London and the South. On a whole range of social questions – but significantly not on political affiliation – the North was more conservative than the South. That this closely mirrors social and political attitudes in Britain generally is certainly worthy of wider recognition. Northern English Muslim communities are as they are in part because of their specifically English regional qualities, not their 'alienness'.

The politics of multiculturalism, therefore, did at one level successfully mediate the assimilation of South Asian communities into British political culture, as the existence of a North/South divide illustrates. However, the form it took was a parallel path which institutionalized marginalization – a very British form of marginalization, and one with particular implications for women.

Community: Cohesion or Division?

Multiculturalism has cast New Commonwealth Muslim and other South Asian communities as ahistorical in character, despite the long and painful intertwining of all our histories over three hundred years and more. Where social divisions and antagonisms are readily acknowledged as existing in the dominant culture, particularly class and gender divisions, the dynamic of change is denied recognition in Muslim communities in Britain. The minority ethnic community, in the multiculturalist perspective, is constructed as static and two-dimensional, like an exquisite Indian miniature compared to the heroic conquest of perspective in dynamic European art. These communities, it is held, lack real politics, because there are no pressing social divisions to require negotiation and the exercise of political skills. In this view, all families are extended, children respect their elders, religious faith is total and unquestioning, and women are veiled creatures living in the shadows. Male community leaders are called upon by multiculturalism to mediate between this community and the authorities, like local elites under a colonial administration. Each side, leader or governor, trades with the other at the margins, anticipating occasional gains but mostly content to recognize their relative power and the boundaries of jurisdiction in each sealed system.

This is a caricature, of course, but it bears a remarkable resemblance to the assumptions really made by the multiculturalist state. 'Ethnic groups' (note that in the language of social policy only darker-skinned people have ethnicity) are presumed to aspire to permanent marginality by their continuing desire to speak the languages of the Indian subcontinent – sometimes known, strangely, as 'community languages' – and by their stubborn attachment to a rigidly hierarchical (but classless) social system. The local state, in particular, reflects ruefully from time to time upon the inherent contradiction between their 'equal opportunities for women' policies and the need to 'respect' minority community autonomy, but this glimmer of awareness of a problem rarely follows from a questioning of their assumptions about the nature of the 'community' itself.

These assumptions are permitted to survive because for the state it is easier to deal with something unchanging represented by authoritative figures who can be co-opted at the margins into existing structures. For the beneficiaries of such patronage the result can be to strengthen their hegemony within the community; the 'friends in high places' syndrome can operate in many cultural guises. Subcontinental systems of patronage and obligation have been able to fuse with British traditions of representation without democratic accountability because those in positions of relative power have found it convenient or rewarding, or both. 'Ethnic absolutism' was thus created and reinforced (see Gilroy, 1987, for a discussion of ethnic absolutism).

The new organic community leadership of shopkeepers and small-business owners was particularly likely to support the ethnicist position, as they had an objective material interest in maintaining the cohesiveness and introspection of the community. Their rise to lower-middle-class status was dependent upon the 'ethnic' and cultural needs of the community, because their shops and businesses supplied the services which white commerce had little interest in providing. The 'ethnic' grocers, clothing stores and specialist or multilingual services, from travel agencies to garages, did not merely serve the community, however; they also offered a highly visible expression of the community's identity and self-confidence.

The same also applies to the later development of community-based professional services, for example medical and legal practices, although their development was also symptomatic of the effects of racism in the professions, whereby doctors and lawyers (etc.) were effectively ghettoized, or compelled to seek to practise in a more sympathetic environment.

Genuine needs on both sides, therefore, meant that ethnic entrepreneurship was effectively promoted by the informal trade barriers of ethnic difference. This is by no means a phenomenon unique to South Asians in Britain. Marginalized or excluded communities have often generated their class or other social differences through a similar process, as any look at the history of African-Americans, or other non-European ethnic groups in the USA, will demonstrate.

In many cities successful entrepreneurs, usually fortuitously, came to develop new markets beyond the community – either by cultivating a growing multi-ethnic client group (like many food stores) or by attracting trade from beyond the locality through specialization. By thus weakening the economic ties that bind the middle class to the community, this has given the impetus in many areas to the middle-class move to the suburbs, in the classic migrant manner. Where such a move happens, it stretches notions of community, and will ultimately weaken the ties of allegiance. In non-metropolitan areas these changes have been happening to a much smaller degree. Where a weaker small-business sector depends more upon the community for its livelihood, the pressure for maintaining a static and conformist notion of community can build up. The threat of 'assimilation' is not only seen to challenge cultural norms, but has material consequences for the fragile emergent middle class. Survival, as well as sentiment, can compel 'community leaders' to seek to preserve or even invent 'the community' to meet their own interests. Diversity is 'bad for business'.

The results of this process of 'sticking together' can be slightly bizarre. Walking through inner Preston recently, I saw a middle-class Muslim family strolling through the narrow cobbled streets, with one of the children riding her pony! There, English suburban middle-class aspirations met terraced-street proletarian stoicism in a way that only migrant experience could synthesize! The serious point is that social processes – including class formation, and the dynamic of gender – when stunted by economic circumstances and the limits that racism places upon social mobility, will produce some strange consequences. One of these consequences is the imposition of a caricature of a particular form of patriarchal society upon still emergent communities.

This caricature is of the social structure of the region of origin. Inevitably, it is a poor fit when it is cloaked over a new and developing community in another continent. 'Settled' patriarchies have the appearance of being settled precisely because they include the spaces women have won for themselves, and because many forms of gender conflict become institutionalized and familiar. In Pakistan, India and Bangladesh, rural women have clear responsibilities and a physical terrain which is theirs to control. Conflict or difference can be countenanced without necessarily having to shake the foundations of social existence. Inverted and invented 'traditionalism' as imposed upon Muslim communities in Britain is not relaxed or self-confident enough to encompass or sanction any significant degree of conflict, precisely because it is felt that it would shake the security of the community.

The picture being painted here is one of the reality of marginalization. Communities still sufficiently new to be insecure have been going through the process of social consolidation in a climate of economic recession and continuing racial hostility, particularly in the North of England. Outside pressures – whether through allure or insistence, from 'yuppie' self-centredness to feminist consciousness – have found Northern England a difficult terrain in which to become established. It should not be surprising that Muslim communities have also demonstrated resistance to political and cultural challenges in this environment.

That there are interests involved in the promotion and defence of static notions of community, or ethnic absolutism, should be expected. So, too, should be the small but growing development of fissures under the surface of the community as its inherent contradictions – the very dynamic of community – are made manifest.

Women, Islam and Ethnicism

Islam provides a fascinating example of how ethnicity, community and gender can collide in strange and unexpected ways. The maintenance of a static notion of community requires an ideology, particularly in the face of a dominant culture which may appear at times to offer more rewards than continued and total allegiance to the community. Islam can provide the intellectual strength and cohesion to that ideology – ethnicism. The existing order in the community is sanctioned both by the way things are said to be done in an ever more mythologized version of the homeland, and by reference to the teaching of Islam. This may be of particular importance for the experience of women, as Islam, like other religions, can provide 'evidence' drawn from the social mores of the time of its historical origin to support particularly oppressive social practices. Islamic law as practised in some (but not all) Islamic states makes the point eloquently.

Islam, however, did not become a world religion by barbarism. For many, particularly those from peasant backgrounds who came to Britain to become working-class, the idea of engaging with interpretations of Islam as an intellectual exercise was as unfamiliar an idea as theological dispute might be to a Catholic peasant in the Minho. But the process of defending community cohesion by an appeal to the value and superior moral distinction of Islam has been capable of evoking a different response from younger people educated in the traditions of Western scepticism. Taught to question by their education, they have questioned both their religion and their community, but not in the ways that might be expected by Western liberals. For some young people Islam, when looked at critically, has appeared to offer a liberation from their parents' narrow conception of ethnic identity in a manner which does not reject the more positive attractions of community. Where ethnic absolutism offers a restricted vision, the global appeal of intellectual Islam offers the possibility of a wider world in which to live. Where an appeal to the 'traditional' or closed community offers the unattractive posture of defensivenes and fear of contamination by Western wickedness, Islam can appear to offer wider opportunities through its capacity to offer inoculation against materialism and sin.

Put simply, an intellectual understanding of Islam, as opposed to simple obedience to a theocracy, must question some of the basic assumptions made by the 'ethnic' community. Questions like choice of marriage partner, or access to education and employment, are answered in divergent ways by narrow ethnicism and broader Islam. Where the conservative community may want to pull a girl from secondary school at the age of fourteen (as happens regrettably often in parts of Northern England), the good Muslim girl who shows unusual devotion to her faith may find it possible to express a desire for higher education or professional employment without risking her position or that of her family.

The Muslim Manifesto produced by the 'fundamentalist' Muslim Institute argues the case explicitly:

> Muslim women in Britain are in a unique position to develop a comprehensive life-style all their own in which they can develop their talents and achieve their ambitions to the full always guided by Islam. (The Muslim Institute, 1990, p. 8)

A secular feminist might see this as self-deluding or inherently contradictory, and indeed, to some extent such criticism is valid; but it must be acknowledged that rebellion by bright young women may take many forms. The ties that bind to one's family and community are strong, and any means of reconciling personal ambitions with emollient relations with family and friends may be attractive. In the case of an appeal to Islam to legitimize educational or social aspirations, the means to a form of personal liberation – albeit qualified – may arise naturally, organically, from one's experience of a community in which strong (and possibly increasing) emphasis is laid upon religion as a stabilizing force in an unstable world.

None of this is to say that the contradiction is thus resolved. Marrying another Muslim, being educated as a Muslim, working as a Muslim: none of these things need be intrinsically stabilizing for the family or community if one's marriage partner is from the same religious group but not from one's own ethnic group, or if the marriage was arranged in too loose a manner, or if one gains 'too much' (particularly economic) independence as a woman through education or employment. In this way Islam is at least a potentially subversive force in the conservative communities of the North of England.

Declaring that a community is 'Muslim' – as opposed to Sylheti or Punjabi, for example – can be a guide to some of the fractures that will emerge as the dynamic of community creaks into gear. Men may have strong material and political, as well as 'moral', reasons for hoping that Islam will work as a brake upon women's independence. Women may find that they can subvert men's intentions by taking male rhetoric about religion, as in *The Muslim Manifesto*, at face value.

It is impossible to say quite how many younger women in the North of England have chosen an Islamist route out of ethnic absolutism. An impression of numbers may be possible, as there is an element of 'youth culture' about political Islamism which manifests itself in dress. 'Ethnic colour' in dress, and the wearing of make-up, appear to be rejected in favour of a more sombre style in which covering one's hair is more important than hiding the shape of one's legs. The inspiration seems to be contemporary Middle Eastern rather than 'traditional' Indian subcontinental Muslim. It is a student's or a professional/office worker's look rather than the dominant style, but as such it is none the less remarkably common.

To describe this kind of Islamist subversion on women's part is not to be wholly sanguine about its benign implications. The fact that political Islamism has some appeal in the North of England is symptomatic of the relative success of ethnicism with a Muslim core in maintaining rigid and religiously legitimated forms of patriarchy in the community. Tensions that must arise out of the experience of any community, let alone one that is still experiencing the shock waves of migration, have to take some form. Religion can be a powerful polarizing force against the attractions of secular materialism in imposing the direction from which dissidence can be expressed. Equally, however, the medium – religion – can become the message.

The Failure of Anti-Racism

It is also the case that the persistence of multiculturalism, ethnicism and Islamism underlines the failure of anti-racism in the 1980s. Anti-racism at its clearest asserted the unity of 'black' people in Britain because of an objective common interest in fighting racism. At the municipal level, anti-racism was a potentially powerful force for facilitating the development of more democratic and accountable political relations between black communities and white authority, as well as encouraging a more democratic political culture to emerge in minority communities themselves. At a basic level politics is about the distribution of resources, and the resources which the anti-racist local state could offer were not insignificant, even in the face of growing hostility from central government. There was an attempt, in some cases, to be explicit about making a linkage between different facets of anti-discrimination: in other words, to avoid the trap of thinking 'all blacks are male, all women are white . . .'

The promise of anti-racism – to offer minority communities a democratic route out of marginalization – was, unfortunately, rarely made explicit enough to be resilient in the face of the hostile political circumstances of the 1980s. Too often anti-racism was not distinguished from – or was mistakenly held to be compatible with – multiculturalism. The proper recognition of a need for black minority autonomy in the development of political strategies and organization too easily became an excuse for not recognizing or engaging with sexism in black organizations. Black women were under strong pressure to be black (or 'authentically ethnic') first, women second, in accepting the primacy of the anti-racist struggle. The white Left was – in some ways rightly – pushed to recognize its racism and leave well alone. In this context of walking on political eggshells, exacerbated by the central government assault upon Labour local government from the mid 1980s on, anti-racism dwindled into a better-resourced form of multiculturalism operating the usual system of patronage.

The débâcle of anti-racism was not merely an interlude in the forward march of multiculturalism. Its influence was real, if limited. The style and rhetoric of anti-racism, stripped of its political content, was plundered by both the state and minority communities, and found a path into the cultural mainstream – perhaps illustrating its potential strengths, had national political circumstances been more favourable. Attempts at creating a visual representation of the multiracial community were central to the practice of anti-racism in its heyday – for example, by paying attention to municipal public-relations and publicity material. This use of 'positive' multiracial images has now become standard practice in some government departments, and has been developed further, and in more complex ways, by the advertising industry. From Community Charge leaflets to privatization share issues, there is now some visual recognition of Britain's multiracial character. This is, in a small way, a token of success for anti-racism.

But the legacy of anti-racism for minority communities, particularly for community leaderships, has not been a depoliticized veneer of inclusion in the image of the national community, but a conscious taking up of anti-racist militancy for ethnicist ends. Anti-racism accelerated the development and practice of some of the skills of political activism, from lobbying to community mobilization, as well as exposing some of the weakness of Left-liberal sensitivity towards minorities. As the agitation against *The Satanic Verses* shows, the 'ethnic activist' has in many respects capitalized upon this heritage, much to the bewilderment and confusion of the white Left.

The new style of activism, stripped of the input (however feebly it was once manifested) of socialist and feminist politics, is often aggressive and macho, both in rhetoric and in action.

Socialists and feminists from within communities are cast as unmilitant gradualists out of touch with the realities of community life or contaminated by alien influences. In this way the 'traditionalism' of the old or lower middle class can be conjoined with the quasi-ethnic nationalism of male youth. There can be no place for women in this kind of politics, yet its lineage is authentically radical.

Fundamentalism

At no point in this analysis of the political influences upon Northern English Muslim communities has it been suggested that genuine Islamic fundamentalism is in itself the key influence. Understood properly in its global context, Islamic fundamentalism has an intellectual rigour and a praxis which are largely absent from the experience of Muslim working-class communities in Britain, as Tariq Modood (1990) has argued persuasively. Rather, as Akbar Ahmed has suggested (*Guardian*, 'Jeans for You, Robes for Me'), when a justification for some practice or belief rooted in 'ethnic' tradition is demanded, there is a kneejerk appeal to Islam as a means of avoiding having to face the question. In Britain, in the context of developments in international politics which have erected Islam in the place once occupied by Soviet Communism, some activists are only too happy to be associated with the glamour of a powerful international force, and the association, however tenuous, makes good copy for the press.

The dangers inherent in this noisily intransigent pose, full of sound and fury and signifying nothing, are well illustrated by an examination of the domestic angle on media news coverage of the 1990 war in the Gulf. From the moment of the invasion of Kuwait in August 1990 reporters began a descent upon the mosques of England, and particularly of Bradford, the capital city of the 'enemy within'. The effects of spuriously associating British South Asian Muslims with a war about oil in the Middle East, particularly one promoted so jingoistically by sections of the popular press, served only to entrench the marginalization of Muslim communities and to fan the flames of popular racism. Yet the relentlessness of media attention (in Preston, not noted as a media city, my colleagues and I were fielding several journalistic enquiries a day about the local community's position at the start of the war) encouraged people unsophisticated in the ways of the media to agree to blood-curdling propositions, and then to become trapped in defence of an ill-considered and politically dangerous position, as happened also during *The Satanic Verses* affair. This has then, all too often, been presented as the view of the whole community. It is no such thing. It is not the view of a homogeneous community, nor is it Islamic fundamentalism.

This takes us back to the position stated at the beginning of this chapter. There is a symbiotic relationship between the state and the dominant culture in Britain, and sections of the leadership and activists in South Asian Muslim communities, which has had damaging effects for the development of the community as a whole, and particularly for women. Its consequence has been a collusion between (unequal) partners to maintain a narrow and static definition of community which severely circumscribes the stage upon which women are permitted to perform as political and social actors. Multiculturalism has provided a mandate for the community 'leadership'. Ethnicism has provided them with an ideology. Islamism has done more, by subverting both multiculturalism and ethnicism. It has done this by conflicting with the former, and shifting the ground from beneath the latter. Women who wish to use their ingenuity can find some space in which to operate in all three of these political arenas, but there are limits – particularly upon working-class women – to how far it is wise to assert an alternative position, or to take independent and autonomous action.

Women and Dissent

Many women reach the limits of 'legitimate' dissent, particularly if their battles are not fought over issues where some

119

resolution or compromise is possible without loss of face for the men involved. Where the argument is over education or employment, for example, compromises which mean some acceptance of the community's 'right' to maintain surveillance over their women at work or study may be struck. Young men in colleges often form an informal intelligence network with a hotline to 'opinion-formers' in the community: reporting, for example, on unapproved relationships, attendance at social events, or even style of dress and 'immodest' behaviour. To reject, rather than accept, the community right to police personal life and choices is to take a much more difficult and exposed step.

Subversive – or, more often, submerged – acts of defiance nevertheless do continue to occur daily in the lives of Muslim women in Northern England. Even in the tightest, most vigilant of communities, women make love, or their own form of war, practise 'illicit' contraception in a variety of relationships, make unlikely friends, have abortions. At the same time the men proclaim – usually, I believe, sincerely – that such things cannot happen in Muslim communities, their own hypocrisies (and the women who share them) conveniently forgotten! But for a woman to choose openly to live as an outlaw in the midst of her own community, repudiating male jurisdiction over the limits of what is communally tolerable, remains so uncomfortable – dangerous, even – that few women in the non-metropolitan North of England are in any position to withstand the pressure to conform. Even quite small degrees of nonconformity may be sufficient to provoke massive pressure – some of it from women themselves, who see the reaction generated by their sisters' defiance as a threat to their own limited freedoms. Domestic violence, even, may be tolerated because the prospect of rejection – not by one man, but by one's whole social world – is felt to be too catastrophic to contemplate. The invisible ties that bind women to the community are very strong, but they are not necessarily accepted without criticism or struggle. To be critical and to struggle, however, is to accept pain.

Ultimately, such unhappiness cannot continue to be submerged. As the claims that there is a static community identity are revealed to be a fiction, so the male leadership's ability to impose their chosen methods of social control over women and girls must be increasingly contested. Real battles are being fought and won. The argument presented here is that such contests have their roots in the material world, and can take many forms. Islam, as a basis for one of those forms, has been appropriated by some on both sides in the contest because it is seen – in present, defensive circumstances – as conferring an uncontestable legitimacy upon two essentially contradictory struggles. It would be a mistake to dismiss out of hand the significance of Islamist 'feminism' in British Muslim communities. It is simply one – currently visible, albeit highly unsatisfactory – route to a limited extension of opportunity for a relatively small number of women.

In the longer term, however, the prospects of a continuing high profile for religion among the socially mobile are not good. For the Northern English Muslim intelligentsia, the limits of Islam as a key to the opportunities of a largely secular society must soon become apparent. It is likely that as that happens, the mode of expression of identity through religion must be modified, and may eventually become little more than a residue, at least as a basis for activism or political mobilization. The language of Islam is, in the present context, addressed to a contest within the community. Social mobility puts a greater focus upon relations with more powerful exterior forces – relations which see legitimacy symbolized in other, more secular ways. The growth of the new Muslim middle class in Britain will continue to undermine Islamism (as opposed to the simple expression of religious faith as an aspect of ethnic identity) by providing other outlets for the expression of class interests.

The real contest will then be revealed as a more fundamental struggle than the one currently expressed, in part, through Islamism. The coming contest will be a battle not against community – as, necessarily, some forms of Islamism have been – but for community. The community that many women, through their struggles to control their own bodies and determine their own lives, want to create will recognizably have emerged from the communities of today. The insecurities of migrant experience generate ambivalent effects. The reverse side of insularity and defensiveness could be solidarity and warmth in circumstances where women's experiences can be freely expressed and legitimated. Social and moral censure against a wife who rejects her husband could in other circumstances, become intolerable of a husband who abuses his family. Rigidity can relax, and surveillance can become concern and supportiveness. These opposites are intrinsic to community, but need a balance in order to be asserted in proper measure. Women are currently the missing balance in the Muslim communities of Northern England.

How long it will take for women's experience to find open expression in the Muslim communities of Britain is difficult to estimate. The forces which resulted in the epithet 'Muslim' being attached to in some ways disparate South Asian communities will retain their resilience as long as a particular and politically intense antipathy towards Islam remains a part of majority political discourse in Britain. There is a clear message, therefore: anti-Muslim 'racism' is bad for women. The unhappy prospect which follows is that in the political climate of the early 1990s it is not easy to see when Muslim communities will feel less insecure and vulnerable.

On the other hand, the social and political processes that can bring about change can be identified and, once understood, should be regarded as an imperative for action. To act requires, in the first instance, an active rejection of the multiculturalist state. The assumption that the same small group of men can always speak for the community in negotiations about the distribution of resources, such as Section 11 funds,[1] must be challenged. Attempts at limiting the choices available to women and girls with regard to social services need to be countered by demands for women to be actively involved in the delivery and structuring of those services. The institutions of the local state, in particular, need to be reminded, forcefully, that not all women citizens are white, and that no community's needs are homogeneous and unchanging.

The more difficult and more crucial area for action lies in interventions in the politics of community itself. Here there is a role for classic pressure politics by women who are able to put their heads above the parapet and draw the flak, but in the short term at least such action will remain a hazardous minority prospect in the communities of Northern England. Those of us within and outside the communities need to concentrate on the informal networks through which women operate in order organically to build up support for effective challenges to the hegemony of the community leadership. The solidarity of women over the politics of the personal sphere needs to be encouraged to emerge from the secret walls of friendship, and to take on a campaigning role.

These things must be done in order to reinvigorate the secular and progressive traditions within South Asian Muslim communities, so long suppressed by multiculturalism and ethnic absolutism. Only in this way can the oppressive practices developed by some communities be challenged with any prospect of success.

Note

1. Section 11 of the Local Government Act 1966 provides substantial resources to local authorities and other organizations for projects to meet the needs of minority ethnic communities. It is a condition of the receipt of Section 11 funds that local communities are involved in a consultation process to confirm the need for such projects before the bids can be received by the Home Office. Usually this process of consultation involves liaison with Community Relations Councils, Racial Equality Councils and other bodies which, in the non-metropolitan North, are largely male-dominated and conservative.

Education and the Muslim Girl

SAEEDA KHANUM

I have come to spend a day at the Bradford Muslim Girls' School. I hail a taxi from the Bradford Interchange and ask to be taken to the school. The Asian taxi driver smiles and turns his gaze away from my face. This subtle difference in attitude is on his part a mark of respect, and a change from the normal flirtatious actions of drivers to a Westernized Asian woman with uncovered hair. He commends me on my choice of school and hopes that I will make a good student.

I am greeted at the school, an old stone building in the city centre, by one of the older girls in a maroon-coloured uniform complete with *hijab* (headscarf). Over thirty girls attend the private middle school at the expense of parents who believe their daughters are getting a good education as well as a strong grounding in Islam. These schools are being set up in this country in an attempt to reproduce the religious and cultural values of Muslim home life. The schools act as daytime custodians, ensuring that Muslim girls do not stray very far from orthodoxy.

The Muslim Girls' School is staffed by a headmistress and seven part-time teachers: two Muslims, two Catholics, two Anglicans and one whom the head, Nighat Mirza, suspects of being an atheist. Costing £100,000 a year to run, the school raises only £28,000 in fees; some of the rest is made up in

124

donations from wealthy individuals and from selling school merchandise, like cards and mugs. The school runs on a huge deficit.

After morning assembly the girls disappear to rooms named after the Prophet's wives and daughters to begin their studies. The classrooms are spartan, small and decorated with posters showing details of prayer, pilgrimage and the life of the Prophet. Lack of adequate teaching staff and equipment, and a narrow range of subjects, indicate that the girls are getting less than a decent education. Although the school has been open since 1984, it was only in 1989 that some girls took GCSE exams in Urdu, childcare and religious studies. In 1990 the curriculum was expanded to include French and English. In 1991 the girls were promised Maths and Sciences. Although things may be changing, Mrs Mirza admits that past students have been cheated of an education: 'Sacrifices have to be made. I'm not sad that those girls left with no qualifications, but proud; they have the satisfaction of knowing that they did something for someone else.'

Nighat Mirza says that she too has made sacrifices. She claims that because of her present job, she will now be regarded as a fanatic by the education Establishment and will be unable to go back into mainstream teaching. While feminists eschew the hijab and see it as a symbol of oppression, Mrs Mirza says she feels liberated by it. She claims it makes her feel confident and gives her freedom to move around in the community: 'No one can see me, I'm private. I have access to all the world. Although shut off from the rest of the world, I have my own window to it.'

Mrs Mirza's teaching career followed marriage and motherhood. At the school she is interested in passing on the values of Islam as well as the benefits of her own experiences: 'I'd like the girls to be good Muslims and aware of their faith.' She dismisses suggestions that by teaching the girls to be good wives and mothers she is placating the demands of male members of the Muslim community. 'By teaching the girls about Islam we are giving them tools with which to challenge and fight for their rights. Empowering women doesn't frighten men but creates a more stable society,' she says. 'Islam teaches us that men and women are equal but different.' The girls are taught to understand the restrictions on their lives, and that Islam is a preparation for the life hereafter. She denies suggestions that the religious teaching in such separate schools consists of little more than teaching the girls to pray and read the Qur'an in Arabic, something they learn quite early on from their parents: 'In religious studies we teach the girls to question and analyse and to follow the commandments of God.'

Islam is said to pervade the whole of the school's teaching. French is taught by Molly Somerville, a charismatic white woman, dressed in shalwar-kameez and wearing earrings in the shape of the continent of Africa. The only presence of Islam in today's lesson is that the walls are covered with press cuttings about the French Muslim Alchaboun sisters Fatima, Samira and Layla, involved in the campaign to allow them to wear the hijab to school. In the afternoon the same classroom doubles up as a room for religious studies, of which the Christian element is also taught by Molly Somerville.

Today, the girls are learning about leprosy. They are told to look up the coverage of leprosy in the Bible – references are given – and in the index of the Qur'an, and compare the two. (No one has the courage to tell Ms Somerville that no such category exists in the Qur'anic index.) The girls then discuss the modern-day equivalents of outcasts; suggestions made include people with AIDS, the homeless, people with disabilities and black people.

Mrs Mirza says she wants her ten-year-old daughter to get the best possible education. Will she send her to the school? Yes, but only if things improve. Her daughter, she claims, doesn't need to come to the school to get the good grounding in Islam because, says Mrs Mirza, 'I can provide that at home for her.' If all other parents could do that, wouldn't separate schools like the Muslim Girls' School become redundant? 'Most other parents are failing to do that these days because they don't have the same background as I do,' she says.

Statistics, however tell a different story. Most Muslim parents don't send their daughters to separate schools but to state schools. Heavy fees may act as a deterrent, but in effect parents still place a value on giving their daughters a good standard of education, if only for the prestige of having an educated daughter in the marriage market.

During the lunch hour, I am surrounded by a sea of maroon uniforms. The majority of the pupils at the Muslim Girls' School have been sent there by their parents and have had little choice in the matter. They are now reluctant to leave, saying they have got used to the school. They agree that they would not be getting an education unless it was compulsory and have reconciled their personal ambitions with the realities of their situation. They say they are educating themselves because they 'might need it one day'. 'If I am lucky I might get married to a man who will let me use my education and get a good job,' says a fifteen-year-old with thick-rimmed glasses.

What do they like about the school? 'We get to learn all about our religion and can pray when we like. There is no racism here. No one here laughs at the way we dress, because we are all the same,' they say. Few dispute the fact they could get the same religious education by going to an ordinary state school during the day and attending a supplementary school run by the mosque in the evenings. They regard the education at the nearby state-run Belle Vue Girls' School with a certain degree of envy and wish they too had more facilities like 'computers, a proper gym and books'. A sixteen-year-old cannot decide whether she wants to be a doctor or a lawyer, but says it will depend on what her parents allow her to do. This strikes a familiar chord with all of them. 'I want to be a hairdresser,' says another. Does she think she will realize her ambition? 'No, because my parents won't let me.'

One tiny fourteen-year-old with freckles has hopes of being a journalist. I take to her immediately. She does not think her dream will come true because 'Asian parents don't allow their daughters to go into such professions.' A moment of silent confusion follows when I point out that they are talking to such a woman.

At the nearby Belle Vue Girls' School, a Bradford comprehensive where most of the girls are Muslim, there are similar conflicts. A group of about a dozen girls, of differing ages, have given up their lunch hour to talk to me about their hopes and aspirations. On one thing they are all agreed: none of them wishes to go to a 'separate' Muslim School. These girls see themselves as the 'lucky ones', for they have been brought up to regard education as a privilege, not a right. They resent the fact that their brothers are encouraged to get qualifications, whereas they have to fight for them every step of the way. No one is sure of the future. 'We all have our own plans, but we don't actually know what will happen,' says one lively seventeen-year-old who is about to sit her A levels.

They see education as a means of empowerment: 'If we don't get qualifications, then the only alternative is marriage.' These girls see marriage as the end of their individual identity, and some describe it as a form of death. One eighteen-year-old is getting involved in as many activities as possible before she gets married this summer: 'My in-laws are sexist and won't let me do anything once I'm married.' Yet she doesn't see herself as being oppressed: 'My parents' choice is my choice. My freedom is in my mind.'

The girls move on to the subject of 'love'. They describe 'romance' as being pampered with 'lots of chocolates, flowers and candlelit dinners'. The eighteen-year-old talks about her relationship with her fiancé, a childhood playmate: 'Before we got engaged, we used to be able to talk to each other. Now if he comes into the room, I go out. I never talk to him. I never look at him.' The other girls are horrified by this state of affairs and vow it will never happen to them. 'We will make sure we get to know the man before we get married to him,' they say.

Community pressure plays an overwhelming role in their

lives, and 'mistakes' made by other women in the community result in more restrictions. 'Asian parents don't understand the concept of individuality; we're always judged by someone else's standards, never our own,' says Farrah, a seventeen-year-old former heavy-metal fan who found her identity at thirteen when she became a practising Muslim. Dressed in a *hijab*, she says Islam has taught her her rights, that she no longer allows people to take advantage of her, and that religion is the dominant force in her life: 'It answers all my questions, makes sense and is perfectly logical.' Muslim women, she adds, are oppressed not because of religion but through a lack of religious education: 'Women have to be educated to use religion as a tool and not leave the interpretation up to men.'

For Asian women teachers, social pressures impose their own particular restrictions and difficulties. The younger generation of women teachers work hard to challenge their students' cultural and religious upbringing and to use their own experiences as a model and a guide. Saira, aged twenty-nine had been teaching in a Bradford state school for one year when a colleague reprimanded her for challenging an Asian girl pupil who said arranged marriages work because there are hardly any divorces. The white teacher accused Saira of 'arrogance' and told her to stop confusing the girl and learn to be more 'objective' about cultural concerns. 'As a black teacher in the school . . .' began Saira. 'You're not a black teacher, you're *a* teacher,' came the response.

This incident, says Saira, highlights the complexities and contradictions of her position: 'As a professional I'm expected to detach myself from the concerns of Asian pupils. However, as an informed insider who has experienced the intolerable pressures the community brings to bear on girls, I feel I have a duty to encourage pupils to hope for more from life.'

Some girls assume that because Saira is young, drives a car, wears Western clothes and teaches a subject other than Urdu, her experiences are completely different from theirs. To them she's distant and totally 'free'. 'This is just one step away from seeing me as an Uncle Tom, a mere token,' says Saira. Asian parents also have different expectations from an Asian teacher. On the one hand, they welcome the fact that Saira is Asian, but they also expect her to police their daughters on behalf of the community. 'Tell me straight away if you see her hanging around with boys after school, won't you?' they say.

Saira's ambivalent relationship with her pupils is paralleled by a story told by Asha, a twenty-four-year-old teacher in a Leeds state school. A stone was recently thrown at her in the classroom in what she describes as a display of 'tabloid fundamentalism'. 'I have an extremely good relationship with my fourteen-year-olds. They love having a teacher who relates to them in both language and experience. On this particular day, a new Asian girl had joined the class and I suppose the others were trying to impress her by seeing what they could do to rile me,' says Asha. 'I turned to the blackboard to write "biased" and felt this stone whizz pass my head and hit the board.' Asha's calm response resulted in the culprit coming forward to confess the full story. The girls had had a meeting during break and collected nine stones each, the size of pebbles, and decided and that if 'Miss' gave a negative response to the question 'Are you fasting?' then they would discharge their missiles at her. All but one lost their nerve.

Asha and another teacher tried to make sense of the episode, and there was talk of bringing parents in to discuss it and reiterate the school's philosophy of tolerance. She now thinks that the girls have an ambivalent attitude towards her: 'Part of them finds me and all I stand for enticing, yet another part of them finds me threatening. It was this conflict and inbred conditioning that made them respond to me in what I regard as a fundamentalist way.'

The education of Muslim girls has less to do with schooling than with the exercise of control by Muslim men over the lives of women in the family and wider community. Generally, control is maintained by monitoring the level and amount of interaction with male relatives and local community. But in the area of schooling, Muslim parents feel that their grip on their daughters' lives is weaker. Single-sex education is preferred by Muslim parents, and nearly always for their daughters only.

While many parents have been content with single-sex state schooling for their daughters, in recent years there has been a growing demand for 'separate' schooling – Muslim schools. This demand is now stronger than ever, not least because of the momentous events of the past decade, such as the *Satanic Verses* affair and the Gulf War. Muslim schools are seen as the ideal way of maintaining a cultural cohesiveness, but demand for such institutions remained relatively muted until the *Satanic Verses* affair catapulted British 'Muslims' into the headlines.

Why did the demand arise in the first place? Was it purely to do with inadequacies in the state education system, or was there a hidden agenda? If so, whose interest was this serving? The demand for separate Muslim schooling in Bradford in the early 1980s did not occur in a vacuum. The political climate created by the campaign for the provision of *halal* meat in schools and the campaign against headmaster Ray Honeyford for his alleged racist comments provided the perfect breeding-ground for such ideas.

The halal meat campaign was fought within the context of debates taking place inside Bradford council as it formulated its multicultural policies. The council's response to discontent among Muslim parents was to construct a multicultural policy based on the special needs of ethnic minority children. In November 1982 Bradford council circulated a memo to head-teachers entitled 'Education for a Multicultural Society – provisions for pupils of ethnic minority communities', calling on headteachers to promote better relationships with parents of ethnic minority children. The memo outlined plans to provide parents with Asian-language translations of school activities; allow pupils to withdraw from religious assemblies with special arrangements for Muslim prayer; allow pupils to wear clothing in accordance with their faith; and provide segregated physical education and swimming lessons.

These early battles were not fought solely on a Muslim agenda, although the Council for Mosques used them to negotiate reforms with Bradford council. The Council – then recently formed as an umbrella organization and an emergent powerful rallying voice for the community – saw one of its roles as mediating Bradford Muslim demands to the metropolitan authority.

A series of articles in 1983–4 by Ray Honeyford, headmaster of Drummond Middle School, Bradford, published in national newspapers and the right-wing journal *Salisbury Review*, criticized the city's multicultural policies. These articles drew allegations of racism. His writing contained phrases such as 'A volatile sikh', 'The hysterial political temperament of the Indian subcontinent', 'A figure straight out of Kipling is bearing down on me . . . His English sounds like that of Peter Sellers' Indian doctor on a day off' and 'Pakistan, too, is the heroin capital of the world (A fact which is now reflected in the drug problems of English cities with Asian populations).'

Honeyford claimed that the education of English children was suffering in schools where there were large numbers of Asian children. These views caused outrage in Bradford when he repeated them in the Yorkshire press in June 1984 and, following a sustained campaign, led by Jenny Woodward of the Drummond Parents' Action Committee, he took early retirement in December 1985.

Although the campaign to oust Honeyford was regarded among black people in Bradford as a considerable victory for parents and other anti-racist activists, they nevertheless found themselves facing a backlash from local racists as well as an onslaught from an unsympathetic press, both local and national.

Ian Jack (1985), in his revealing article 'A Severed Head' (*The Sunday Times Magazine*), described how popular racism surfaced at a football match when Bradford's Asian Lord

Mayor, Mohammed Ajeeb, went to receive a cheque for money raised for families of victims of the Bradford football stadium fire: 'As his shoes touched the turf a cry broke out. "Honeyford!" shouted a couple of thousand Bradford football enthusiasts, all of them white, "Honeyford, Honeyford, Honeyford!" The Lord Mayor's speech could not be heard. For possibly the first time in British history a football crowd invoked a school headmaster as a hero.'

Another effect of the 'Honeyford affair' was to reinforce the siege mentality of Bradford's Muslim community. The effect of this was paradoxical: faced with institutionalized racism, the community became defensive as it tried to hold on to its culture, but in turn this defensiveness made it internally repressive – as a patriarchal culture, its cohesiveness is threatened when its female members interact with the outside world. The concept of *izzat* (chastity and honour) is central to Islamic culture. However, the burden of upholding the *izzat* of family and community rests solely on the female members, so *izzat* is maintained by controlling women. Methods to control women are different from those that control men. Women's lives are effectively policed – often quite crudely – while for men, preserving honour and chastity is mostly a question of exhortation to self-regulation and 'good' behaviour. The solution of separate schooling preferred by religious fundamentalists finds an echo in the fears of parents who want to hold on to their culture and control their daughters' sexuality.

Asian parents often face conflicting tensions when it comes to making choices over their daughters' education. An educated daughter, particularly one in the socially prized professions such as medicine, law or teaching, is infinitely more marriageable than one who has a poor education or one who is not educated. However, education leads to independent thought, and hence to a desire for actual independence.

Choices in education reflect class, background and aspiration. Where parents are able to provide a strong sense of cultural and/or religious identity at home for their daughters, they are more likely to want them to acquire educational qualifications; they may be satisfied with the existence of single-sex state schools and supplementary evening schools in religious instruction and be reluctant to support Muslim schools. But where there is an apparent cultural deficit (such as when parents are unable to instruct children in the teachings of the Qur'an, possibly because they themselves are not educated) or where less value is placed on Muslim daughters' standard of education, then Muslim schools, where at least total segregation and Islamic teaching are guaranteed, become attractive. Judging by the background of most of the girls who attend the Muslim girls' schools in Bradford and Batley (West Yorkshire), these types of schools are more attractive to lower-middle- and working-class families. Wealthy visitors to Britain from Arab countries do not send their daughters to private Muslim schools, preferring to send them instead to English public schools.

The idea of Muslim schooling for girls as a radical solution to the perceived deficiencies of state schools had already been on the agenda for a decade. In the 1980s in Bradford the idea never really got off the ground, floundering because the council's education concessions, wrested by community campaigns, proved to satisfy most parental demands. However, in 1983 an abortive attempt to set up separate schools was made by the pressure group the Muslim Parents' Association.

Tensions came to a head in Bradford council when, during the debates about multiculturalism, the Muslim Parents' Association began its bid to take over five state schools with an overwhelming majority of Muslim pupils and run them as voluntary-aided Muslim schools. The Muslim Parents' Association wanted to set up Muslim schools at five existing state schools in Bradford: at the Belle Vue Girls' School, Whetley and Green Lane First schools and Drummond and Manningham middle schools. The MPA proposed to run the schools on Islamic lines but would not bar other children. It was estimated that this ambitious scheme would cost about £12 million. Abdullah Patel, a member of the MPA, was reported to have said confidently, 'Money is no problem.' He added that all he had to do was lift a telephone and any of the Muslim states in the Middle East would be willing to help (*Guardian*, 19 February 1983).

Bradford City council decided to put the proposal to public consultation, claiming that most Muslim parents were opposed to it. At one of the schools earmarked for the change, teachers took matters into their own hands and conducted a ballot among the girls. Pupils at the predominantly Muslim Belle Vue Girls' School overwhelmingly rejected the proposal. All the fifty teachers at Belle Vue, including Muslims, vowed to find other jobs if the plans went ahead. Polls taken later by the Commission for Racial Equality within Bradford schools and the community also found little support for the idea of separate Muslim girls' schools. The then prominent Bradford Asian Youth movement also voiced its objections.

The plans for separate schools (rejected by the education committee in September 1983) forced Bradford to speed up its educational reforms to cater for minority needs and so maintain good race relations. This in turn weakened the Muslim Parents' Association's case for separate schools. Ironically enough, at the time, the Council for Mosques opposed the demand for separate schooling and opted for a compromise, accepting Bradford council's concessions on school dress. In public the Council for Mosques said the proposal had not been thought out properly. Other Asian organizations said the idea smacked of 'educational apartheid'. Privately it was rumoured that the Council for Mosques decided that 'tactically' the time was not right to pursue the campaign because of the atmosphere created by the Honeyford affair.

In all these campaigns the Council for Mosques played a central role in the negotiations, using the tensions between the community and the city council to wrest concessions which fulfilled its agenda too. It supported the state's multicultural banner in the *halal* meat controversy, and flew the anti-racism banner to join in ousting headmaster Ray Honeyford from Drummond Middle school.

After the failed attempt by the Muslim Parents' Association

to 'buy' the five schools and run them as voluntary-aided Muslim schools, a short-term compromise was found. The Bradford Muslim Girls' School came into existence in 1984 when the Muslim Association of Bradford bought a former DHSS office in the city centre and converted it into a private school funded by fees and private donations.

Several unsuccessful attempts have been made in the past few years to get voluntary-aided status for the Bradford Muslim Girls' School and other schools like it up and down the country. Surplus places available at other local schools is often the reason given for not awarding voluntary-aided status – as in the case of the Islamia Primary School in the London Borough of Brent and Zakaria Girls' School in Batley, West Yorkshire.

Although far from perfect, the apparent acceptance of state schools today among Bradford Muslim parents and the gains in the city's multicultural policies since 1984 have come under attack from renewed demands for separate schooling, perhaps indicating that the issue was never really resolved. In 1984, in an interview (Ian Jack, 1985), Liaqat Hussein from the Council for Mosques gave the orthodox Islamic perspective of threat to the community's religious and cultural well-being. The struggle, he said, is between Islam and godlessness, which in the schools takes the form of coeducation, Darwinian theory, female emancipation and 'Muslim girls running away with non-Muslim boys': 'There's no such thing as freedom in religion. You have to tame yourself to a discipline. We want our children to be good Muslims, whereas this society wants children to be independent in their thinking.'

The Satanic Verses affair put Muslims on the defensive about their religion and culture, and Muslim men (in particular) on the offensive in their desire to control Muslim women. This in turn has put 'separate' Muslim girls' schools firmly back on the agenda – only this time, in fundamentalist eyes, Rushdie and all he represents have become a symbol of the struggle between Islam and godlessness. Despite his Muslim faith, Rushdie's professed 'godlessness' is unpalatable to most ordinary Muslims. Rushdie has, in effect, become a nightmarish role model from which the Muslim community and its impressionable young women must be protected.

A culture besieged in this way throws up its own notions of what a 'good Muslim woman' is – or should be. Religion becomes a substitute for a kind of cultural conformity. In practice Islam has come to represent what is allowed rather than what is possible. For women the idea of *izzat* has become more blatantly a means of social control, and Muslim schools have become the perfect institutions for exercising that control. Similarly, Muslim fundamentalists, like those of other religions, have misappropriated the word 'freedom'. Freedom to explore one's own potential as a human being – intellectually, socially and sexually – has come to mean being 'permissive' and therefore morally corruptible.

However, the argument in favour of separate schooling finds strength in its aim of gaining parity with other religious denominations and is in keeping with provisions enshrined in the 1944 Education Act: minority parents should be accorded the same rights under law as Christian and Jewish parents in their demands for voluntary-aided schools under the policy of equal opportunity.

According to Department of Education and Science figures (January 1988) about a third (32 per cent) of all state schools have voluntary status (under the 1902 and 1906 Education Acts) and are denominational. The pupils at these schools account for 23 per cent of all pupils being educated in state schools: there are 4,768 primary and 233 secondary Church of England schools, 1,863 primary and 421 secondary Roman Catholic schools, and 16 primary and 5 secondary Jewish schools. There are also a handful of Methodist schools. Apart from the few Jewish schools, there are no voluntary-aided schools of ethnic minority faiths, although there are a small number of Muslim, Seventh-Day Adventist and Orthodox schools in the private sector.

But the 1988 Education Reform Act has established the dominance of the Christian religion and undermined any notion of sufficiently catering for the religious needs of minority children. It has led to an increase in the popularity of supplementary schools where Muslim and other faiths seek to redress the balance. The overall low achievement rate of black children from some minority groups in state schools strengthens the hand of the separatists, who believe that only in separate schools can pupils get a positive religious and cultural education. This non-racist environment, coupled with higher teacher expectations, should increase pupil confidence and performance.

The counter-argument is that an increase in separate religious schooling will result in racial segregation. The creation of minority-faith schools will undermine multicultural or anti-racist education by absolving other state schools from carrying out such policies. Finally, there is the division along class lines: the creation of Muslim schools will be more attractive to working-class than to middle-class families. Politicians, including the Labour Party leadership, are divided over the issue of separate schooling. Those most vocal in their support for the idea also happen to have a large number of Muslim constituents. Others want to see the abolition of state funding for all separate religious schooling.

While attempts to gain voluntary-aided status for independent Muslim schools (totalling 26 in Britain) have failed, religious fundamentalists may have found a way of overcoming that hurdle. The opt-out legislation of the 1988 Education Reform Act gives state schools grant-maintained status and gives parents and governors control over the school. If the majority of these parents and governors in a school are Muslim, then the school can become, in effect, a state-funded Muslim school. At the time of writing, it remains to be seen whether this strategy will succeed.

However, very few have acknowledged the 'hidden agenda' behind the demands of religious fundamentalists: an attempt to stifle dissent and exert absolute control over the lives of women in the community. It is no accident, nor is it an act tinged with racism, that Muslim religious schools are referred to not as 'Islamic denominational' schools but as 'separate' or 'segregated' by those who have a particular idea of the kind of community they want to foster – both those who want the schools and those who oppose them.

The issue of education and the battle for young minds has become a matter of vote losses or gains in areas where there is a large minority community. The education of Muslim females has become a pawn in a power struggle. Can the self-appointed and often fundamentalist community leaders deliver the much-needed Muslim vote to either Conservative or Labour? Maybe, but only if their religious and cultural demands are met, particularly in the education arena. However, this claim has yet to be put to the test. Where Muslim parents have been forced to express their opinion they have tended to support the existing state school, not the idea of a 'separate' school. For example, in 1991 an attempt to organize an 'opt-out' at Willowbank Primary School in Glasgow failed amid accusations that campaigners had not made it clear that their aim was to set up a Muslim school ('Signing up for pupil segregation', *Guardian*, 5 November 1991).

Male Muslim 'leaders' are willing, it seems, to go to any lengths to achieve their goals. In January 1989 Muslim parents in Batley, West Yorkshire, enlisted the help of the right-wing organization Parental Alliance for Choice in Education. PACE, whose patrons include Baroness Cox and Norris McWhirter, is the offspring of the right-wing pressure group, the Freedom Association. PACE fought and won the court case for the twenty-six white Dewsbury parents (1988) who withdrew their children from a state school where 85 per cent of the pupils were Asian, in order to be allowed to send them to another, predominantly white, school.

Batley Muslim Parents, under the guidance of German convert Sahib Mustaqim Bleher, hope that PACE will win them their battle for state aid for the Zakaria Muslim Girls' School. Bleher has said that the co-operation between PACE and the Muslim parents is an 'interfaith alliance against multiculturalism, as what is at stake is not race but culture and religion'. The alliance, he admitted, is one of convenience, not a political marriage: 'We have different religions but both are preferable to some kind of secularistic mishmash.'

There has been virtual silence from Muslim girls and women over the issue of Muslim schools. In the poll taken in 1983 at the Bradford Belle Vue Girls' School the overwhelming majority of pupils and teachers rejected the proposal to turn the school into a 'separate' Muslim school. Another poll taken at the time by the CRE within Bradford schools showed a similar result. At the time of writing there are no indications that Muslim girls and women are preparing to voice their demands either in support for or in opposition to Muslim schools, but if the movement for separate schools continues at its current pace, or increases, those who object to it will be under increasing pressure to speak out and make their views known.

Note

A version of the first part of this chapter appeared in *New Statesman and Society*, 25 May 1990.

Double Exile:
Iranian Women and
Islamic Fundamentalism

MARYAM POYA

*I*ranian women are among the largest group of political exiles in Britain (Rouhifar, 1989). Their experience in Iran – first under the Shah and then under Khomeini and the Islamic state – is an important weapon for women in Britain against fundamentalist propaganda. In a women's conference which took place in London in summer 1991, after the Gulf War, in a workshop on women and fundamentalism, British women found themselves unable to answer the claims of Muslim fundamentalist women who participated. The multiculturalist consensus (see the Introduction to this book) prevented them from challenging these women. The presence of an Iranian woman exile not only made clear what had happened and is happening to women under Khomeini and under the Islamic state, but also allowed an open discussion about the position of women under a fundamentalist social order.

Between the mid 1960s and the mid 1970s, a large number of young Iranian women entered Britain as students. Britain was then a different society. The existence of radical movements – especially the women's movement and the struggles against racism – was encouraging. Many women became involved in the women's movement and the student movement and publicly participated in organizing against the repressive regime of the Shah. They soon became known to the Savak, the Shah's secret police, and found themselves exiles in Britain; many who went back to Iran were imprisoned, tortured and executed.

When one talks with Iranian women living in Britain, it soon becomes clear that although they lead full and rich lives here, it is their experiences in Iran which continue to be of most formative importance. And what continues to happen in Iran continues to affect them emotionally, with an intensity that nothing that happens in Britain ever could. In this, they are no different from many other women living in exile in Britain – except that they are even more so. Many of them have become doubly exiled – first from the Iran of the Shah, and then from the Iran of Khomeini. More than any other group of exiles they have borne the hopes and then the terrible disappointment of a revolution that at first seemed magnificently promising and then immediately turned on its head, when the source of power moved from the people to God – or, rather, to the fundamentalist leaders who assert that they represent God's will.

This chapter will explore the development of the political consciousness of anti-fundamentalist exiled Iranian women living in London: growing up in the Shah's Iran, becoming politicized, fighting for the revolution, escaping from fundamentalist Iran and, for many, continuing their political struggle in Britain. For this purpose I interviewed four women: Alma Gharehdaghi, a member of the caring professions; Mandana Hendessi, a researcher and writer on women's issues; Mana Sarabi, a student; and Parvaneh Dezfooli, an artist. This chapter would not have been possible without their contributions. Their stories are unique, but they also represent the experiences of many others. These common elements are emphasized in this chapter.

To understand the experiences of these women, however, it is important first to examine, albeit briefly, the contradictions of economic, political and social developments in Iran which shaped their political socialization.

Twentieth-century Iran

The formation of a 'modern' state in Iran coincided with the country's rapid integration into the world economy. The Qajar dynasty (1785–1925) introduced secular courts, army and education. Modern economic activity created a modern middle class. The economic and political power of the traditional middle class, with its close link to Islamic law (sharia law) and the clergy, was undermined but not destroyed. The new state synthesized modernism and traditionalism, in response to the new social formation. Moghadam (1991) calls it a neo-patriarchal state, a modernized patriarchy; however modern the form of state and its institutions, it remained deeply rooted in patriarchal values and the social relations of religion.

The two opposing classes formed an alliance against the Qajar Shahs, who were destroying the wealth of the nation by giving economic concessions to foreign countries. Although they had different objectives – the modern middle class desired a fair chance against foreign capital and the clergy desired the return of religious power and tradition (Abrahamian, 1982) – their alliance resulted in the victorious Tobacco Protest of 1891–2 and the Constitutional Movement of 1905–11.

Women participated in these movements and struggled for their liberation, as the coexistence of modernity and traditionalism in the state maintained the influence of religious laws, especially in the sphere of women and family. Women did not gain any political rights in the Constitution, for it declared that only men have the right to elect and be elected (Sanassarian, 1983). But women's involvement in the Nationalist and Communist movements of 1915–18 paved the way for many women to break away from the domestic sphere. Many became active in social and political activity as teachers, journalists, founders of women's schools and women's clubs, and as political speakers. Girls' schools were particularly attacked by the Islamic clergy as, by allowing women into the public sphere, they weakened the clergy's power to control their lives.

The Pahlavi dynasty (1925–79) centralized the state and intensified the process of secularization through modern economic and political development. Economic development was based on oil production under the ownership and control of an authoritarian neo-patriarchal state which never allowed any form of democratization. Although the power of the clergy was undermined more than it had been under the previous dynasty, the interrelationship between religious and secular ideologies continued. In the sphere of women and the family, marriage and divorce came under civil rather than religious jurisdiction, but polygamy, *sighe* (temporary marriage), custody of children and inheritance rights carried on aspects of *sharia* law.

The socioeconomic development of this period also opened the way for women in education and employment. However, the Shah's 'modern' state associated changes with the 'modern' woman (Najmabadi, 1991; Hendessi, 1991); therefore only a small number of women who constitute the modern urban middle class benefited from these developments. Traditional middle-class women did not participate in the labour market. On the one hand, their contribution was not essential to the family; on the other, the heavy weight of tradition and religion segregated them from the public sphere. A small number of rural and urban working-class women did enter the modern production of traditional industries which needed female labour – such as textiles, foods and pharmaceuticals – but illiteracy and economic hardship, as well as tradition and religion, did not allow them to benefit. According to official statistics, even in 1976–7, just before the 1978 revolution, only 11.6 per cent of rural women and 53.7 per cent of urban women were literate.

The contradiction of this form of uneven and unstable economic, political and social development led to the rise of the Nationalist and Communist movements of 1945–53 (Zabih, 1966; Abrahamian, 1982). The threat they posed resulted in the nationalization of the oil industry and the CIA coup. During the 1960s and 1970s, resistance to the regime continued to grow. Despite dictatorship and persecution of any form of opposition, a relatively effective movement of workers, students and guerrilla armed struggle developed (Poya, 1987a; Bayat, 1987). Finally, in 1977–8, a popular revolution overthrew the Shah's regime. Women played an important role in all the resistance and revolutionary movements (Azari, 1983; Tabari and Yeganeh, 1982).

These movements were divided into secular and religious camps. From 1965 to 1978 Khomeini led the religious opposition from exile in Najaf, a holy city in Iraq. In his declarations opposing the Shah's regime he did not separate Islam from nationalism, so secular Nationalist and Communist leaders were attracted to his views. They acknowledged Khomeini's domination of the opposition movement and followed his leadership during the 1978 revolution. After the revolution, however, Khomeini clearly opposed all secular movements. By 1981 all forms of Nationalist and Communist movements were defeated and banished.

Khomeini's doctrine of government was based on the theory of the 'governance of the religious jurist' [*wilayat al-fagih*]. It advocated an ideal traditional Shi'i society, in which Islam is a religion and a state – an Islamic state applying the principles of sharia law to all aspects of social and economic life (Bakash, 1985, pp. 38–40; G. Rose, 1983, pp. 166–88).

If the Shah's state synthesized modernity and traditionalism, Khomeini synthesized fundamentalism of Islamic ideology with traditionalism. As exiled women in this chapter argue, the Shah's state, especially during the 1960s and 1970s, entitled women to some reforms which allowed the development of new ideas, and encouraged the struggle for liberation. Despite political repression and the continuation of traditionalism women, to a limited extent, experienced some aspects of the women's liberation which was occurring in other parts of the world only. Khomeini's state, however, took away all entitlements from women and any new ideas in relation to women's lives in the twentieth century. The ideal woman under the Islamic state had to follow the path of Fatimah and Zainab, the Islamic female saints of the traditional seventh-century Shi'i society.

In the absence of any alternatives, Khomeini's theory of changing the 'corrupt' capitalist and Communist systems gained political credibility in the eyes not only of the most deprived sections of Iranian society, but of many Muslims around the world, who could identify with Khomeini's Islam as a way of liberation. He promised them that the Islamic revolution and the establishment of Islamic states would favour the *Mustasafin* (the 'downtrodden'), by paving the way for an independent society based on equality, fraternity and social justice; and free from hunger, crime and foreign domination.

But the slogan 'Neither East nor West' and the bitter reality of the eight years' war with Iraq resulted in Iran's isolation from the international economy and politics. However, Khomeini's death and the end of the Iran–Iraq War paved the way for a reformed Iran. Economic progress and development through opening the doors to both East and West has begun a contradictory process of change from fundamentalism to pragmatism, which has created disillusionment among the supporters of the fundamentalist system. The pragmatist economic policies in favour of private and foreign capital are seen as an eventual return to a position not unlike the one which existed before the 1979 revolution (Poya, 1987, 1990, 1991).

Reform has even appeared in relation to some aspects of the sharia law on women and family. As the population increased by ten million despite eight years of war with Iraq, polygamy and temporary marriage have now been discouraged, and even abortion and contraception are permitted under religious law. Although after the establishment of the Islamic state women were forced out of the paid workforce through early retirement and redundancies (Moghadam, 1988; Afshar, 1989c), during the war economy (1981–1988) a large number of women were encouraged to work unpaid behind the front lines to prepare food and clothes for the men at the front line. After the war, however, many women were employed and re-employed in paid work, as their contribution to maintaining the family became a necessity in the light of rising inflation and male unemployment.

Despite these pragmatist policies, however, the *sharia* law on women and family remained in force and has intensified women's oppression and subordination through segregation and seclusion. Sexual segregation and seclusion have led to an increase in arranged and temporary marriages (Haeri, 1989). Divorce and custody of children are the exclusive rights of men, and women's rights to work, to travel and to choose their place of residence are subject to male permission. Although women can obtain some of these rights from their husbands, their implementation can be denied in a number of ways: the necessity of male permission and witness; the withdrawal of husbands' decisions at any time; the use of force and violence against women – all on the basis of the principle that women are the morality-keepers of the family and society. Although in the Islamic state this ideology constitutes the official law, it is not specific to it. It was deeply rooted in the secular state of the Shahs, and even among the radical nationalists and socialists.

Politicization

The exiled women I interviewed were involved in all these processes of development and change, resistance and control, hope and disillusionment, which have been part of their lives since the 1960s and 1970s. As I explored their politicization with them, it soon became clear how powerful were the contradictory messages they received at home concerning womanhood.

As Mandana describes:

'A dual role was expected from women by religion and the state . . . they were sent to participate in the Shah's "White

147

Revolution" . . . they worked in the private and public sectors of the economy. But at the same time they had to be devoted mothers and wives.

'I could see my mother as a victim of this ideology. She worked full-time outside the home and was expected to be a devoted wife and mother inside the home. That made her feel guilty . . . under enormous pressure. She was expected to be modern, independent, free, and on the other hand to be a good manager of the home, a devoted mother and wife. These contradictions were reflected in her relationship with me. She wanted me to be a virgin because my future was dependent on getting married to a man who was superior to me and this was possible only if I could attract such a man with my virginity. She even made me go through the degrading virginity test, as I had a friend who happened to be a man. The contradictory dual ideology imposed by religion and the state forced her to degrade me and herself.'

And Mana says:

'Despite my secular education, all my life I was told that the most important thing in my life was my virginity. I did not even know what exactly was a sexual relationship and virginity. When I was sixteen I had a sort of a relationship with a young man. For years I was scared by the idea that I might not be a virgin. I was paranoid, to the extent that when I went for my entry examination for a teacher's training course and I heard that the examination also involved a virginity test, I wrote nothing on the answer sheets in order to fail.'

The politicization of these women was affected by the limited availability of progressive literature and poetry on gender, class and racial issues. Women like Alma, an Iranian Azerbaijani, and Parvaneh, an Iranian Arab, were motivated to join political movements because of national pride and the experience of national discrimination. In Iran, the Kurds, the Azerbaijanis, the Turkomans, the Arabs and the Baluchis are ethnically distinct from the dominant Persians. Alma was very moved by the poems of Forough Farokhzadi, 'who spoke boldly and honestly about her sexuality and intimate feelings as a woman', and Parvaneh was influenced by the Iranian Azerbaijani writer Samd Behrangi, whose stories expressed the conflicts in society, class and racial inequalities – all the themes around which the radical resistance movements have emerged. Heroic women's participation in the national struggle also played an inspirational part. Alma tells of an Azari woman, Sarieh, who participated in the 1946 fight against the Iranian central state which overthrew an autonomous Azerbaijani national government:

> 'Sarieh resisted the central government's troops for five days on her own and did not surrender. Just before her execution she said, "You have not won. Those who betrayed will only be remembered with hatred. Children of Azerbaijan will revenge my blood and our blood will nourish the tree of freedom."'

The process of politicization, however, takes time to mature, and life in adolescence was full of contradictions. Parvaneh says:

> 'Many friends were in jail and under torture. Many were executed. I was anti-Shah, but there was no concrete political guidance for my generation. [For a while] I found religion as a way of survival. I was not fundamentalistically religious. I prayed, but I wore a miniskirt. I fasted, but broke my fast with a sandwich and a Coca-Cola in the cinema. I found religion fulfilling and securing my life. I did not like the religious implication that women should stay at home. I did not want to stay at home. I wanted to be educated and be an artist.'

Throughout the 1960s and 1970s a large number of Iranian women who became active within the women's movement and the student movement in Britain were particularly attracted to the ideology of the armed struggle against the dictatorial regime of the Shah.

Alma remembers:

'The belief in the armed struggle was the dominant belief on the Left. However, the Fedayeen had a particular attraction to me. In the guerrilla movement, women were engaged at all levels of activities . . . This was a great leap forward, as women were recognized in their own right, as independent social and political beings. They were no longer just sisters, wives and mothers who were to provide moral and practical support for their menfolk; women were also encouraged to take part in the struggle.'

However, this 'great leap forward' was still far from satisfactory, because of the limitations of the political struggles in which the movement was engaged. The revolutionaries failed to observe and analyse the contradictory changes which were taking place in Iran. Blindly, they followed their formulae for liberation and socialism, failing to relate to the majority of the population, who were affected by the contradictions of economic and sociopolitical development. They did not relate to class, gender and racial inequalities in society except in an abstract way, as was the case with religion and religious values.

This continued also during the revolution. As Alma observes:

'As a whole, the revolutionaries were isolated from the working class and the oppressed sections of society, which facilitated the easy takeover of power by the conservative clergy. Generally the Left became even more isolated as they failed to understand the dynamics of the change in society. They alienated many people by their constant vacillations, mistakes and negligence in defence of democratic rights and women's rights, which were heavily under attack by the regime.

'In general there was ignorance and disinterest in women's

issues. Most male comrades felt threatened and considered them divisive and jeopardizing to the unity of the movement. A few of us who stressed the importance of the issues affecting women's lives were branded as extremists and separatists. The task was just to raise the slogan of equality and liberation of women and wait until the victory of socialism.

'During this period [of the revolution] many women's organizations were set up by women who were affiliated to various Left organizations. But unfortunately they were controlled from above by their political leadership, who dismissed women's struggle as insignificant and compromised with the fundamentalist regime. The excuse was that women who struggled for their liberation were only a bunch of middle-class women who had nothing in common with the working-class women. For working-class women, they argued, these petty feminist demands did not matter. Unfortunately the women on the leadership of these organizations remained loyal to the mainstream politics of their organizations. Therefore the task of struggling for women's issues which was so heavily under attack by the fundamentalist Islamic state was weakened and was finally destroyed by the victory of fundamentalism and its values.'

Mana agrees:

'When the first attacks of the fundamentalist regime began with attacks on women's rights, we were not prepared. Soon, we were driven to a defensive position and finally, we were defeated bitterly. We talked about women's independence and freedom, but fundamentally there was neither a real understanding of nor real belief in struggle for women's rights. Feminism was a dirty word. It meant only being anti-men. Our political education was mainly concerned with class struggle, and the struggle against imperialism and dictatorship. If we had appreciated the importance of women's issues, the level of our struggle and the scale of our defeat could have been different. We could perhaps have attracted a number of women who were absorbed into fundamentalist ideas.

'No doubt, the ideological and physical attacks on women and women's rights were so severe that all forms of organizations were smashed. But we are partly responsible for our defeat. When compulsory veiling was imposed, some "Left" organizations such as the Tudeh Party instructed their women to comply with the Islamic regulations. Their women sold their papers and publications while wearing the compulsory veil. Many of us didn't. We were beaten up but we didn't until they began to arrest us, but by then our movement was divided. By 1981, when some of us understood that there was a need for struggle on women's issues, it was too late.

'In many political and cultural gatherings, women didn't and still don't talk. They say, "All the good and important things have been said by men." Women believe that "men know better". In these gatherings men ignore women. Whether women discuss something of value or talk nonsense, they are ignored. Even when women are invited to these gatherings in order "not to be male-dominated", they are ignored. Men don't argue with women; they consider their contributions and their ideas worthless.'

Many politically active women gained valuable experience, trying to free themselves from racial, class and gender inequalities. They paid the heavy price of becoming exiles; but they found not only that the political movement did not tackle the importance of women's subordination, but that activists also discriminated against women at a personal level.

Parvaneh's story illustrates this:

'I became an exile in Britain as I became known to the Shah's secret police. During the revolution my husband and I went back to Iran. We felt that our struggle against the Shah's system was fruitful. In the first year of the revolution my daughter was born. Soon the attacks of the Islamic state began.

I was very frightened as more and more were arrested, tortured and executed.

'Finally, it happened to me. One day my daughter and I were arrested. They were also looking for my husband. I was kept in solitary confinement with my daughter for many months. I was tortured in front of my daughter and witnessed my little girl being tortured in front of my eyes. They threw me in a sack and whipped me with cables and chains. They threw women in the sack in order that the male torturer would not see the woman's body. They broke my little girl's leg in front of my eyes. I survived and never told them my husband's hiding place. He safely left the country. The prison authorities decided to release my daughter. She was given to my mother, who soon died in her grief for me. My daughter was left to my sister, as her father started a new life and forgot all about us.

'I felt desperately frustrated and sad. I could see that many women, as political prisoners' wives, remained loyal to their husbands for years. They never left them. They were there every visiting time, they gave them every support they could give. They tolerated the frustration and difficulties of living on their own with their children. They tolerated the authorities' insults and threats. They coped with financial and social problems, but remained political prisoners' wives. Their love and support made their husbands' imprisonment and torture more bearable. But for many women prisoners, the husbands were not there, even those whose lives were not in danger.

'Children of the political prisoners were always looked after by mothers and sisters, allowing men to find a new life. This hurts very deeply, even now that I am free, united with my daughter, and out of the country. I am still loyal to my political belief, but I have lost all illusions with political groups, as women's subordination to men in religion, in society and even within the opposition movement indicates that women's lives have little value.'

Escape and Second Exile

Alma decided to leave Iran again:

'I felt I was nothing but a subhuman in that society. I felt angry and bitter about all the political organizations in Iran: their limitations, vacillations and betrayal, which helped the consolidation of the fundamentalist Islamic state. I therefore escaped from Iran. Those who organize political escapes charge massively. They charge women more, as they believe women are more trouble. The journey took two weeks. I travelled through poverty-stricken border villages: no roads, no electricity, no water and no toilet facilities. I witnessed how fifty-five years of economic development by the Shahs of the Pahlavi dynasty haven't touched these areas . . . Some others joined me. To cross the border and reach our destination we had to run, to climb mountains and ride horses in the mountains. We had to go through areas which were under the control of the Revolutionary [Islamic] Guards. We had to cross the border in the dark of the night and the freezing cold of the mountains. Several times we had to return to the village and start the journey all over again, as the conditions for crossing the border were not suitable. In one of these return journeys I had to ride a horse up a mountain so steep that I could see only the sky in front of my eyes. Once I fell off the horse and was injured. All my bones were aching and I was unable to move. I tried to keep my morale high. There were a few men who were frightened and their morale was very low. One even decided to return halfway through, as he found it was impossible to continue. This would have endangered his own life as well as those who were helping our escape. Because I was injured they organized a bath for me in the women's hut. Women warmed up their scarce water, they surrounded me and, while giggling at my naked body, bathed me in tub. I finally managed to escape alive.'

Coming back to Britain for Alma meant starting a new life in exile, determined to continue work politically as well as working with refugees and exiles in Britain:

'Back in Britain, all I had was a suitcase full of books which I had left with a friend and some money in the bank. I started a new life in exile. I studied and worked. I now work in a caring profession. In this capacity I have met many Iranian political refugees, many single mothers. Political repression shattered many families. They escaped the repression in Iran but here they feel displaced, irresponsible, guilty and hopeless. They feel that they have left their friends and comrades dead, in jail or under terrible repression. Language and traditional barriers make them alienated. They also feel humiliated because many within the welfare state show their hostility by delaying their rights, implying that taxpayers' money should not be spent on refugees. Therefore the refugees feel too proud to use the social services and hide their problems. I always remind them that the people of the developing countries have a claim on the wealth which has been accumulated here – our oil has been exploited for years to build the enormous wealth here.'

Mandana says:

'In 1980 I joined the Iranian Women's Solidarity Group in Britain. Our main activity was to expose the Islamic laws against women under the Islamist state. I then became active in the International Solidarity Front for Iran. This was an organization to help the Iranian political refugees. In 1985, in the International Women's Conference in Nairobi, at the end of the UN Decade for Women, I became a woman in exile, as I, alongside other Iranian women, actively exposed the sufferings of women under the Islamic state.

'As a researcher for the Housing Campaign for Single People I work around homelessness among young women, and sexual abuse as a cause of homelessness. As a journalist I worked for many years with refugee women. In this capacity I experienced and exposed the bitter struggle of many Iranian women against fundamentalism. In 1989 I interviewed an Iranian woman in exile who successfully struggled to gain custody of her daughter. After divorce her husband kidnapped her three-year-old daughter and, without her knowledge, returned her to Iran, in order to use the *sharia* law which advocates that girls after seven years of age and boys after two years of age belong to their fathers. The woman is a refugee in Britain. She could neither go to Iran to bring back her child, nor could she get a court order against him. She contacted other women. She found that there were many women in her circumstances where husbands use the fundamentalist approach of sharia law to take the children away from their mothers. She found that in 1989, twenty-one cases of child-kidnapping had taken place in America, and thirty-three in Europe. Through an active campaign, women exposed the kidnapping of their children by their fathers and raised this issue within international organizations such as Amnesty International, the United Nations and the Red Cross. They have succeeded in bringing back seven of these children to their mothers from Iran, amongst them her daughter.

'Another case I have been engaged in is that of an Iranian woman in Japan who has been refused refugee status. If she returns to Iran she will be stoned to death according to the law of *zina*, adultery. This woman joined her husband, who had Japanese residency, in Japan. After a while they separated without getting divorced. As a result of a relationship with another man, she now has a child. The Japanese authorities refuse to give her residency because her husband has left Japan. In most countries, residency is given to women because of their husbands and they do not consider a woman's case independently. If she returns to Iran she could be executed according to the *zina law*, as she is married to an Iranian man and has an "illegitimate" child by another man. But the Japanese refuse to grant her refugee status because they do not consider this law a basis for granting refugee status. I am therefore actively involved in the campaign to save the lives of such women by pressurizing international organizations to recognize the threat to women's lives under Islamic laws and to change international law to consider these cases for granting refugee status.'

The experience of exile as a result of political struggle makes Parvaneh determined to continue the struggle and hope for a future generation:

'Here in Britain, I study and work as an artist. I have begun a new relationship and have another daughter. My second child is important to me because I feel that I lost so many years of my life in prison away from my first daughter. I missed her growing up. When they took her away from me she was a baby, and when I was reunited with her she was a big girl. I missed seeing her losing her teeth and lisping. I missed seeing her going to school for the first day. I missed her laughs and her cries in that stage of her childhood development. I want to see those years in my second daughter.

'I think fundamentalist ideas which also existed under the Shah's system, and have been intensified under the Islamic state, distort women's development sexually, intellectually and emotionally. Women are given a role which is not natural, and it represses their ability and potentialities. Part of my struggle against fundamentalism is to bring up my daughters free of fundamentalism and all the fear which is attached to it for women. I don't want my daughters to suffer my bitter experience of fundamentalism. I want my daughters to gain all that I lost as a woman.'

The Importance of the Anti-Fundamentalist Struggle

One question which preoccupies all these anti-fundamentalist women is why so many women in Iran have been supporters of this sexual apartheid regime. Alma explains:

'A large number of women from the deprived sectors are attracted to this apartheid system. This is partly because of the humiliation and deprivation they experienced during the Shah's regime. Unlike the minority upper- and middle-class women who enjoyed a certain degree of prosperity, many of whom adopted Western lifestyles, the majority of women from

157

the deprived sections of society were debased, degraded and neglected. Hence they envied and detested the other groups and their Western lifestyle. The Islamic regime exploited such sentiments and won the women to its side. These women became the staunch supporters of the Islamic regime. The regime declared them the guardians of the Islamic society and the upholders of the society's new morality and values. These women are the symbol of Islamic womanhood and advocators of sexual apartheid.'

This empowerment is not just symbolic. The Islamic state provided material and ideological interests for these women, and allowed them to become visible.

Mandana says:

'I know of a woman whose activities were confined to preparation of food for Islamic gatherings such as Sofreh, which are exclusively women's gatherings within the home. After Islamization, she extended these activities to public work. She began to work voluntarily within the Islamic organizations such as Bonyade Mostazafin. [The Foundation of the Oppressed]. She became visible and gained prestige. Moreover, she was not in a contradictory position, as this was just an extension of her activities in the private sphere of the home and she was not expected to be modern. She became the symbol of the good woman, a real Fatimah [the symbol of motherhood and devoted wife] and Zainab [the symbol of woman fighters] at the same time. For many women, fundamentalism ended the contradictions of modernity.'

However, many women who struggled to free themselves from the class, racial and gender inequalities of the Shah's system did not find sexual apartheid a form of liberation, even if it did give a number of them the opportunity to benefit materially from the ideological implications of the Islamic state. Alma, as we have seen, felt 'subhuman'. Mana remembers:

'Many times I was arrested in Iran in the streets for not complying with compulsory veiling "properly". I was asked by the fundamentalist woman who arrested me:

"Sister, how could your heart allow you to let the eyes of a *namahram* [strange] man look at your body? How could you make him guilty of sin?" I was dying to ask her: "Sister, why in your eyes am I guilty of his sin? Why is it that I am not only sinful for not being ashamed of my own body, but also guilty because a man harasses me by looking at me as a sex object? Why am I responsible for his faults, and why is it me who is driving a pure man to sin? Why do you see your value and your power in what you do for men, and for this you deny your own body and your visible presence?" I couldn't, though. If I had, I would have ended up in jail.'

Parvaneh says:

'I feel that with all its limitations, political activity helped me to bloom like a bud, to overcome my fears and realize my potentialities. The task now is to struggle against fundamentalism.'

What is this fundamentalism that needs to be struggled against? There are many definitions of the concept (see the Introduction to this book). For me, however, the best definition is Alma's:

'I use the terms fundamentalism and fundamentalists specifically for the Islamic state in Iran and those who share the same beliefs and values. Fundamentalism is about absolute control over the female body and mind. It is about the segregation and exclusion of women. The regime in Iran is founded on sexual apartheid as well as dictatorship and repression.

'Under the apartheid system of the Islamic state, women are directly segregated and secluded by the laws of the state. There is no way out. They are limited to the rights, roles and tasks that the state sees fit for them.

159

'Sexual apartheid is expressed in Islamic law. According to the *Ghesas* law, the value of a human being is based on her/his price. The price of a man is equivalent to 100 camels, but the price of a woman is equivalent to 50 camels. According to the *Ghesas* law a man can kill his wife in a case of Zina. Men who commit adultery can be set free if they admit to their sin, or if they manage to escape while they are being stoned to death. But these exemptions do not apply to women. According to this law, women are categorized in the same rank as children and the insane. According to Khomeini's book *Hallolmassael* [Analysis of Problems], Article 2412, married women cannot go out of the house without the permission of their husbands. The wife has to obey and facilitate his sexual pleasure, except during menstruation. According to Islamic law, women are dirty during this period and they should be avoided. They are not even allowed to pray. When their cycle finishes, they have to bath and ask God for forgiveness and cleanness.'

The need to struggle against the fundamentalism of the state is also a struggle against values embedded in ourselves, says Mana:

'Our movement against fundamentalism was defeated because what was imposed on us was already part of us. Even among anti-fundamentalists, women are identified with chastity, virginity and dignity – with getting married, having legitimate children, being a devoted wife and mother. We don't have these definitions for men. If we could free ourselves from these fundamentalist concepts of womanhood, we could then face the fundamentalist women who feel powerful under the Islamic regime by implementing state power – that is, by being active within the Islamic organizations and punishing other women for not obeying Islamic law. We will then be able to ask them: "How could you feel powerful by denying your own existence? How could you feel powerful by being ashamed of your own body, and be proud of covering it from head to toe?" What we need is a women's movement which absorbs all women from

Left to Right, from atheist to religious fundamentalist, to discuss women's issues, to tackle women's issues and not to allow political boundaries to separate us. This is where we may achieve a new concept of womanhood.'

Conclusion

The message of the four exiled Iranian women who have been quoted in this chapter can be summed up by the claim that the fundamentalism of the Islamic state in Iran is about absolute control over the female body and mind. It is about the subjugation and exclusion of women, based on sexual apartheid as well as dictatorship and repression.

The roots of this form of fundamentalist ideology can be traced back to the secular state of the Shahs, and can also be found in the minds of radical nationalists and socialists. As a result, many women who went through the contradictory process of socialization and politicization under the Shah's system were torn between two symbols of womanhood: the modern woman of the public sphere and the traditional wife and mother. The establishment of the Islamic state resolved this contradiction, especially for those who benefited materially and ideologically from the rise of fundamentalism and became the advocates of sexual apartheid, even though it denies them any equality with men within Islamic law.

Most importantly, the worsening of women's situation under the Islamic state has had material effects. Many women whom I interviewed in Iran, especially the new generation whose socialization process has taken place under the strict social control of the institutions of the Islamic state, have accepted their position. They feel more comfortable under the veil and being segregated in the workplace, universities and buses. It seems that social control has led to self-control – the values have been internalized, so it is not just a question of Islamic state repression. The lack of feminist consciousness within the radical Nationalist and Communist movements never allowed them to raise women's consciousness on women's issues.

Under these circumstances, being in exile can fulfil a very important role in the political struggle against fundamentalism, as Mana points out:

'If I couldn't discuss the class and gender inequalities in Iran with the women who supported the Shah's regime and Khomeini's regime, maybe in exile we could discuss these matters without fear of execution and torture. We must discuss together our fears, such as motherhood, childbearing, childrearing, love, especially in exile.'

Could the existence of an organization such as Women Against Fundamentalism help in this way? Many Iranian exiled women, as socialists and feminists, are involved in this movement. As the largest group of political exiles in Britain, their experience under the Shah's state and Khomeini's state is very important in understanding and struggling against all forms of fundamentalism and fundamentalist propaganda. However, many others, even with strong socialist and feminist ideas, are ambivalent about the British Left and feminists. They feel that a form of sectionalism and sectional interests prevails even within these movements, overriding the struggle of women against fundamentalist issues. Issues such as the multiculturalist consensus and fundamentalism, which are debated in a purely British context, can marginalize exiled women. Fundamentalism is viewed as a legitimate form of identity politics. The terrible experiences of those who do not see it within this framework are ignored. These are important issues which could be discussed within the Left and feminist movements as a way of removing obstacles and involving many more women in the struggle against all forms of fundamentalism.

Secular Spaces:
The Experience of
Asian Women Organizing

GITA SAHGAL

*T*his chapter is about the encounters of two women's groups organizing within the framework of anti-racist politics during the 1980s and 1990s. Southall Black Sisters was founded in 1979. About two years later, the Brent Asian Women's Refuge was established. From the moment of their birth, both groups were engaged in battles within their communities and with the state. In the process they developed a critique of their own point of origin within anti-racism, but also of multicultural policies which prepared the ground for fundamentalism. I came to Britain from India in 1983, and have been involved with both groups since then. My account is based on my own observations and those of friends and colleagues. It is, in a sense, the story of our encounter with British identity politics.

When I arrived here, I was struck by unexpected similarities to politics in India as they relate to issues of pluralism and multiculturalism. They were all the more remarkable for not being noticed as political similarities. This could be because the rhetoric employed to discuss them on the Left was very specifically British – borrowing from black consciousness and using the language of anti-racism. It was also because the language of multiculturalism disguised political decisions as self-evident 'natural' truths about minorities. To question

163

them was to challenge the basis on which the idea of pluralism and diversity had been constructed.

Southall is in Outer West London, the largest area of Asian settlement in Britain. It is a pluralist area in many senses of the word. Different communities coexist, though the population is largely from the Punjab, a region that straddles both India and Pakistan. All the major religions of the Indian subcontinent are represented there: Hindus, Muslims, a small number of Christians, and Sikhs, who form the majority. A wide range of political opinion is also represented. Asians have been active, particularly on the Left. Over the years, a number of men have been elected as Labour councillors. They have also worked in trade unions and Left groups. Recently, Southall elected an Asian M.P. Indian politics is widely represented – from the Congress Party, which has ruled India for most of the post-Independence period, to the various branches of the Communist movement. Various factions of the Sikh fundamentalist movement for the separate state of Khalistan has a strong support in Southall. Political pluralism also ensures that opposition to the rise of fundamentalism comes from secular voices within the community.

Brent, too, is a very plural borough. The Asian population there came to Britain from East Africa. Most are Gujaratis with a Hindu background. The politics of caste associations are more noticeable in Brent than they are in Southall. So are the activities of well-endowed Hindu temples. (The media, however, have focused more on the activities of Muslim fundamentalist groups who are setting up separate schools.) Again, the opposition to Hindu fundamentalism came from within Hindu communities, reflecting not only a diversity of opinion but strong political opposition.

Class stratification – particularly the development of a petty bourgeoisie and a rapidly growing professional class – also ensures that different sections of these communities have ceased to have common interests on a range of issues such as the education system.

The pluralism of Brent and Southall resembles most

strongly aspects of Indian civil society, which operates a kind of secularism which has grown out of Indian social and political conditions.

Secularism in Britain and India

While Indian understandings of secularism have a British colonial history, they bear very little resemblance to contemporary discussions in Britain about the nature of the secular state or of secularism as an ideology.

References to secularism in Britain usually describe a state of mind rather than a constitutional fact. Britain is assumed to be a secular society because most people's lives are not governed by religion. It's also argued that secularism is a militant, evangelical form of atheism imposing a rationalist discourse on all citizens of the state. Some of secularism's defenders, as well as its critics, assume that it replaces religious modes of thought and imposes the separation of religion from everyday life. This alien form of thought, it is argued, would destroy the way of life of religious minorities in Britain. It is thought that religion sanctions and guides all conduct, even in the secular sphere, and allows minorities no independent political views or social existence.

Unlike Britain, India is constitutionally a secular state. There, secularism, far from being an atheist imposition, is seen as the only guarantor of the rights of religious minorities. All politicians who want to be seen to safeguard or defend such rights appeal to the Constitution. On the other hand, Hindu fundamentalists who want to impose their version of political Hinduism have condemned the secular state for allowing minorities special privileges and for failing to defend Hinduism and impose its ethos on all true Indians.

Both the strengths and the limitations of Indian secularism derive from its mission to protect religious minorities. In order to fulfil this mission, their collective rights are recognized and they are treated as a homogeneous unitary category. The insertion of gender issues upsets this consensus.

Secularism, Fundamentalism and Women

The modern Indian state, like the British colonial regime before it, has often been the instrument of the preservation and ossification both of customs and of legal concepts which were codified from imperfectly understood religious texts. Enshrined in the law, they have been given a new lease of life. In many respects, secular Indian attitudes to minorities and social policy related to them resemble multiculturalism in Britain. In both Britain and India the existence of a women's movement has challenged the assumptions on which policy-making towards minorities is based. In India, this is seen most clearly in the arguments on personal law that took place during the 1980s. In Britain, the existence of autonomous black women's groups has raised profound questions about the multicultural consensus and the limitations of anti-racist politics over the last ten years.

By organizing autonomously within the black women's movement, Asian women drew on and challenged both the feminist and anti-racist movements. Both Southall Black Sisters and the Brent Asian Women's Refuge reached beyond the narrow allegiances of one caste or community of origin. SBS, in fact, started as both an Afro-Caribbean and Asian group. Their own notions of diversity meant that they formed, in effect, secular groups, operating within a framework of religious tolerance which would be recognizable to secular opinion in India. Women coming to these centres have been radicalized by their clash with the social mores of their families and communities when they tried to leave intolerably violent relationships. Their critique of religion is based on their own experience. It threatens the boundaries of secularism – usually defined as a secular public sphere, and private religious practice, and demands a redefining of the concept.

Although Asian politicians in Britain have on occasion tackled fundamentalists within their communities, they have seldom chosen to do so in defence of women's rights. They have tended to choose those issues which had a clear political agenda, where they could avoid being seen to attack the central tenets of the religion itself. Khalistan is a separatist movement, which threatens the Indian state. The rise of the Hindu Right threatens Centre and Left political parties. The campaign on schools in Southall demonstrated both the strengths and the limitations of this form of secularism.

In India, different fundamentalist movements have had a profound impact on the behaviour of women. This is most noticeable in minority groups where fundamentalism combines powerfully with secessionist movements to forge new forms of group identification. In Punjab and Kashmir, women have had to change their clothes – either forcibly, or as a matter of political choice. They have begun to wear more 'traditional clothes'. In Kashmir, this means that they have taken to the veil even where they have not traditionally worn one. In Punjab, there are reports of a headmistress being shot when she pleaded for more time for her students to convert from wearing dresses to *shalwar-kameez* (traditional Punjabi dress regarded by fundamentalists as 'Sikh' clothing, although it has always been worn by Punjabis of all religions). Girls on the campus of Chandigarh University, in the Punjab, have been threatened and beaten if they have been seen in jeans.

These movements have all found their echoes in Britain – both in the activities of young men on the streets of Asian communities such as Southall and Bradford as they attempt to control their sisters, and also in the higher reaches of social policy, which is steeped in a common sense, with colonial antecedents, of how to manage and control an alien people while maintaining social peace.

Where other ex-colonial powers like France adopted policies of assimilation, British colonialism in South Asia and parts of Africa retained and reinvented aspects of religious law governing property and family matters. This history partly explains the attractions of multiculturalism as a specifically British policy, though it is usually assumed to have been invented no earlier than the 1960s in response to the influx of immigrants from the old colonies. Grappling with unfamiliar social groups meant that policy-makers in education or the social services made very reductive choices about the attributes of a particular minority group. A complex web of political, social and cultural considerations, which helped to form a particular identity, has often been reduced to purely religious values, emanating from conservative opinion within the community. In this way a harassed social worker in an area like Southall, telling a young Asian woman that she should conform to her family's desire to marry her off, may quite unwittingly be following in the footsteps of some colonial forebear.

The Personal Law Debate in India

From the early period of British colonialist rule in the eighteenth century, the political imperative of stable rule and the use of the law as an instrument of administration led to a massive effort to codify indigenous law. This was done by referring to religious texts as though they were the basis of the whole legal system, and largely ignoring the role of changing custom and practice, as well as the role of legal interpretation.

Individuals who came before the courts were forced to construct themselves in new ways:

> Under the colonial state, the category of 'Muslim' or often 'Muhammadan', took on a new fixity and certainty that had previously been uncommon. In theory, each individual was linked to a state enforced religious category. Identities that were syncretic, ambiguous or localised gained only limited legal recognition; for the most part, litigants were forced to present themselves as 'Muhammadan' or 'Hindu'. Courts repeatedly faced the problem of accommodating the diversity of social groups within these two categories. (Anderson, 1990)

The Indian Constitution displays some of the tensions of the British inheritance. Though the directive principles of the

Constitution enshrine the idea of a uniform civil code, personal laws for Hindus, Muslims and Christians have been retained, governing such rights as inheritance, marriage and divorce.

The Hindu Code Bill, introduced a few years after Independence, reformed laws for Hindus governing inheritance rights and divorce. For the first time Hindu women were given rights in property owned by the extended family. Polygamy was abolished and divorce introduced. Yet this legislation – which had challenged Hindu orthodoxy, threatening land rights and other forms of patriarchal control – was never repeated to alter personal law for minority women. So a rationalist ideal of treating all citizens equally before the law coexisted somewhat uneasily with the idea that the rights of religious communities should be preserved by maintaining different laws in the private sphere – the family.

Large minorities such as the Muslims are seen as an important block vote, because although a secret ballot exists, individuals are usually assumed to vote according to caste or community loyalty. For the elected government of India, even more than for the autocratic British Raj, it has become imperative not to reform the internal arrangements of Indian religious minorities.

In the 1980s personal law became the focus of a massive mobilisation of Muslim opinion, to defend 'Islam in danger'. Shah Bano, an elderly Muslim woman who had been deserted by her husband, was granted a small amount of alimony under a provision of the Criminal Procedure Code. Subsequently, Rajiv Gandhi's Congress government introduced a Bill known as the Muslim Women's Bill, restricting the rights of Muslim women applying for relief under the Criminal Procedure Act. They would be forced to apply to nearly moribund shariat courts on all matters governing their matrimonial status. This Bill, which was rushed through at great speed, caused outrage. It was seen as a blatantly cynical attempt to court the Muslim vote. It led to widespread protests, including protests from what is known as 'secular Muslim' opinion in India, who felt betrayed by the limitation of their rights. One Muslim member of the Cabinet resigned. But Muslims – including women – supporting the Bill mobilized in huge numbers. Feminist organizations also arranged protests against the Bill and demanded a uniform civil code. In some cases, they alienated Muslim women by couching the debate in terms of Muslim 'backwardness' rather than the desirability of general reform; this forced some Muslim women to start thinking about organizing autonomously.

But among the most vociferous in speaking out against the new law were the Hindu right-wing party, the BJP, who used a modernist rhetoric to express their opposition. They demanded to know why Muslims were treated as a special category with rights denied to other Indian citizens. They, too, demanded a uniform civil code, but for them this meant asserting the essentially Hindu character of the country. Uniform meant uniformity of custom and practice.

The Congress government's position on the Muslim Women's Bill had been seen as particularly iniquitous because they had acted against a form of Hindu revivalism in the western state of Rajasthan. In 1987, the Congress government had passed a law outlawing a modern revival of the practice of sati – burning widows on their husbands' funeral pyres. So the government was seen to act against the demands of Hindus. In other words, it was acceptable for the government to legislate against the 'traditional' practices of Hindus while preserving – indeed, re-establishing – Muslim practice.

Sikh separatists in Punjab had already demanded a Sikh personal law. Although the government rejected their more secular demands concerning the control of river waters and other issues, they considered this one. When fundamentalists cannot control a state, the control exercised over women, which helps them to maintain patriarchal control over land and inheritance, becomes crucial.

Fundamentalism and Multiculturalism in Britain

In 1986, 'Bandung File', a series on Channel 4 television, investigated extreme right-wing Hindu revivalist or fundamentalist groups who had set up apparently innocuous 'cultural' organizations in Britain. Two organizations were cited: the VHP, known as the Vishwa Hindu Parishad, and the RSS, the Rashtriya Swayamsevak Sangh, known in Britain as the HSS. They had been granted funding on the grounds that they wanted to promote Indian culture – a culture which was always defined as exclusively Hindu. The programme looked at the background of these groups in India, where, at that time, the RSS particularly had a history of involvement in large-scale communal riots – that is, riots between religious groups, in their case directed mainly against Muslims.

In Britain, these groups were seen as a legitimate target for state funding, as they appeared to cater to a community need. The councils which funded them were largely Labour-controlled. Ken Livingstone, former Leader of the Greater London Council and a scourge of the Right, found himself somewhat shamefacedly defending his administration's record, saying that GLC officers were not always aware of the antecedents of the groups they funded. On the face of it, the grant applications seemed unexceptional. He did not mention that the mailing lists of the Ethnic Minorities Unit were made up almost wholly of religious organizations which would very probably have failed the GLC's tests of anti-sexist or equal-opportunities policies, had these been applied to them.

'Bandung File's programme first made the link between these 'cultural' organizations and the Ramjanmabhumi issue. Ramjanmabhumi means birthplace of Rama, a major Hindu deity whose life is described in the popular epic the *Ramayana*. Hindu fundamentalists have been promoting Rama as a historical rather than a mythological figure, whose birthplace is a matter of historical fact rather than popular tradition. In the northern Indian town of Ayodhya, on the supposed site of Rama's birth, a mosque was built in the fifteenth century by a Muslim ruler, Babar, who founded the Mughal dynasty. Hindu fundamentalists have been fighting for the greater part of this century to reclaim the site from Islam and build a large temple on it.

The VHP converted the issue from a series of obscure legal wrangles to a highly publicized political campaign with international dimensions. They organized a series of marches all over India about the right of Hindus to build a temple on this sacred site. They also held prayer meetings to bless bricks which were sent to build the temple. This was a completely new ceremony. Hindu congregations abroad took part in fund-raising and brick-blessing, urged on by the VHP. The 'cultural' work done by the VHP enabled the political party of the Hindu Right, the BJP, to use the struggle for Ramjanmabhumi as a major plank of the 1991 election campaign. Since the BJP began to campaign on the issue, communal riots among Hindus and Muslims have spread, even in areas not previously affected. Hundreds of people have been killed, with Muslims being driven out of their homes all over northern Indian.

Although the VHP did not campaign publicly in Britain, religious ceremonies such as blessing bricks would normally be viewed by multiculturalists as a legitimate activity to preserve a culture and some links with the homeland. It took secular Indians, in both India and Britain, to point out that the BJP was constructing a new 'tradition'. Far from preserving Hinduism, they were trying to turn it into a mirror-image of the religion they most hated. By politicizing the cult of Rama, the Hindu Right were transforming Hinduism into a monotheistic religion with a single, paramount, sacred site.

Multiculturalism and Women

While Ken Livingstone's GLC was funding right-wing Hindu groups, it was also supporting some of the early self-organization efforts of black women. It continued to do this in spite of considerable scepticism and sometimes active hostility in the labour movement and outside. In London, the control of a small number of community leaders over the lives and politics of their community has never been complete. It has always been contested, and their right to represent the community has been challenged.

The GLC and other councils never seemed entirely clear about why they were funding black women's groups. Some of them clearly had a commitment to equal opportunities and autonomous organizing which would enable black women to set their own agendas. For others, the principle of autonomy was akin to the 'separate but equal' policies of multiculturalism. Black women or groups of other ethnicities had to be separate, it was argued, because of their 'special needs'. They were simply 'different'.

An example of this was the funding of the Brent Asian Women's Refuge by Brent council. The first management committee was composed of women who, while they recognized that domestic violence was a problem, were trying to contain it within the Asian community. For them, the refuge was a breathing space from which women could be reconciled back into the family. The women they hired, who had been politicized through the anti-racist movement, regarded an Asian women's refuge as a necessity because of the racist structures and mentalities of the British state and within socialist and feminist groups, including Women's Aid. Their position with regard to the role and function of the refuge was feminist. They refused to organize reconciliations, saying they would not reproduce the family pressure from which women had escaped. They were fighting for women to be able to make truly autonomous decisions.

Councillors were quite bewildered when they were presented with these arguments. Surely the reason for funding an Asian refuge was because Asians were different: their family structure was tightly knit and complex, and they had their own methods of dealing with these things, never really revealed to outsiders. Eventually the workers, with the support of residents of the refuge, won support for their position and formed a new management committee.

Councils seldom questioned whether the funding they

offered to other groups conflicted with their support for women's groups. Sometimes this was because different political committees carried out their functions with complete disregard for consistency in council policies. The 'cultural' activities of religious groups were usually funded through Ethnic Minority or Race Equality Units, while women's groups were funded by Women's Committees. It's very likely that if there had not been a 'hundred flowers bloom' approach, black women's centres would never have been established in the first place.

Groups with longer links with the local state demanded their closure on the grounds that they were destroying the 'culture and traditions of the community'. Surprisingly, in Brent and Southall, the most vocal complaints and lobbying did not stem from religious institutions, which did not make their disquiet public through the local press or council meetings, so that they did not jeopardize their funding. It was secular, political organizations which used culturally based arguments to attack the existence of women's organizations. One of the Asian Labour councillors who had voiced strong public criticism of Brent council and the GLC for funding the Hindu Right was said to be very hostile to the setting up of the Asian women's refuge. Similarly, in Southall the most organized hostility came from Asian men within the Labour Party and from the Indian Workers' Association, who used their lobbying skills to campaign against institutions they believed were a threat. The secular Left, then, has never been a natural ally of women's struggles within Asian communities – and the most powerful arguments it has attempted to harness are based on religious sanction, appeals to 'tradition' and 'culture', and a denial that feminists are an authentic voice from within the community.

Every political tradition, no matter how new, constructs its own version of authenticity. Community leaders tried to delegitimize the activities of young radicals by calling them 'outsiders', while feminists were placed beyond the pale because of their challenge to tradition. This was very painful for black women who had seen their own struggle as intrinsically allied to the general struggle against racism and fascism. The anti-racist movement itself elaborated myths of origin by which it raised its own flag of authenticity. The Southall case shows how the same events could produce very different politics – all of which were in some way exploring and validating different subjective identities which would come, in time, to clash within the tradition of anti-racism.

Myth of Origin

Southall Black Sisters was founded in the heat of mass activity against racism. The Institute of Race Relations booklet *Southall: The Birth of a Black Community* begins: 'On April 23rd, 1979, a whole community took to the streets of Southall to protest at the invasion of its town.' The National Front was holding a meeting at the Town Hall with the backing of the Conservative-controlled council. The police turned up in huge numbers to allow the meeting to go ahead, and brutally attacked the crowds which had gathered. One man, Blair Peach, was killed; 700 were arrested and 342 were charged.

Women, both young and old, were active on that day. Some of them contributed to the work of the defence campaigns formed to challenge the draconian sentences handed down to the defendants. Six months later, a small group of Afro-Caribbean and Asian women were to form Southall Black Sisters. It was the first critique of that moment of absolute community unity.

Southall: The Birth of a Black Community presents the events of 23 April 1979 as the culmination of the long process of building a black community in Britain. It records the previous struggles around housing, education, employment and immigration which helped to form modern Southall. Yet in concentrating on the factors which unified the community and treating that unity as a linear progress, it obscured the very real divisions within the area. It also obscured the fact that although 23 April may have represented Southall's most heroic moment, it also sowed the seeds of the problems which were to become more evident as time passed.

Two contrasting points of view in *Multi-Racist Britain* (Cohen and Bains, 1988) present opposing analyses of that moment. The first shows how some anti-racist politics became intimately bound up with questions of ethnic identity, and laid the foundation for the justification of fundamentalist movements by anti-racists. Tuku Mukherjee's piece is a description of his involvement with the young men of the streets, who were the potential recruits for gangs. Many of them were later to see 23 April as their day when they went out to beat the fascists off their streets. They formed Southall Youth Movement after the murder of a young man, Gurdip Singh Chaggar, by fascists in 1976. Mukherjee captures the sense of territoriality and the siege mentality of these youths. He quotes Balraj Purewal, who emerged as one of their spokesmen:

> 'In a multi-racist society we have nothing to lose. We have taken on board the fact that we are under siege, and our only security is our understanding and acknowledgement of what it means to be Black. Any other position would be a pathological escape from realism.'

While Black was a political colour, the development of a sense of self was intimately bound up with a reassertion of ethnic identity. As early as 1979, Purewal had said:

> 'I'm a Jat. I reckon the amount of racist violence I've seen in school nobody will ever realise in their lifetime. And as I'm a Jat Sikh I feel we must learn how to organise, how to survive and, even more important, how to retaliate.'

The dominant group in Southall are Jat Sikhs. It is in this group that the support for the Sikh fundamentalist movement demanding the separate state of Khalistan is strongest. Of course, there are also Jat Sikhs on the Left who have risked their lives to oppose the rise of the Khalistani movement, both in India and in Britain. Mukherjee sees in the heritage of the Jat Sikhs an almost mystical identification with the past, out of which the future would be forged:

> For in the wider context, Southall has emerged as not just another Black community but as the sacred centre of the Khalsa Sikh. A historical legacy of struggle rooted in the plains of the Punjab and the Sikh psyche is being reclaimed as the birthright of a new generation.

In another piece for *Multi-Racist Britain*, Harwant Bains presents a more differentiated view. He stresses the pull of conservatism among upwardly mobile Southall families. Class stratification in Southall and the emergence of a class of small businessmen have led to increasingly different perceptions of social and political issues among Southall people. Bains argues that far from being perpetually militant, 'the majority of Punjabis are also seeking economic assimilation – they wish to become an integral if subaltern, fraction of British capital.' The events of 23 April 1979, and again in 1981, represented a coming together of different class forces who would at other times have been in conflict:

> A bourgeoisie protecting its material stake in British society and an under-class defending the territorial integrity of the community . . . However central the riots were to the myths of origin elaborated by the Southall Youth Movement itself, the immediate consequence was to increase the level of political involvement only amongst the minority of youth who were already politically active.

Among the youth who became active during this period were the young women who founded Southall Black Sisters. Their existence was partly a rebuke to the sexism of the Southall Youth Movement, but they remained active in the defence campaigns and other anti-racist work on housing estates.

While critical of the idea that the black community can be

treated as an undifferentiated whole, SBS has remained loyal to the group's myth of origin in the struggles of the community. By the mid 1980s the membership of the group had completely changed, but in spite of efforts to marginalize them they continued to take an active part in the annual commemoration of the killing of Blair Peach by the Special Patrol Group.

Although the critique of oppression within the community was fairly muted in public in the group's early days, it was present from the beginning in discussions and the first attempts to organize support for women facing domestic violence. In 1980 SBS women picketed the home of Dhillon, who had burnt down his house with his wife and five daughters in it. Earlier, they had supported women strikers in the Chix factory.

But there was also time for exploration. Avtar Brah, one of the early members, has written:

> We made a conscious decision to move beyond a sloganism and develop solidarity on the basis of a mutual understanding of both the similarities and differences in our experience as Asian and Afro-Caribbean women and then translate this understanding into practice. None of this was easy. (Southall Black Sisters, 1990)

Their work was made more challenging because they had rejected the option of constructing an identity based on a common ethnicity, and moved beyond the community groups whose foundations were rooted in caste and religious politics of one particular community. Like some of the more radical groups formed in the struggles of the late 1970s and early 1980s, their language was largely secular. As Parita Trivedi wrote in *Feminist Review* (Autumn 1984):

> Asian women have consistently come together on a common platform, regardless of country of origin, caste, religion. To do otherwise would be suicidal.

Stirrings of Fundamentalism

The need to find a common identity within the anti-racist project led many black feminists, particularly socialists, to locate black women's oppression and exploitation in the racist structures and mentalities of the British state rather than within the institution of the family. Women who wanted to discuss aspects of family oppression publicly could be castigated, both by feminists and by male anti-racists, for incorporating their experience into the discourses of racism, which saw Asian women as perpetual victims. At the same time, the search for their roots meant that many black women were ambivalent about making a political critique of religion, or of those who were using religion to 'find out where they came from'. Although they were trying to map the articulations of race, class and gender in their theoretical writing, they insisted, in fact, on the primacy of racism in structuring all of life in Britain.

As they evolved, SBS and the refuge broke with that tradition within black feminism, developing critiques based on their members' experiences within their own communities; but the most direct threat to anti-racists lay in taking on some of their central myths. Pragna Patel, a worker in SBS, criticized the police for criminalizing young Asian men, but she also warned of the uncritical acceptance of youth militancy (Southall Black Sisters, 1990).

The young men themselves, particularly those associated with a gang known as the 'Holy Smokes', have developed a style which allies black consciousness to Sikh identity. Since 1979 their chief usefulness in anti-racist terms was supposed to lie in their ability 'to smash the fascists off the streets', and so protect the community from attack. Yet they have singularly failed to organize against racist activity in estates surrounding Southall. They are more likely to engage in inter-gang battles, and to protect the social mores of the community by the organized scapegoating of vulnerable single women. In Birmingham, there is a similar group called Sher-e-Punjab,

179

the Lion of Punjab. They have gone to discos and dragged girls out of them. They also find girls who are trying to leave home and bring them back to their families, and it has been alleged that they attack men from outside their community who have gone out with 'their women'.

As Pragna Patel has argued:

> Youth activity generates a culture which appears autonomous from the rest of the community. Yet, as the experiences of women indicate, that culture is a mirror reflection of values sanctioned in the family and the community at large. This calls into doubt the arguments of community leaders that 'gang' activities are somehow 'alien' manifestations of moral corruption and lack of respect for authority and discipline. (Southall Black Sisters, 1990)

Young men like these, from similar backgrounds of anti-racist struggle, were successfully mobilized in the campaign against *The Satanic Verses*. Analysts on the Left, particularly, have situated their rebellion in a failure of anti-racist politics. Yet the language and demeanour of militant Muslim and Sikh youth are clothed in the rhetoric of anti-racism. Admittedly, it is the bombastic street rhetoric of anti-racism, not the talk of its policy-making committees, but it is no less genuine for that. A crude anti-imperialism is combined with a specifically religious and ethnicized form of black identity. And when there is no white fascist enemy in sight – indeed, often when there is – young men, particularly in groups, appoint themselves the moral police of the women in their ambit.

In some cases, the mixture of traditions meshes in a peculiarly British way. Young men who claimed to be associated with the 'Tooti Nung' gang prided themselves on their greater eclecticism, having absorbed soul and other black musical taste. Their counterparts in 'Holy Smokes' (they'd named themselves 'Baby Smokes') tended to prefer bhangra, which was originally a Punjabi folk dance transformed in Britain into British Punjabi pop. At the same time as rejecting the British state, they were asserting identities which, for all their nostalgia for an imagined past, could only have been constructed in contemporary Britain.

Meanwhile, in the orthodox Muslim campaign against *The Satanic Verses*, the older leadership was also being accused by the British media of not being sufficiently assimilated into the 'British way of life'. Yet their campaign was steeped in the language of multiculturalism. Demands to extend the blasphemy law were, in effect, a plea for equal rights within a pluralist but Christian state.

There was a complete rejection – a rejection of secularism and secular values which would loosen the grip of religious control. Common to movements transforming from a quietist position in relation to the state to a public evangelical platform was a strong critique of the moral degeneracy accompanying the collapse of religious values. This was it – not a challenge to the British state, or even the 'British way of life', but an attempt to discipline the pious, whip the faithful within the congregation into line. To recognize this would be to see that the control of women was at the heart of the fundamentalist project.

But the most significant failure is the failure to connect the international networks which provide ideological ballast and direction to British discontent. Muhammed Siddique, one of the leaders of the anti-Rushdie campaign, active in the evangelical sect the Jamaat i Tabligh, has said that he first heard about *The Satanic Verses* from Muslims in India, where an Indian Opposition MP demanded a ban on the book to embarrass the government. The government quickly complied.

The activities of Hindu fundamentalist groups have not come to public attention in Britain, because they have concentrated on raising resources and gathering support for the Ramjanmabhumi campaign among Hindus. The sanctified bricks sent back to India return them symbolically to a pan-Hindu fold, transcending caste and region, which the Hindu

Right is trying to create both culturally and politically in India. The active support of wealthy Hindus settled abroad is crucial.

In India it is widely supposed that the idea of Khalistan itself originated among Sikhs settled abroad, particularly in Canada and Britain. While this may be an oversimplification, nostalgia armoured with discontent abroad is a powerful weapon in keeping separatist movements alive in the homeland. As long as the activities of pro-Khalistanis in Britain – such as battles for control of the *gurdwara* (Sikh temple) committees or physical attacks on individuals such as the editor of a Punjabi paper – are within the Punjabi and Sikh communities, the media have not focused much attention on them. Not surprisingly, they are not very concerned with the effects of extreme polarization within Asian communities.

In 1989, the campaign against *The Satanic Verses* had the odd effect of turning us into evangelicals. In SBS, we felt that our right to dissent was threatened. We wanted to defend the institutions we had built up and try to extend the critique we had developed of multiculturalism, and its responsibility for promoting conservatives and fundamentalists. It was much easier to do this in Women Against Fundamentalism and in all sorts of fora up and down the country than on our own home ground.

We went to address a meeting of the Southall Labour Party with considerable trepidation, for at that meeting would be people who had, over the years, tried to shut us down. We were astonished when, instead of the hostile reaction we had expected, we were congratulated on the stand we had taken.

Local politics in Southall had a great deal to do with this. People were divided in their attitude to the Sikh separatist movement for Khalistan. While some on the Left – including some within the Labour Party – were said to be sympathetic to the movement, many others had actively opposed it. Those with affiliations to the Congress Party had supported the Indian government; others had condemned the state's atrocities against the Sikhs as well as opposing separatism. It was clear that even those politicians who were not going to take the risk of supporting Rushdie themselves were happy to hear a secular point of view defended.

The Schools Campaign

In early 1991, SBS joined a campaign to oppose an effort by some parent–governors to take two high schools – Villiers and Featherstone – out of local-authority control. This process, known as 'opting out', had been encouraged by the Tory government under the Education Reform Act, 1988. Their rhetoric was to devolve more power to parents. They provided a new route for those who had previously tried to set up independent religious schools. The option of taking over an existing school and changing its ethos (even though, officially, the 'character' of a school could not be altered for five years) was more attractive than trying to establish a school from scratch. In addition there were financial incentives from central government, while the local Tory-controlled borough of Ealing was looking for ways to reduce local government spending and cut the poll tax.

Mukherjee and Bains had both mentioned an earlier proposal by a *gurdwara* in Southall to set up an independent Sikh school. For Mukherjee, this represented an opportunity for Southall Youth to learn 'where they were coming from' and to ground themselves in their cultural heritage, while Bains saw it as a sign of the growing distrust of the quality of state education among some conservative parents:

> But here again we see a double standard in responses to educational discrimination. The issue of 'acculturation' is raised primarily in relation to girls' schooling – for girls are to be the 'bearers' of traditions, whereas the issue of academic failure is raised apropos boys – for they alone need exams to prosper. (Cohen and Bains, 1988)

The 1991 opting-out campaign started when Sikh parents were approached to sign a petition saying 'Save Our Sixth Forms'.

The organizers were careful not to argue explicitly on religious grounds. Instead, the campaign situated itself in opposition to the educational reorganization which was planned throughout the borough. Parents were alarmed that they might lose sixth-form education altogether.

The campaign appeared to be headed by a few parent–governors, with support from some Asian teachers. Parents who were approached said that they recognized people who were active in a local gurdwara. When talking to parents, these people aroused fears about whether their children would be safe in the wider world outside the school. At this stage, the campaign gathered enough signatures to ask for a ballot of all parents in the school. Many parents still did not realize the implications of what they were signing, but their discontent about the quality of education and their fear for their daughters' safety had been awakened.

The campaign to defend the status quo was called 'Southall Save Our Schools'. Members of the Indian Workers' Association, the Indian Workers' Federation, the Southall Monitoring Group, Southall Black Sisters, some Labour councillors and prospective parliamentary candidates, and some parent–governors and local teachers took part. Organizations which had a history of hostility to each other came together because of the threat to the future of Southall as a plural society. Southall SOS concentrated on the long-term implications for the schools if they opted out, trying to make the educational changes accessible to parents.

But there were two arguments which were not addressed at all in the campaigning material. There was silence on the religious thrust behind the opting-out campaign and the sectarian way it had developed. The fear that the real agenda was to turn the schools, in the long term, into Sikh schools was not mentioned. Secondly, the campaign was reluctant to raise gender issues at all, though both teachers and pupils acknowledged that it was one of the major issues at stake. 'It's the girls they're after,' said one of the teachers privately.

SBS workers tried to raise these issues within the campaign, but failed to get them inserted in the literature. They did succeed in discussing them on the doorsteps when they mobilized extensively, going from house to house. Women who used the centre – some of them parents themselves – campaigned with them.

Once demands for a ballot had been achieved, the opting-out campaign produced a series of well-designed leaflets. The bogeys they raised were that in the new, more impersonal system, where sixth-formers would attend local colleges, the children would run away from home, there would be problems for parents, and families would split up.

The leaflets also said that rumours that the schools would be turned into denominational schools were baseless. They promised that the new governing body would be more representative of local parents – Hindus, Sikhs, Muslims and others. This was a new construction of people living in Southall, purely on the basis of the religious communities from which they came. Since Sikh parents would be by far the most numerous group, it implied that they should be in control.

When SBS canvassed parents about their views, most were firm in rejecting the control of religious establishments over local schools:

> 'We came here to educate our children. We don't want our girls going around with their heads covered.'

> 'If it's anything to do with the *gurdwara*, I want nothing to do with it.'

The assumptions of the anti-racist Left meant that they viewed the whole campaign through the prism of race. At a conference on education, the key issue had been identified as racial discrimination in the education system, and the solution was parent power. They were untroubled by consideration of the complex new changes in the Education Reform Act, by the fact that 'parent power' had been adopted as a Tory slogan. It could be a very problematic slogan, if it meant a severe curtailing of the rights of children, particularly girls. To raise these issues would be to question the thinking that Southall was 'a community in resistance'.

In an area like Southall, where the education system is relatively popular and some schools have good examination results, it is possible to defend their record. But it is dangerous to try to ignore fears and discontents where they do exist. When the anti-racist Left in Southall silenced itself on the question of religion, it fell into the assumption that most people in Southall actually wanted to be guided by religious diktat. Instead, they were hostile. In the parental ballot, Southall parents overwhelmingly rejected opting out. In Villiers, 93 per cent of those who voted voted against opting out; in Featherstone it was 76 per cent.

Domestic Violence and its Effects

Southall Black Sisters took an active part in the campaign on schools, because years of fighting around issues raised by the experience of domestic violence had alerted the group to the hidden agendas of orthodox religious control and fundamentalism. In 1984 the suicide – apparently by hanging – of Krishna Sharma led to pickets of her inquest and demonstrations outside her husband's house. Later, the murder of Balwant Kaur by her husband in the refuge was followed not only by a campaign to ensure his conviction, but by the raising of wider issues by a coalition of groups called Network of Women, culminating in a demonstration in summer 1986 (Southall Black Sisters, 1990).

The latest campaign, launched in 1990, was to obtain the release from prison of Kiranjit Ahluwalia, who had killed her husband after suffering ten years in a violent marriage. This has led to work with a number of other women's groups to make demands to change the law on homicide so that it reflects the experience of women. To the charge that feminists were presenting Asian women as constantly victimized, there have been two answers: first, broadening the struggles to take on issues applicable to all women, regardless of racial background; second: campaigning very vocally; singing songs in different languages in public; briefing MPs in private. Asian women were presenting the media with a new view – far removed from the images of either passivity or drabness with which Asian women and feminism respectively have been saddled.

What effect did the experience of domestic violence and of being involved in a women's centre have on women's consciousness? Women getting together at the refuge or centre often discuss their experience of violence and its effects on their lives and thought. Asian women from different religions and widely varying class and educational backgrounds come together in these spaces. Yet they have no difficulty in expressing or sharing key concepts with each other – particularly those women who share a common spoken language such as Hindi or Urdu.

Attempts to discuss religion are usually far removed from theological niceties or differences in religious observance or belief. Instead, wherever it starts, a discussion on either religion or domestic violence rapidly reaches the same point. From their own experiences, women draw conclusions about the nature of their society and its expectations of them – expectations which many have tried to fulfil for years, with tragic results. Their sorrow and bitterness are hard to witness.

A key concept is izzat – the notion of honour. While *izzat* is a code which affects men and women in different ways (for instance, it can be used to describe family honour at stake in a land dispute) and has a greater or lesser prominence in the social structure depending on community, region or class, the idea is commonly understood. Most women who have escaped from violence in the family have broken one of the codes of *izzat*: that the honour of the family rests on the woman's behaviour.

This is why all the women who heard it were able to identify immediately with the speech taped by Kiranjit Ahluwalia in prison. It was played at the launch of her defence campaign in June 1990, which demanded that she, and other women serving life sentences for the murder of their violent partners, should be released immediately. Kiranjit indicted not only her husband's violence, but also the code of *izzat* for keeping her in bondage for ten years:

> 'My culture is like my blood – coursing through every vein in my body. It is the culture into which I was born and where I grew up, which sees the woman as the honour of the house. In order to uphold this false "honour" and "glory" she is taught to endure many kinds of oppression and pain in silence. In addition, religion also teaches that her husband is her god and fulfilling his every desire is her religious duty. A woman who does not follow this path in our society has no respect or place in it. She suffers from all kinds of slanders against her character; and she has to face much hurt entirely alone. She is responsible not only for her husband but also his entire family's happiness.'

None of the women felt that Kiranjit's final desperate act – throwing petrol at her husband as he slept – was unreasonable. As her peers, they could have judged her. They themselves had left home, and many had gone into hiding. But they chose not to judge her harshly, saying instead that they knew what she had faced and that any of them could have done the same. They knew what it had cost them in terms of lost honour and family support to leave violent marriages. Typically, like Kiranjit, they had tried several times before ending up at the refuge or women's centre. They would have tried to get relatives to mediate for them. Some might have tried a place of worship, where the outcome was nearly always unsuccessful.

They had been through the process where they had been seen as 'good' as long as they were prepared to put up with the marriage, then seen as transgressive and therefore 'bad'. Over a period of years, some had carved out a place for themselves again within their communities. But these upheavals made them clash with the roles in which they had been brought up – and, indeed, to which they may have aspired as young women.

The Dutiful Wife

Though these women may have had different names for the role of the good wife, all understood the Hindu concept of *dharma*, or the right path. This was the term used for religious duty by Kiranjit, who is herself a Sikh. One Hindi term for husband is *pati-dev*, or husband-god. The complementary term for wife is *dharma-patni*, or righteous wife. The idea of service to your husband as if he were your god is embedded in the language itself.

The prime example of the *dharma-patni* is Sita in the epic *Ramayana*. Sita was the wife of Rama; as the embodiment of the perfect Hindu woman, she followed her husband into his fourteen-year forest exile. While they were there she was kidnapped by Ravana, a demon king. Rama and his brother fought a long war to get her back. Finally, Rama was victorious. But after his triumphant return home to Ayodhya (celebrated as the festival of Diwali), there was trouble ahead for Sita. According to one version, a *dhobi* – or washerman – complained that she could not still be pure, since she had been in Ravana's clutches for so many years. So Sita agreed to go through a trial by fire, an *agni-pariksha*, to prove her purity and save her husband's honour. But though she passed the test, Rama would not keep her because he feared popular disapproval. On a pretext he had her abandoned, pregnant, in a forest.

Sita's story is an early caution of the dangers of populism, and its power to maintain the boundaries of acceptable behaviour.

Millions of young Hindu women grow up with this story. There are many versions of it, and even the most commonly accepted are subject to different interpretations, but oppositional viewpoints that have often survived in traditional forms are less commonly given space in more modern versions.

The two great Hindu epics, the *Ramayana* and the *Mahabharata*, have been shown as two long-running television serials in India. BBC2 has screened the *Mahabharata* here, and both have circulated widely on video in Britain. When they were transmitted in India on Sunday mornings it seemed as though the whole country came to a standstill to watch. Their effect is incalculable. Political commentators in India argue about whether they have fed into the progress of the Hindu Right. Certainly, the BJP has come to its own conclusions by getting the actress who played Sita into Parliament as a BJP MP.

Sita is already a more powerful model of behaviour for women than Rama is for men. With the political development of the Rama cult, it seems probable that the image of his consort will only be reinforced. And the dominant image of Sita today, from television, is both kitsch and submissive.

A Politics of Desire

Kiranjit Ahluwalia's story was a horrific example of a phenomenon very common to other women who have experienced domestic violence. She was not a victim of fundamentalist control, merely of patriarchal oppression buttressed by popularly understood, codified religion. It was not the exercise of religion according to a text which she challenged, but custom and practice which determine and sanction behaviour.

This was the most common experience of religion for most women who came to Southall Black Sisters or the refuge, but some were more explicit about the changes that had been taking place within their religions. A Muslim woman said, 'Weddings used to be a time of celebration. Now, we cannot dance or clap our hands.' For her, the growth of fundamentalist attitudes was signified by the increasing control exercised on people by religious bodies, intent on purifying 'tradition' and rooting out un-Islamic practices, which have become common all over South Asia as different religious and cultural traditions have fused. Apart from increasing the power of the mullahs, it also simply took the fun out of life:

> 'Men never think that women have desires and longings of their own. Why should we contain them? I have tried to get a divorce from my husband for the last ten years, but the mullah said I must be reconciled to him. Why should I live with a man I don't love?'

> 'James Joyce was my inspiration. My parents were trying to marry me off when I was taking A levels. I clutched *Portrait of the Artist as a Young Man* to myself and said over and over again, "I will not submit".'

Two women: both involved with the women's centre, both with a personal politics born out of struggle, both struggling to retain a sense of self. Their language has much in common, but one is a devout Muslim who has been on a hajj, while the other is an atheist feminist who has rebelled against her religious background, which she describes as 'born-again Hindu'. One of the few places where such women can meet is in secular spaces such as the refuge or a women's centre like Southall Black Sisters. They are important because they are places where conversations about religion are possible – conversations which are not necessarily limited to simply a pro- or anti-religious point of view. When women disentangle religion from social expectation, they arrive at surprisingly varied views – from complete rejection to an intensely personal belief.

Critics of secularism accuse feminists of imposing their world-view on a group of unsuspecting victims – ordinary pious women. They ignore practicalities, such as the difficulty of imposing an entirely new moral order on a woman whose primary aim is to seek legal advice and counselling. They also ignore the self-denying ordinance that many feminists practise by refraining from discussing their own views and politics with their 'clients'.

Many women's centres are secular in their conduct rather than specifically in their aims or their constitution. Welcoming women from different religious backgrounds, they create the space to practise religion as well as challenge it. This is peculiarly difficult for multiculturalist policy-makers to grasp. Having abandoned an egalitarian ideal for a policy of recognizing cultural differences, they tend to have to codify, implement and reinforce these differences (as British colonialism did in relation to family law). For instance, a well-meaning social worker, enquiring into cooking arrangements in the refuge, was told that there were two kitchens. 'Ah, yes,' she said knowledgeably, 'one vegetarian and one non-vegetarian.' 'No,' we said, 'one upstairs and one downstairs.'

The distinction is important. The fact that the refuge does not run separate kitchens for people with different diets does not mean that women who live there are expected to abandon their dietary restrictions and adopt a homogeneous diet. They cook for themselves and follow whatever diets they choose. They are expected to respect each other's patterns and taboos, but this is sorted out informally among the women, who decide which shelves in the refuge will be used for what purpose, or which cooking utensils will be restricted to certain uses. Making these decisions is a very small part of the process of living in the refuge, which serves as a very overcrowded home for women and their children, sometimes for many months, before they move on. The workers do not impose particular diets or forms of behaviour on individuals based on assumptions about their religion or community. So if women want to challenge the norms to which they are expected to conform, they can do so without disapproval. Their experiments may range from cutting their hair to trying alcohol or eating meat. Paradoxically, the non-Asian women most comfortable in the refuge were North African Muslim women, who were able to carry out their religious observances such as fasting during Ramadan without hindrance or ridicule.

This was the context in which it was possible to see an intense reaffirmation of belief as well as a rejection of it:

'I used to be a very good religious wife, as was expected of me. I was deeply religious and had a shrine in my room at which I used to worship. When I decided, after much praying, to leave my husband, I couldn't stand it any more. I took the shrine outside and threw it away. I can no longer believe. I can't go to the temple any more. My children go with their friends because they have fun, but I don't.'

'A Muslim woman will observe what is expected of her. She will pray five times a day and fast at Ramadan. But she will no longer be the slave of man.'

'I am proud to be a Muslim. I have become a Muslim to a much deeper extent, since I left home. But now it is not imposed on me.'

What are the differences between these women and their fundamentalist counterparts? We have discussed in other chapters the ability of fundamentalist movements to posit a strong separate role for women, sometimes in opposition to the tenets of their own orthodoxies. Does secular feminism offer anything stronger than a powerful critique from within a religious framework? The answer lies in practice rather than looking at theoretical arguments. Many of the groups who argue for reform within a religious framework are reluctant to go beyond the limits of the permissible. Even if reformist configurations of religion stretch these limits, they do not, for instance, usually extend to explicitly endorsing lesbianism, or a rejection of marriage or a childbearing role for women. In other words, women don't have permission to be 'bad'.

All the women who claimed that their belief had been strengthened by hardship saw religion and the private rituals surrounding it as a refuge rather than an empowering experience. For some women, being pure in observance helped them to deal with their anguish over their marriages and their own sense that they had failed to live up to the standards that they had wanted to meet. To be pious was to avoid the charge that in the eyes of the world you were dishonoured, because your intentions had remained pure.

There is clearly a difference between authoritarian prescription – in which limits, while being shifted from the old orthodoxies, are still clearly defined – and women who use their beliefs and, indeed, their texts to construct a very personal view of religion. One woman used the same language as the verse in the Qur'an which is usually interpreted as the reason why women should dress modestly and cover their bodies. She said: 'Life is so precious, we should live it to the full.' For her, the notion of preciousness was to be used not to conceal but to enjoy life and embrace its pleasures. Although she sees herself as deeply religious, her views would be threatening both to orthodox Muslims and to the new fundamentalist evangelicals, because they would not be able to control her.

Yet even orthodoxy can assimilate some exceptional women. The notion of *sewa*, of service, can be used to accommodate unorthodox behaviour. So that after years of disapproval, a Hindu family may explain their daughter's feminism as a form of *sewa* and take pride in her self-sacrificing nature and her contribution to the general good: 'She won't marry because she's married to her work. She wants to do good and help others.' A somewhat embarrassing testimonial for a woman who is dedicated to the language of autonomy; but a convenient way of maintaining family honour in public and re-establishing harmony within. These are some of the ways in which members of Southall Black Sisters have healed rifts in their families and been accepted again.

Conclusion

The assaults of more than ten years of Thatcherism have pushed some sections of the Left in Southall into essentialist positions to maintain their ideological purity. Ironically, many socialists have jettisoned a class analysis, which would necessitate seeing a conflict between different interests in an area like Southall, in favour of the familiar slogans about defending the community as a whole. The spirit of 1979 is relentlessly recalled, but not the complex message that it has for us today. The slogan of defending the integrity of the community is as likely to be dangerously retrograde as it is to be progressive. It is the context that decides this, not a knee-jerk reaction to a formula. Early anti-racism – particularly the kind which was informed by a socialist politics – never intended to substitute ethnic and religious organizing for a broader transformative politics. But its most enduring legacy appears to be not the analysis of the roots of racism in the British state, but a defence of the politics of identity.

It is not surprising that these politics should have acquired such resonance among Asians settled in Britain. There has been a failure of hope, both for older people who had expected to return to their countries of origin, and for the young who know no other reality than the one into which they were born and what they have forged for themselves, coupled with the pressure from powerful evangelical groups offering them a ready-made identity authenticated by an appeal to religion.

Anti-racism and multiculturalism elevated the twin values of the 'authentic' and the 'subjective'. For feminists this was familiar, though sometimes conflicting, territory. The concentration on the subjective voice sometimes prevented them from challenging the versions of authenticity that were presented to them.

Among the few people who have challenged that discourse on its own terms are those with alternative histories of the religion and politics of the countries of South Asia. Among the feminists who have successfully confronted the new constructions of 'authenticity' are those who used the conflicting evidence of their own subjectivity to present a different version of 'reality'. In addition, groups like Southall Black Sisters and the Brent Asian Women's Refuge have attempted to reformulate both feminist and anti-racist theory through the activities they undertook.

It's not surprising, then, that the schools campaign, an important turning point in Southall's history, was fought by a wide coalition which included a strong presence of men whose politics were formed in part by the nationalist and socialist movements of South Asia, and feminist women. Just as a coalition of very different forces had come together to protect the community against external assault in 1979 and 1981, so all the groups with secular traditions mobilized to defend themselves against a threat from within. But although they admitted privately that they were fighting to maintain Southall as a plural society, most were unwilling to be precise about the nature of the arguments with which they were engaged. Without using the words, they had fought to maintain secular values, but had not wished to be seen in a head-on collision with religious establishments. So the battle was fought covertly, and the challenge only half met. Again it evoked similarities with India, where secular opinion is particularly sensitive about tackling religious belief.

For SBS, the campaign was an opportunity to test, in a public arena, issues that had been debated for nearly two years in Women Against Fundamentalism. It also symbolized acceptance by people who had campaigned against the group's existence. Whereas most people would assume that the price of challenging fundamentalism would be exclusion from the community, for SBS it created a common ground for acceptance and recognition. Significantly, the defence of secular values, however covertly it was conducted, was seen as an electoral asset by those politicians who associated themselves with the campaign.

But the schools campaign also contains a warning. The refusal to make the gender issue explicit implies that many of the campaigners were hoping to confine their argument to making a case for defending educational standards – in other words, the future of the boys. There are no guarantees that they would be able to attract widespread political support if they were fighting specifically about women's issues – though defeat, even over these issues, would not necessarily be inevitable.

The difficulty for secularists, particularly those who have embraced a pluralist ideology rather than being complete atheists, is that they cannot offer a complete identity to people in search of their roots. With the breaking down of the traditional distinctions between public and private spheres, the idea itself is in the process of redefinition. Secularists can, however, raise awkward questions: for instance, about how the experience of domestic violence and the challenge to family values have radicalized many women. But their involvement in Southall Black Sisters or the Brent Asian Women's Refuge has not made women into clones of the feminists who run these projects. The engagement with the depth and complexity of the response to religion is just beginning. It is only in a secular space that women can conduct the conversation between atheist and devotee, belief and unbelief, sacred and profane, the grim and the bawdy.

Note

This article could not have been written without the years of practical activity in which the women of the Brent Asian Women's Refuge and Southall Black Sisters have been involved. I am deeply indebted to them for creating the space to engage politically and theoretically in otherwise desolate times. Ali Hussein, Kavita Punjabi and Kelwyn Sole also discussed the ideas in this piece, as did Raju Bhatt whose ironic good sense has sustained me greatly over the years.

Jewish Fundamentalism
and Women's Empowerment

....

NIRA YUVAL-DAVIS

*O*wing to the specific history of the Jewish people, Jewish fundamentalist movements (and the position of women inside them) embrace forms of religious fundamentalism common among both majorities and minorities both in the West and in post-colonial countries. Two different perspectives and political interests have determined the definition of Jewish fundamentalism as reflected in the literature: the Messianic Zionist *Gush Emunim* and its satellites (Lustick, 1988) and the individualistic spiritual *khazara bitshuva* ('Born-Again') movement (Kaufman, 1989). I share with Lustick his political definition of fundamentalism:

> A belief system is defined as fundamentalist in so far as its adherents regard its tenets as uncompromisable and direct transcendental imperatives to political action oriented toward the rapid and comprehensive reconstruction of society. (p.6) [For comparative purposes, see our own definition of religious fundamentalism in the Introduction to this book.]

Jewish fundamentalism is not, therefore, just about being, or even becoming, Ultra-Orthodox, and is not necessarily present everywhere where a Jewish community exists. At the same time, examination of some of the *khazara bitshuva* movements, especially the one led by the Lubavitch Rebbe, reveals that they are fundamentalist movements in the political sense as well. Individual redemption in the Jewish religion is but a means towards collective redemption. Although these different forms of Jewish fundamentalism developed separately and often with antagonistic interrelationships, they have deeply affected each other and cannot be fully understood without each other.

The Lubavitch Women's Organization (the most active 'missionary' movement in contemporary Judaism) published a book aimed at women, trying to convince single American Jewish women that they should 'return' to Judaism. The Hebrew expression is *khazara bitshuva* – return to repentance; for everyone born to a Jewish mother is Jewish according to the *halakha* (the religious law) – even if they never practise or believed in the Jewish religion. As the *mitzvot* (commandments) which women have to practise in Judaism all relate to their roles as wives and mothers (single girls do not even have to cover their hair), and as early arranged marriage is the normal practice among the Ultra-Orthodox, the task of targeting single women is not as simple as it could have been had Judaism been aimed at individual (gender-neutral) redemption. The argument used in the book emphasizes the collective nature and collective responsibility of the Jewish people, which transcends even their gender differences:

> Every Jew – no matter what one's physical, spiritual, sexual or marital status – critically affects every other Jew, the world and G–d Himself, so to speak. (Shaina Sara Handelman, 'On Being Single & Jewish', Lubavitch Women's Publication, 1981, p.5) [Orthodox people avoid using the full name of God and therefore use G–d instead.]

While this is an elegant formulation which has obviously been effective among single 'returning' women, the different construction of men and women in Judaism is crucial. It is no coincidence that the second article in the above collection is called 'Changing Careers' and claims that:

> Shifting gears from the contemporary professional world to the traditional roles of wife and mother can be unexpectedly fulfilling. (ibid., Abstract in the Table of Contents)

The following twenty-eight articles deal with women as Jewish wives and as mothers.

In this chapter it is virtually impossible to do justice to such a complex background, as well as to explore the ways in which women are empowered and disempowered by the Jewish fundamentalist movements. I shall therefore resort to wide generalizations, drawing only in very general terms the history of British Jewry, as well as that of the major fundamentalist movements which have affected it. I shall then concentrate on issues relating to women's position and empowerment within these movements and, in particular, on factors which push women towards and away from Jewish Orthodoxy.

Britain has not spawned a unique or even particularly intense Jewish fundamentalist movement. However, the effects of Jewish fundamentalist movements which have emerged both within Israel and within the USA, and have been operating in Britain, are transforming the character of British Jewry. At the same time, it is impossible to understand fundamentalist activities in Britain without analysing them within the particular context of British multiculturalism and state structures.

British Jewry

Stephen Brook (1989) sums up the contemporary situation of British Jewry:

> British Jewry, like the waters of an estuary, is tugging in innumerable directions simultaneously. While declining in numbers, it is growing in Jewish awareness. Its religious

structure is becoming increasingly polarized, as the various synagogal bodies adopt irreconcilable positions on interpretations of Jewish law and on such crucial matters as Jewish status. Loyalties to Zionist causes and principles that twenty years ago seemed unproblematic to most Diaspora Jews are now under severe strain. Religious authoritarianism is on the increase while the rate of assimilation into the non-Jewish community continues unabated. (p. 36)

Unlike many other ethnic minorities in Britain, Jews as a whole (except Orthodox Jews in Hackney during the last few years) have remained outside the British 'Race Relations Industry'. One reason is the particular construction of the 'Industry', which emerged mainly as a response to immigration from Britain's imperial domains (Yuval-Davis, 1991). Another reason, however, is the continued reluctance of most Jews to be 'unnecessarily' visible, so as not to become an easy target for discrimination and *numerus clausus* (quotas which used to limit the number of Jews who could have access to higher education in Tsarist Russia).

A further reason is the fact that, despite several debates in the British Parliament regarding the legal status of Jews in Britain, no agreement was ever reached on the subject, so that Jewish legal and political rights were achieved largely as a side-effect of rights given to Catholics and other non-Established Churches during the eighteenth and nineteenth centuries. This, of course, applies to the Jews who settled in Britain from the sixteenth century onwards. Before that period there were no Jews in Britain for about three hundred years; and earlier, their legal position had been very clearly delineated. Jews first reached Britain during Roman times and settled in large numbers in England after the Norman occupation. In medieval times they constituted what Abraham Leon (1970) has called 'a people-caste' and fulfilled specific socioeconomic roles within the feudal estate society. They were excluded from agriculture as well as from the city guilds, so their occupations were necessarily concentrated in the money economy, from pawning to the poor to lending huge sums to the aristocracy.

In this way they enjoyed a certain autonomy as a community (*Kehila*) and the patronage of the feudal lords. But their position also made them vulnerable. They were exposed to pressures and antagonism in periods of social and economic crisis, both from above (especially when they were owed large amounts of money by the lords) and from below (where they represented to the masses both the extractor of money and the religious 'Other' – the demonic 'Antichrist').

Things came to a head during the Crusades, both as a result of general social destabilization and religious mobilization and because of the heavy economic burdens the campaign imposed. After a period of persecutions and pogroms, and with the weakening of the economic resources of the British Jewish community, Jews were expelled from Britain in 1290 by a royal decree from Edward I – the first of a series of Jewish expulsions which took place in Western European countries, with the general rise of mercantile capitalism and national bourgeoisies.

The first group of Jews to arrive in England again was composed of those expelled from Spain at the end of the fifteenth century. However, Jews started to arrive in larger numbers in England only after the establishment of the Commonwealth. During the seventeenth and eighteenth centuries, both Sephardi Jews (originating in Spain and Portugal) and Ashkenazi Jews (originating in Germany) settled in Britain. But the biggest influx of Jews took place towards the end of the nineteenth century and at the beginning of the twentieth, when they escaped persecutions and pogroms in Eastern Europe, the last part of Europe to emerge into modernity. Jewish refugees continued to arrive in Britain before and after World War II, but their numbers were greatly reduced by a developing machinery of immigration controls. The first law of this kind – the Aliens Act 1905 – was prompted as a direct response to the Jewish immigration from Eastern Europe (S. Cohen, 1988).

It is difficult to estimate the exact number of Jews in Britain, since there have been no ethnic (until 1991) or religious questions in the British census, and as fewer and fewer Jews are associated with the organized Jewish community. An additional difficulty is the great controversy about 'who is a Jew' (Yuval-Davis, 1987). Waterman and Kosmin (1986), who conducted a statistical and demographic study of contemporary British Jewry, estimate their number to be around 330,000.

Although Jews can be found in virtually every part of Britain and in every class group – from poverty-stricken East Enders to members of the lower aristocracy – there are still certain demographic trends which characterize British Jewry. They are mostly concentrated in Britain's large cities, especially in certain parts of Greater London; the percentage of those who have achieved high levels of education is somewhat greater than among other sections of the population; and a higher proportion are either self-employed or professionals.

The organized Jewish community is formally led by the Board of Deputies, which includes delegates from various synagogues and other Jewish organizations, such as charity and community organizations. It has 460 delegates who meet on a monthly basis, and in between the organization is run by the Executive Committee and by ten committees organized around issues such as Israel, education and youth, Jewish defence, Shechita (ritual slaughter), public relations and parliamentary relations (Brook, 1989). While the Board represents a wider constituency than it used to do in the days when the Cousinhood (the Jewish aristocracy which used to intermarry: Bermant, 1971) used to dominate it, it is still far from being representative of the Jewish community as a whole. It has no relation to Jews who are not members of any established organization (including some 'alternative' synagogues), nor does it include formal representation from the Ultra-Orthodox. In the controversy regarding appropriate reactions to anti-Semitic attacks, the Board of Deputies has always taken the line that minimiziing and turning attention away from such attacks would be best – although this might be changing gradually, given the recent upsurge of anti-Semitic attacks in Britain, and much more so in other parts of Europe.

Jewish education in Britain is usually associated with the different kinds of synagogues – Orthodox and Progressive. About half of Jewish schooling is carried out by part-time, after-school and Sunday schools, and half in full-time Jewish day schools. In 1967 only a third of Jewish education occurred in full-time schools (Waterman and Kosmin, 1986); this growth in full-time Jewish education can be explained by two factors: the growth of the Ultra-Orthodox sector, and parents' desire to withdraw their children from general state schools – either because of anti-Semitism or, just as often, because they consider that the academic and social atmosphere in the Jewish schools is of a higher quality.

Given his title, one might be misled into thinking that the 'Chief Rabbi' is the supreme religious authority in British Jewry. However, classical Judaism did not recognize religious hierarchy. Rabbis acquired their reputation and followers according to their religious knowledge and their charisma. This latter was especially prominent among the Hassids (a populist religious movement which grew up in Poland during the eighteenth century). For them, charisma could also be inherited. Originally, the Chief Rabbi was simply the rabbi of the biggest synagogue in London, and his title was given to him as a result of the British state's need to have a religious representative. Even today, the Chief Rabbi represents the mainstream modern Orthodox synagogues – the United Syn-agogues – but not Sephardi Orthodox, Liberal, Reform, the Federation, Independent or Ultra-Orthodox. When Stephen Brook talks about the process of polarization which takes place among British Jews (1989), he is talking about their gradual drift away from the mainstream Judaism of the United Synagogues.

On the one hand, upwardly mobile Jews have been moving

to the suburbs, where they have often chosen to join liberal/ reform synagogues in order to avoid the cumbersome daily observance rules which constitute the basis of Orthodox observance (the Jewish adult male is supposed to follow 613(!) different *mitzvot*). Assimilation becomes a dominant pattern in a neighbourhood which lacks a support network of kosher food shops and a synagogue within walking distance (observant Jews are forbidden to travel in a vehicle on the Sabbath), and has a class-homogeneous but religiously and ethnically mixed population. This assimilation can take place either on an individual basis, accompanied by secularization, or on a more collective basis. Liberal and reform synagogues have constructed kinds of Judaism which are much more compatible with Protestant denominations and do not intrude significantly (except on Jewish holidays) into the daily lives of their adherents.

On the other hand, more and more Jews who grew up in the United Synagogues strand of Judaism are moving towards a more Orthodox lifestyle. Again, this movement can be on an individual or family basis, when they become *khozrim bitshuva* ('born-again Jews'), or on a more collective basis – when the synagogue's rabbi, or the Jewish school, develops a much more Orthodox style. One cause of the latter is the general growth of the Ultra-Orthodox community, a result of the average large size of their families. The post-World War II generation in Britain has reached adulthood and produced large numbers of Jewish scholars who became available to serve as teachers and sometimes as rabbis in the United Synagogues' institutions. Much of the United Synagogues' Jewish education took place in part-time, after-school and weekend lessons which could not compete scholastically with the products of full-time Jewish education. Moreover, the difference between the United Synagogues and the Ultra-Orthodox was a question of degree rather than one of religious ideology; therefore the United Synagogues proved themselves vulnerable to Ultra-Orthodox self-presentations as representing '*the*' valid version of Judaism.

This essentialist notion of Judaism has also proved effective among those individuals who became *khozrim bitshuva* and was used by Jewish fundamentalist movements in their attempt to impose their version of Judaism on other Jews. (In a recent survey among Ultra-Orthodox in Israel by Professor Ben Zion Hochstadt, quoted in *Ha'aretz*, 9 December 1990, only 2.9 per cent of those asked agreed that other Jews have the right to lead moral lives without following the religious *mitzvot*.)

Jewish Fundamentalist Movements

It is difficult, especially in Israel, to determine which Orthodox movements are fundamentalist and which are not. In a sense they all are – both those who define themselves as Zionist and those who do not (except, probably, the small groups of the extreme anti-Zionist Neturei Karta and the Satmar Rebbe Hassids, who consistently continued to oppose the Israeli state and to boycott any participation in its politics). Although Zionism generally presented itself as a modern alternative to Orthodox Jewishness, the two were never completely separated (Yuval-Davis, 1987). The Zionist movement needed the legitimation of Orthodox Judaism for both its claims on the country and its claim to represent the Jewish people as a whole. The Orthodox movements used the Israeli state both to gain more resources for their institutions and to impose as many religious practices as possible on Israeli society. Central to their strategy was the control of women's position in Israeli personal law (Yuval-Davis, 1980).

While the instrumental approach to the Israeli state has been common to all Orthodox movements in Israel, it has intensified in recent years as their position as the balancing power in Israeli government coalition-building has grown. Recent figures, for instance, show massive growth in both the number of students and the state financial support of *yeshivot* (higher religious study institutions), at a time in which higher education institutions in general suffered massive cuts in their budgets and very small growth in their numbers (Amiram Cohen, *Al-Hamishmar*, 28 December 1990). A similar situation exists in pre-school and primary education (*Hadashot*, 6 December 1991).

Some of the Orthodox – although by now a minority among the religious voters in Israel – have been actively Zionist. The religious ideologue during the early days of Zionism was HaRav Kook (Lustick, 1988), who saw the Zionist settlers, secular as they were, as instruments in the hands of God. He considered building the Israeli state as a necessary step, a precondition for the return of the Messiah.

The Messianic element is central to contemporary fundamentalist Jewish movements, both in Israel and in the Diaspora. Although the individual motivation of people who become *khozrim bitshuva* is often totally subjective and personal, Judaism is a communal religion. The general political message of these movements as a whole is Messianic; therefore, 'the Promised Land' – Israel and the Occupied Territories – is central to them. In all versions, the ultimate aim is constructed in terms of the coming of the Messiah, in which all these splits within Jewish existence would heal – the people of Israel would be in the land of Israel, in a state of Israel, with the Messiah as its ruler. While most Orthodox rabbis have learned to treat Jewish Messianic movements very suspiciously (owing to some painful historical moments such as the Shabtaic Jewish Messianic movement – let alone Christianity, which started that way as well . . .) and consider all those who declare themselves Messiahs to be false, the active role of promoting the coming of the Messiah has been a major mobilizing power among Zionist fundamentalists.

Gush Emunim (the Block of the Faithful) was the earliest manifestation of this tendency. Headed by Rabbi Moshe Levinger, they initiated the project (illegal, at first) of Jewish settlement in the Occupied Territories, especially near the Jewish holy places. In their actions, the settlers, many of whom were the product of the Israeli state religious educational system, combined Zionist pioneering myths with religious practice, and produced a new mode of Jewish religion in which the 'Land of Israel' gained a cardinal importance; its control and settlement by Jews became a precondition for the arrival of the Messiah (Lustick, 1988). These ideas followed from the ideology of HaRav Kook. However, Gush Emunim intensified them, and took upon itself the role of initiating settlements (albeit in the Occupied Territories), which used to be the vanguard role of the kibbutz movements. Their vision is total, and there is no space in it for any recognition of the national aspirations of the Palestinians, nor any compromise or negotiated peace with the Arabs.

Like other influential social movements, Gush Emunim was not a homogeneous body. Especially since the Likud Party's rise to power in 1977, it has become more an umbrella organization, parts of which cannot easily be distinguished from the general right-wing annexationist bloc within Israeli politics. Its most extreme wings, however, turned themselves into paramilitary units terrorizing and counter-terrorizing the Palestinians, as well as threatening to resist by force any attempt by Israel to withdraw from the Occupied Territories.

The major distinction between Gush Emunim and the other major Zionist Messianic fundamentalist movement, the one which used to be headed by Rabbi Meir Kahana (who was shot dead in 1990 while conducting a meeting in New York), has been more sociological than ideological. While most of the supporters of Gush Emunim have come from middle-class Ashkenazi homes, Kahana supporters have often come from poor and marginal homes, whether in Brooklyn, New York – where the movement first emerged – or in Israeli slums and development towns, where it later acquired a growing number of supporters (Mergui and Simonnot, 1987).

Kahanism has added a populist fascist style to the Messianic message, and was the first organization to call for the expulsion of the Palestinians from Israel (not just from the Occupied Territories) and for a law which would forbid any Jew from having sexual relations with an Arab. As Professor Israel Shahak has noted (1990), its main contribution to Israeli political discourse has been to introduce an alternative moral system, 'religious rationalizations for their thirst for violence, bloodshed, cruelty and plunder' (p. 4). In Kahana's religious teachings there is a notion of 'God as being personally offended by the presence of Arabs on Holy soil' (ibid.).

British Jewish youth have been affected by these Messianic movements in Israel, especially members of right-wing or religious youth movements such as Betar and B'nai Akiva. Paradoxically, however, their influence in Britain was curtailed in the 1980s because of the nature of their ideology – the zealous immigrated to Israel, and those who remained had to adopt a more pragmatic approach and became incorporated into mainstream Jewish political and religious life. As in Israel and the USA, however, the political message of these movements has moved the political discourse within the general Jewish community to the Right.

The missionary fundamentalist Jewish movement which is growing most rapidly – both in its numbers, and especially in its influence among Jews in Britain – is that of the Lubavitch Hassids. Although it shares with the previous movements opposition to Israel's withdrawal from the Occupied Territories, it does not define itself as Zionist and sees in the land of Israel only a part of its overall Messianic project, one which concerns the entire Jewish people.

The most important project for the Lubavitch Hassids is to convert all Jews to observe the *halakha*, as this is perceived as a precondition for the arrival of the Messiah – something which is expected very soon. Indeed, the personality cult around Rabbi Salman Schneerson, the Lubavitch Rebbe, has been called blasphemous by some other, non-Hasidic rabbis (like the Rav Shach in Israel), as it is claimed that the Lubavitch Hassids see in their rabbi the coming Messiah. The Lubavitch Hassids, more than any other branch of Judaism, are active in the forefront of *khazara bitshuva* – the Jewish equivalent of 'born-again' Christians.

Unlike Christianity, however, the Lubavitch and other Jewish missionary movements are not interested in any outside converts, only in those they define as Jews – those who were born to Jewish mothers. The notion of collective responsibility, which is linked to self-definition as 'the chosen people', dictates that all Jews should be made to see the light and start keeping the *mitzvot*. For this purpose, the Lubavitch movements send emissaries all over the world (recently they have been very active in the former Soviet Union, especially in places where only small Jewish communities survived). They not only take over synagogues and build Jewish 'community centres', but also stand on street corners and in railway stations, and have even developed *mitzvot* tanks – vans in which they go into Jewish neighbourhoods and persuade people to pray or keep other commandments. They practise entryist strategies, and their members are now also active in mainstream (United Synagogues) Jewish schools and synagogues. At the same time, they also maintain separate organizational and financial frameworks, among students and in local groups, in order to keep control over their movement.

The modern and technological sophistication of the Lubavitch movement cannot be demonstrated better than by the launch of a forty-city satellite link-up on the eighth day of Khanuka (a Jewish holiday), when Lubavitch Hassids everywhere (including University College, London University, which has a Hassid member of staff in the Hebrew Studies Department), listened to their Rebbe predicting redemption and the imminent coming of the Messiah (*The Guardian*, 15 December 1990).

The Lubavitch Rebbe is not the only Jewish religious leader who is interested in *khozrim bitshuva*. Many other rabbis have established organizations and educational frameworks for this purpose, although none of the others is as explicitly missionary as the Lubavitch Hassids.

One of these organizations, active in London, is Project Seed, which originated in the USA. It is active mostly among those who are already synagogue members, and it concentrates on religious study in pairs (*khavruta* – the traditional system in *yeshivot*): one knowledgeable Jew studies with a less knowledgeable one, in this case the *khozer bitshuva*.

The director of the Project in London told me about an important innovation in their method which they have established in Britain: weekend seminars. The *khozrim bitshuva* gather for a weekend in a country hotel, and in this way the organizers can work with and influence the families as a whole – because, as she told me:

> Although most of our *khozrim bitshuva* are men, we have come to know that unless we can draw the wife to our side, to involve her in the project as well, there is almost no chance that the *khazara bitshuva* of the husband would be permanent. The women are the foundation of the family.

Women, then, have a crucial role to play in the 'Khazara Bitshuva' movement. As in other fundamentalist movements, their conformity to the role allocated to them by the fundamentalist social order is crucial and central.

Women and Judaism

The position of women in Judaism depends, of course, not only on the particular religious ideology within which they are operating but also on their class position and other sociological determinants. Although all Jewish Orthodox would claim that there is an inherent Jewish position on women, their degree of freedom and empowerment varies from one community to another, a function of the different interpretations which are given to common laws. The difference between a middle-class professional American woman, say, and a poor housewife in a development town in Israel is immense, even if both are Orthodox, married and have four or five children. Similar – although probably somewhat less striking – differences also exist among Orthodox Jewish women who live in Britain, from different neighbourhoods and in different class positions.

However, these differences are not only contextual but also

depend on different constructions of the religious duties themselves. A somewhat superficial yet illustrative example of this are the variations concerning women's dress.

Women and men are forbidden to 'cross-dress' – for a man, to wear women's clothes; for a woman, to wear men's clothes. Women who wear trousers and walk in Ultra-Orthodox neighbourhoods in Jerusalem are cursed and sometimes even stoned. When I went to interview college girls from B'nai Akiva, the Zionist Orthodox youth movement, I saw many of them wearing not only trousers but even jeans. When asked, however, they claimed that these jeans were made especially for women; therefore they did not 'sin'.

Even more subtle differences can be seen in varying Orthodox trends concerning the covering of women's hair. Married women (but not unmarried women) are required, by ascribed modesty, to cover their hair. The different fashions vary from shaving their head and covering it with a tight scarf to shaving their head and going out wearing a wig (often more glamorous than their previous natural hairstyle), to wearing a wig outside over their regular hairstyle which they uncover at home, to just covering their hair with a scarf.

Given that there is supposed to be 'the right Jewish way' for every facet of women's (and men's) lives, from cooking and cleaning to sexuality and contraception, and – according to the Satmar Rebbe, at least – for women's (not) driving, it is amusing to hear how different practices are claimed as 'the only valid way' to keep these *mitzvot* by the different religious trends, especially the most extreme. The Lubavitch, however, like other good missionaries, show greater flexibility, to enable new 'converts' to adhere more easily to the *mitzvot*. Their approach is – at least for 'beginners' – that even fulfilling one commandment can make a crucial spiritual difference. They quote Maimonides, who wrote:

> If he [each person] fulfils one commandment he turns the scale of merit in his favour and in favour of the whole world. (Lubavitch Women's Publication, 1981, p. 5)

There are some basic inequalities in the position of men and women in Orthodox Judaism that crosscut all trends. Women are not counted as part of a Jewish 'public'; they are not allowed to lead prayers, to become rabbis, dayans (judges) or hold any other public religious position; their evidence is not acceptable in court and they cannot – unlike men – obtain a divorce against their spouses' will, even if their case is conceded to be just.

In their daily prayers every morning, Jewish men pray: 'Bless Thee that did not make me a woman'. Women pray: 'Bless Thee that has made me according to Thy will' . . . Orthodox Jews, however, claim that women's position is not inferior to men's but different, and equally important. Since the rise of the feminist movement, a lot of energy has been expended to show that in actuality the Jewish woman's position is 'really' even more important and powerful than the man's. For example, concerning the above prayer, one of the *khazara bitshuva* organizations, Project Seed, teaches in its courses that it is actually a sign that women are of a higher 'Madrega' (stage) of spiritual standing and proximity to God. The men have to work harder, and therefore have so many religious duties, in order to be able to strive for spiritual ascendance. Women already have it without needing to work that hard. Their 'proof' is that in this prayer men are mentioned after animals and slaves and before women. It is true that in the Bible women are generally mentioned in the same breath as animals and slaves . . .

Some of the women I interviewed found great comfort in this interpretation of the morning prayer, especially since they are so excluded from any signs of 'proximity to God' in other religious rituals. Some of the Ultra-Orthodox women I have interviewed mentioned 'Simkhat Torah' (the joy in the Bible) as the most painful moment of their exclusion as women. This is the last day of the holiday Sukot, during which the Bible scroll is taken out of its cupboard in the synagogue and the men dance with it and kiss it. But women are not even allowed to get near it.

Women cannot go near and be touched by their husbands during (and seven days after) their monthly period. Only then, and after taking a ritual bath (the *mikve*), are they considered purified enough to be touchable again. Proto-feminist explanations for this argue that this is a proof that Jewish women are not just sex objects for their husbands. This might be so, but it is also a very improbable coincidence that the two weeks in a month in which men can have sexual relationships with their wives are those in which the woman is most likely to become pregnant. Moreover, such an argument can hardly explain the fact that when a woman gives birth to a baby boy she can be purified after forty days, whereas when she has a baby girl she is untouchable for eighty days.

The religious commandments which are specific to women relate to her duties as a wife, a housewife and a mother. As Rachel Adler points out (1983), women's specific *mitzvot* are done for the sake of their families, unlike those of the men, which are done as separate individual Jews or as part of the Jewish public:

> A woman keeps Kosher because both she and her family must have Kosher food. She lights the Sabbath candles so there will be light, and, hence, peace in the household. She goes to the Mikve (ritual bath) so that her husband can have intercourse with her and she bears children so that, through her, he can fulfil the exclusively male *mitzvah* (commandment) of increasing and multiplying. (p. 13)

Women, therefore, are constructed as the guardians of the Jewish home, which is the foundation of the Jewish people.

Fundamentalism and Women's Empowerment

The construction of women as wives and mothers, and the drudgery of domestic labour, were at the heart of the feminist rebellion of the 1970s and 1980s. It is interesting to look, in this context, at the elements within Orthodox Jewish practice which have attracted women, some of them with a feminist 'past', to become (and remain) *khozrot bitshuva*. From interviews with such women several points emerge, some of which are common to both men and women *khozrim bitshuva* and some specific to women.

The first reason many of the *khozrim bitshuva* – both women and men – have given me is:

> 'At last, I know who I am. I know what it is to be a Jew. Before that I knew I was different from the others, but I did not know how . . . And when I went to a reform synagogue, it all looked so artificial to me. Here there are finally people who can teach me who I am, who really understand about Judaism.'

Since the Jewish emancipation and the break-up of 'classical Judaism' in eighteenth-century Europe, the question of 'who' or 'what' is a Jew has become a major debate – is Jewishness a religion? Is it a nationality? Is it a culture? Is it a race? Jewish experience has been heterogeneous in different countries, and a confusing variety of movements and ideologies, developed both by Jews and by non-Jews, attempted to answer this question (Yuval-Davis, 1987; Evron, 1988).

The delegitimization of open anti-Semitism since World War II has enabled assimilation on a much wider scale, but the sense of being different and 'the Other' has continued to be reproduced. Jews who are not Israelis or religious often feel that their identity has boundaries but no content. Zionism has offered an easy 'modern' way of being Jewish via identification with Israel. However, in the developing political reality of post-1967 Israel, this has gradually become more difficult, as a non-critical support of Israel became morally more and more problematic. Ultra-Orthodox Judaism offers the illusion of authenticity, homogeneity and an ahistoric, unchanging Judaism, at least until the arrival of the Messiah. The rise of missionary fundamentalist movements has supplied the necessary bridges to enable Jews who have not grown up in

215

Orthodox homes to join Orthodox Jewish communities and to feel that they 'know who they are'.

Part of the attraction of that knowledge is that it is composed from a duality of security and challenge. The sense of security derives from its offer of a total way of life, in which there is always a right way to approach and do everything, from the most profound to the most trivial things in life. And if one is confused and does not know what the right way is – the rabbi is always available for prescription. This gives a reassuring sense of framework and discipline for those *khozrim bitshuva* who previously suffered from a sense of insecurity and anomie. It is a welcome antidote to what they believe to be the malaise of our time: the meaninglessness of a life where everything is permitted.

Ultra-Orthodoxy also provides challenge, for one is always striving for a higher degree of spiritual achievement – both by practising more of the 613 commandments and through perpetual religious study:

> For me, the Gemora [part of the texts of the religious code, the Talmud] represented the greatest intellectual challenge I had ever encountered. My graduate and doctoral work were minor swells to the Talmud's majestic waves. (Schwartzbaum, 1988, p. 192)

Although for women studying the Talmud was traditionally forbidden, this has changed, especially among the missionary groupings. As the director of the Lubavitch women's centre explained to me:

> 'Traditionally girls were not taught the Talmud. There was a fear that by learning too much of analytical texts, they would lose their natural sensitivity and delicacy. However, these days, they lose it anyway by secular education, so they can just as well study the Torah [the Bible]. Recently the Rebbe said that secular education had improved so much that girls can now study anything in the Talmud. However – they still cannot

become rabbis; this involves not only intellectual knowledge but another element which comes from G–d and helps the rabbis to answer the questions from the people. Women do not have this element – but they have an element men do not have, which helps them to look after children. And who says that to be a rabbi is more important than to bring up a family?'

The emphasis in Jewish Ultra-Orthodoxy is on the 'natural' difference between men and women. They were created differently, and they have different religious duties and life careers:

'When I sometimes become tired and fed up with cleaning the house, I remember that this is not just a dreary cleaning – it is cleaning of a Jewish home and it's part of how God wants me to worship Him.'

'In every other society I think it is not fair. But in my society it is fair that when both the man and the woman work out all day, the woman comes home and does all the cooking and cleaning. Because my husband doesn't come home and watch the telly – he studies the Torah. And we were taught that that's what gives eternity for women – that you encourage the men to learn and you remove the petty worries in their life.'

In addition to containment and clarity of gender roles, Jewish Orthodox lifestyle often offers its *khozrot bitshuva* an escape from loneliness. Many of the women (and men) I talked to described the feeling of warmth that encompassed them when they first started to spend their Sabbath with an Orthodox Jewish family. They were treated as part of the (usually large) family, they participated in the Sabbath meal, the ritual, the festivity, the togetherness.

As the Jewish family is the foundation of the Jewish community, 'the unit of Jewish existence' (Meiselman, 1978, p. 16), a lot of energy is expended in the Orthodox Jewish community in arranging marriages. Lonely single women who become *khozrot bitshuva* gain a chance to have families of their own: 'Before I "returned" I never met any men who were not afraid of commitment.' The sense of community and mutual help and support goes beyond the family cells. Because Orthodox Jews need to live within walking distance of their synagogue, there are always other Jewish Orthodox families around, who provide vital networks of mutual support. Since one of the religious duties is to give 10 per cent of one's income (and many also interpret this as 10 per cent of one's time) to charity work, there is always somebody to help when a baby is born, when somebody is ill or in any other crisis, even when there are no other family members around – for sometimes the parents and siblings of *khozrim bitshuva* break off relations (although often the break-up is only temporary, and often the parents are later drawn closer to Orthodoxy).

The naturalization of the sexual division of labour, in terms of religious duties, in the family and in the community, creates a very strong separate women's community. Moreover, because of the system of arranged marriage and the fact that except on Sabbath and holidays, husbands and wives spend very little time together as a rule, a lot of the emotional bonding is between women. Debra Kaufman (1989) (and, in a much less reserved way, Tariq Modood in relation to Muslim fundamentalists [at a conference in Warwick, April 1990]), has pointed out a similarity between the sense of empowerment of Jewish women fundamentalists and that of radical feminists:

> Like women-centred feminists, many *ba'alot tshuva* and indeed other women of the new religious right celebrate gender differences. For many radical feminists and for newly orthodox women, women represent a source of special strength, knowledge and power. (p. 18)

For me, such a view mixes form with purpose, separateness with segregation, autonomy with male-defined women's space. It is easy to talk about women's empowerment as emanating from their difference without relating to the actual reality of their lives. It is not only about warmth and smiling faces and a sense of solidarity.

The other facet of the warmth and support is the harshness directed against 'deviants' who do not adhere to the very strict rules of internal authority and closed ranks. In a recent well-publicized case in Stamford Hill, the rabbi did not come to the support of a family whose children were allegedly sexually assaulted by a Yeshiva Bocher, a rabbinical student, who acted as a babysitter. When the frustrated family decided, after a long time, to complain to the police, they were denounced as 'Moysers' – 'informants' – and hounded out of their home, and their children out of their school.

There is no Orthodox Jewish 'battered women's' refuge, and family conflicts are usually handled by the rabbi, who attempts to re-establish *shlom bayit* – domestic peace. Recently, however, the Jewish Marriage Bureau has started to train volunteers to become marriage guidance counsellors, for the need has become so acute. In a case of physical violence (as well as failure to provide for her material and physical needs, including sex), a Jewish woman has the right to claim a divorce (but the husband cannot be forced to give his wife a divorce against his will). However, the conception of what constitutes acceptable social relations between husband and wife is very narrowly determined. There have been cases in Israel (where the religious divorce courts have legal validity) in which women have been declared to be 'rebellious women', and therefore denied maintenance, because they refused to sew buttons on their husbands' shirts, or to do other domestic chores. The fact that the husband was living with another woman at the time was not considered a good enough reason for the wife to refuse to fulfil her domestic duties . . . (Aloni, 1976; Hecht and Yuval-Davis, 1978).

Social workers who work among Ultra-Orthodox Jews, as well as the Ultra-Orthodox women with whom I talked, reported many cases of physical and mental exhaustion and extreme post-natal depression among Ultra-Orthodox Jewish women who bore many children in conditions of serious overcrowding and inadequate housing.

As in other cases of oppression, however, it is not those who are most oppressed who rebel. The women whom I interviewed, who broke away from Jewish Orthodoxy during the process of becoming feminists, did not grow up under these extreme conditions (although their families were often far from being affluent). Their reasons for breaking away were much more emotional and ideological. It is interesting, however, that I did not find any feminists who grew up in Ultra-Orthodox homes in East London. This might be owing to the shortcomings of my snowballing sampling methods. It might also, however, be owing to the system of almost complete social control which applies in these homes and this community. In my discussions with women who grew up in Ultra-Orthodox homes, they described to me how rebellious girls express their rebellion by making contact with boys, and therefore end up being married and with children even earlier than the others. They claimed that breaking away happens – although again not often – more among boys, despite their greater visibility due to their clothing and hairstyle. Orthodox girls in the British climate, after all, wear similar clothes to other girls, and they are not required to cover their heads before marriage. While it might be more difficult for the distinctly garbed boys to consume 'forbidden fruit' such as cinemas, secular libraries, etc., the girls are kept closer to home, and the familial and community control over them is still apparently greater than over the boys.

The women I interviewed who had broken away had regular contacts as girls with non-Jews or non-Orthodox Jews as a result of having at least part of their education in regular state schools or non-parochial Jewish schools. In other words, they were exposed – at least to some degree – to *Weltanschauungen* other than the ones they grew up with.

Rebelling against such close control was one of the major factors mentioned by those who have broken away from

Orthodoxy: 'I wanted to live my own life, to find my own way. It was very warm in the family bosom, but too often suffocatingly so . . .' This stifling feeling was not just the familial control, nor were the strict rules and regulations of observance always the most difficult things to bear. Dena Attar (1985) describes being caught between, on the one hand, being encouraged to do well in her Hebrew and religious studies, and, on the other, realizing that there was no point at all to her success in learning the Hebrew or the special musical symbols of the prayers: she would never be given any opportunity to practise them:

> Judaism, I realized, actually required little of me apart from domestic obedience, and some authorities maintained that girls in a proper religious home ought therefore not to be taught Torah at all – all we needed to learn was our place. (p. 2)

And that place itself, she felt, was devalued. Every Friday night, the men sing to their wives the *esheth khayil* psalm (verses from the Proverbs praising the virtuous wife and mother), which she felt was patronizing and actually drew attention to the secondary status of women:

> If you thought about the words – 'A woman of worth, who can find? Her price is far above rubies . . .'. Clearly the poet was setting housewives impossibly high standards.

(When, some years ago, I spent a Sabbath with the Bostonne Rebbe, the Rebbe and his Hassids sang the psalm when the women were not even there to hear it; they were in the kitchen busy finishing the preparations for the meal.)

But for Dena, the most worrying and stifling elements were the lists of terrifying punishments included in the prayers of repentance on the High Holy Days. They trapped her in fear and guilt.

When she was seventeen, in the year before she broke away, she wrote a poem:

> Tree you have grown old
> I have no more use for you tree
> for your insolent arms sky groping
> reach wrapping folding intruding
> into my own close held my-life
> I remember days without you tree . . .
> no stifle-green swaying possessing . . .
> tree I have grown old
> have grown old grown apart
> have no more no more use for you tree. (p. 3)

It was not easy to break away. One of the women I interviewed described her feeling of dread in the beginning:

> 'When I danced for the first time with this tall handsome
> Catholic boy, I was sure I was going to be struck down by
> God. Nothing happened. It was all crap.'

God did not strike them down, but a high price was extracted
from them nevertheless. Contact with their families was
sometimes broken for a long time, and one woman was almost
prevented from going to university as a result. 'Coming out'
as a lesbian or marrying a non-Jew are considered to be the
hardest of all. What might bridge the way for reconciliation
are the grandchildren who, being born to a Jewish woman,
would still be considered Jewish according to the *halakha*. But
the worst of all, according to Dena Attar, is the sense of loss:

> The tree is gone and will not grow again. I don't want to put
> in a new one. I would rather learn to live with the view of a
> more open landscape, bare as it might seem, and with the
> sense of loss – for security, familiarity, for the religious
> calendar of fasts and festivals and for music most of all – which
> I don't suppose will ever quite go. Even relative freedom costs.
> (p. 6)

In other words, a sense of loss of the things which attract *khozrot bitshuva* to become observant.

What can the acquired freedom give those who have broken away from Orthodoxy? As with the main character in the novel on Christian fundamentalism, Jeanette Winterson's *Oranges Are Not the Only Fruit*, the sense of being stifled and of being cast in a different mould from that demanded by the religious Orthodoxy can be particularly enhanced by developing a different sexuality from the norm – not just lesbianism, but also a wish to remain single and/or not to become a mother to a big family. Freedom to become 'different', then, has been essential. Getting in touch with the feminist movement has played a significant role in the lives of many of the women who have broken away from religious Orthodoxy.

Not surprisingly, however, some of them can be critical of attempts by other Jewish feminists, who have come from liberal or assimilated homes, to develop a Jewish feminism which draws on the traditional framework, while eliminating anything which is explicitly offensive to women but does not challenge the whole patriarchal framework. Unlike them, the Jewish feminist liberation theologian Judith Plaskow has claimed (1991) that to transform Judaism into a non-patriarchal religion would require a revolution as extensive as the one which transformed Judaism from a religion that sacrificed animals in the Jewish Temple in Jerusalem into the abstract monotheistic system of classical Judaism which has developed during the last 2,000 years.

Some of the women I interviewed, however, go even further and see feminism as inherently incompatible with any religious order. One of them, Gail Chester, wrote an article on the subject (1983) entitled 'A Woman Needs a God like a Fish Needs a Bicycle'. What offends these women is not, however, just the patriarchal element in Orthodox Judaism but also its particularistic nature:

> I wanted to be part of a wider, freer world in which no one would be judged or valued on the basis of their race, religion

223

or degree of observance. My one mistake, of course, was in thinking the rest of the world might live up to those expectations . . . (Dena Attar, p. 4)

Another woman told me:

'What started my questioning, even more than God, was the question of Israel. Discovering that non-Jews were also living there and what happened to them.'

As we have already discussed in the Introduction to this book, minority women often face the dilemma that the same particularistic collective identity which they seek to defend against racism and subordination – and from which they gain their empowerment to resist dominant oppressive systems and cultures – also oppresses them as women and can include many reactionary and exclusionary elements. In the Jewish case the picture is even more complicated, because the same collective identity which constructed them as a persecuted minority is also the one which, via the hegemony of Zionism and Israel, links them to a collective identity which is racist and exploitative of others. This is true even in most contemporary Jewish identities which do not see themselves as Zionist (the Satmar Hassids are an honourable exception). The search of the Lubavitch *khozrot bitshuva* for a secure identity not only raises pertinent questions about the kinds and limits of any empowerment they could get in man-made spaces, but also puts them in a position which supports the kind of Messianism that is racist and expansionist. This is so even if they never move to Israel, and even if they never make the connections themselves.

God, the religious laws, and Israel are all connected in Jewish Orthodoxy – definitely in its contemporary fundamentalist versions. And the reproduction of the system depends on women, their co-operation and their hard work (Yuval-Davis and Anthias, 1989).

The creation of a Jewish home is no small task. It requires much more than the burdens of childbearing, childrearing and menial household tasks. For to create a Jewish home is to create a new link in the chain of Jewish existence and tradition. (Meiselman, 1978, p. 16)

It might be appropriate, therefore, to finish this chapter with a few excerpts from the songs the girls in the Lubavitch Youth Movement sing (found in song sheets at the Lubavitch Women's Centre):

'Oh mother, oh graceful queen
Your life your sacrifice supreme
So royal such holiness therein
Tell me please where do I come in.
  Daughter dear it doesn't take much
  To share a smile a soul to touch
  The role the goal of a Jewish mother
  Set aside yours for another.'

'Father, father, how can we return once more
The guards are all surrounding the door.
  Children, children, Torah you should learn
  Then Biyas Hamoshiach [the coming of the Messiah] you will
    surely earn.'

'G–d will save Zion and will build cities in Judea
and the descendants of His slaves will inherit them
and the lovers of His name will dwell there.
  How happy we are, how good is our fortune
  How lovely is our fate and how beautiful our heritage
  How happy we are, Jews we are, Lubavitch Hassids we are
  of our Lord, our teacher, our Rebbe.
If you would build everywhere the House of Lubavitch,
I shall show you the House of Lubavitch in Zion.'

[The third quote was translated by me from Hebrew. The first two songs are originally in English.]

The different themes in the different excerpts are not linked in the songs. But *we have* to make the link.

Note

I would like to thank all the many people who helped me to obtain material relevant to this chapter – they are too numerous for me to mention them all here. In particular I would like to thank all those within the Jewish Orthodox community who agreed to supply me with material and to be interviewed, even knowing that I do not share their world-view. I am not mentioning any of their names, to avoid associating them in any way with this chapter. But I would like to mention by name some of the friends who helped me, knowing that I do share some of their views: Dena Attar, Julia Bard, Gail Chester, Neil Collins, Ora Davis, Sue Katz, Janet Kufperman, Rami Levy, Pragna Patel, Israel Shahak. The responsibility for the chapter and its views, however, is all mine.

Bibliography

Abrahamian, E., *Iran, Between Two Revolutions*, Princeton, 1982.
—— 'Khomeini: Fundamentalist or Populist?', *New Left Review*, no. 186, 1991.
Adler, R., 'I've Had Nothing Yet So I Can't Take More', *Moment*, no. 8, September 1983.
Afshar, H., 'Three Generations of Women in Bradford', paper presented at the CSE conference, 1989a.
—— 'Education: Hopes, Expectations and Achievements of Muslim Women in West Yorkshire', *Gender and Education*, vol. 1, no. 3, 1989b.
—— 'Women in the Work and Poverty Trap in Iran', *Capital and Class*, no. 37, 1989c.
Aloni, S., *Women As Humans*, Mabat Publications (Hebrew), 1976.
Althusser, L., *For Marx*, Allen Lane, 1969.
Anderson, B., *Imagined Communities*, Verso, 1983.
Anderson, M., 'Islamic Law and the Colonial Encounter in British India' in S. Malhat and J. Connors, *Islamic Family Law*, Graham Trontron, 1990.
Anthias, F. and N. Yuval-Davis, 'Contextualising Feminism: Gender, Ethnic and Class Divisions, *Feminist Review*, no. 5, Winter 1983.
—— *Racialized Boundaries: Race, Nation, Gender and Class and the Anti-Racist Struggle*, Routledge, 1992.
Arkush, S., *Operation Judaism: Fact Pack*, Operation Judaism, 1990.
Attar, D., 'The Selfish Tree', unpublished paper, 1985.
—— 'The Portable Cage', *Trouble & Strife*, no. 19, 1990.
Azari, F., 'The Post-Revolutionary Women's Movement in Iran', in Azari, F., ed., *Women of Iran*, Ithaca Press, 1983.
Bahar, S., 'A Historical Background to the Women's Movement in Iran', in Azari, F., ed., *Women of Iran*.
Bakash, S., *The Reign of the Ayatollahs: Iran and the Islamic Revolution*, I. B. Taurus, 1985.
Bayat, A., *Workers and Revolution in Iran*, Zed Books, 1987.
Bermant, C., *The Cousinhood*, Eyre & Spottiswoode, 1971.
B'nai, Akiva Hadracha Magazine, vol. 6.

Bowker, J., *Worlds of Faith: Religious Beliefs and Practice in Britain Today*, Ariel Books, BBC, 1983, (chs 8 and 9).

Britten, M., *The Single Woman in the Family of God*, Epworth, 1982.

Brown, T., *Ireland: A Social and Cultural History, 1922–79*, Fontana, 1981.

Browne, N., *Against the Tide*, Gill & Macmillan, 1986.

Brummer, A. and P. Clarke, 'The Time of the Brooklyn Messiah', *The Guardian*, 24 December 1990.

Brook, S., *The Club – The Jews of Modern Britain*, Constable, 1989.

Brooks, B., *Abortion in England: 1900–1967*, Croom Helm, 1988.

Bunreacht na hEireann (Constitution of Ireland), Article 41, Government Publications Office (Dublin), 1937.

Burman, R., 'The Jewish Woman as Breadwinner: The Changing Value of Women's Work in a Manchester Immigrant Community', *Oral History Journal*, vol. 10, no. 2, 1982.

Burtenshaw, R., 'Censorship of Information on Abortion in Ireland', *Women Against Fundamentalism Journal*, no. 2, 1991.

Calley, M., *God's People*, Oxford University Press, 1965.

Campaign Against Racism and Fascism/Southall Rights, *Southall: The Birth of a Black Community*, Institute of Race Relations and Southall Rights, 1981.

Campbell, B., *Iron Ladies*, Virago, 1988.

Centre for Contemporary Cultural Studies, *The Empire Strikes Back*, Hutchinson, 1982.

Chalfant, P., E. Robert and C. Palmer, *Religion in Contemporary Society*, Mayfield Publications, 1981.

Chester, G., 'A Woman Needs a God like a Fish Needs a Bicycle', in S. Maitland and J. Garcia, eds, *Walking on Water*, Virago, 1983.

Chhachhi, A., 'The State, Religious Fundamentalism and Women', unpublished paper, 1990.

—— 'Forced Identities: The State, Communalism, Fundamentalism, and Women in India', in D. Kandiyoti, ed., *Women, Islam and the State*, Macmillan, 1991.

Cohen, P. and H. Bains, (eds) *Multi-Racist Britain*, Macmillan Education, 1988.

Cohen, S., *From the Jews to the Tamils: Britain's Mistreatment of Refugees*, South Manchester Law Centre, 1988.

Commission for Racial Equality, *Schools of Faith*, Commission for Racial Equality pamphlet, 1990.

Connolly, C., 'Splintered Sisterhood: Anti-Racism in a Young Women's Project', *Feminist Review*, no. 36, Autumn 1990.

Connolly, C., *Washing Our Linen: Year of WAF*, Feminist Review no. 37, 1991.

Cooper, C., 'That Cunny Jamaica Woman!', in K. Owusu, ed., *Storms of the Heart*, Camden Press, 1988.

Coote, A and B. Campbell, *Sweet Freedom: The Struggle for Women's Liberation*, Basil Blackwell, 1982.

Corish, P.J., *The Catholic Community in the Seventeenth and Eighteenth Centuries*, Helicon History, 1981.

Cupitt, D., 'Back to Basics: Reflections on the Rise of Religious Fundamentalism', *Marxism Today*, April 1991.

Curtis, L., *Ireland: The Propaganda War*, Pluto Press, 1984a.

—— *Nothing but the Same Old Story: The Roots of Anti-Irish Racism*, Information on Ireland, 1984b.

Curtis, L.P., *Apes and Angels: The Irishman in Victorian Caricature*, David & Charles, 1971.

Daly, M.E., *Social and Economic History of Ireland since 1800*, The Educational Company, 1981.

Davidson, R., *West Indian Migrants*, Oxford University Press, 1962.

Elwell, W., ed., *Evangelical Dictionary of Theology*, Marshall Pickering, 1985.

Encyclopaedia Britannica, 'Birth Control', *Macropaedia*, 15th edn, vol. 2, Benton, 1984.

Enger, G., *Birth Regulation and Catholic Belief*, Sheed & Ward, 1966.

Evron, B., *A National Reckoning*, Dvir Publishing House (Hebrew), 1988.

Finlay, F., *Mary Robinson: A President with a Purpose*, O'Brien Press, 1990.

Fogarty, M., L. Ryan and J. Lee, *Irish Values and Attitudes: The Irish Report of the European Value Systems Study*, Dominican Publications, 1984.

Foh, S., *Women and the Word of God: A Response to Biblical Feminism*, Christian World Publication, 1979.

Foster Carrol, T., *Women, Religion and Development in the Third World*, Praegar, 1983.

Gilroy, P., *There Ain't No Black in the Union Jack*, Hutchinson, 1987.

Haeri, S., *Law of Desire: Temporary Marriage in Iran*, I. B. Tauris, 1989.

Hecht, D. and N. Yuval-Davis, 'Ideology Without Revolution: Jewish Women in Israel', *Khamsin*, no. 6, Pluto Press, 1978.

Hendessi, M., 'Migration and Marriage', *Nimeye-Digar*, no. 12/13, Autumn/Winter 1991 (in Persian).

Hendessi, M. and N. Fielding, 'The Unquiet Grave in Teheran', *New Statesmen and Society*, 13 January 1989.

Holden, P., ed., *Women's Religious Experience*, Croom Helm, 1983.

229

Hollenweger, W., *The Pentecostals,* SCM Press, 1972.

Honeyford, R., 'Multiracial Myths', *The Times Educational Supplement*, November 1982.

—— 'Multiracial Influences', *The Salisbury Review*, Summer 1983a.

—— 'Multiethnic Intolerance', *The Salisbury Review*, Summer 1983b.

—— 'Education and Race – An Alternative View', *The Salisbury Review*, Winter 1984a.

—— 'Do-gooders Doing a Disservice', *The Times*, May 1984b.

hooks, b., *Ain't I a Woman?: Black Women and Feminism*, Southend Press, 1981.

Horowitz, M., *Rabbi Schach*, Keter (Hebrew), 1989.

Hyman, A., *Muslim Fundamentalism*, The Institute for the Study of Culture, 1985.

Hynes, U., 'The Great Hunger and Irish Catholicism', *Societas*, vol. VIII, no. 2, Spring 1978.

Irish Information Partnership, *Agenda*, 5th edn, Irish Information Partnership, 1987.

—— *Agenda*, 6th edn, Irish Information Partnership, 1990.

Irish Press, 'Hierarchy's Statement on Contraceptives', *Irish Press*, 26 November 1973.

Irish Times, 'Irish Protocol on Abortion', *Irish Times*, 10 December 1991.

Irish Women's Abortion Support Group, 'Across the Water', *Feminist Review*, no. 29, May 1988.

Jack, I., 'A Severed Head', *Sunday Times Magazine*, 15 December 1985.

Jackson, P. Conroy, 'Women's Movement and Abortion: The Criminalization of Irish Women', in D. Dahlerup, ed., *The New Women's Movement: Feminism and Political Power in Europe and the USA*, Sage, 1986.

Jenkins, D., *The British, Their Identity and Their Religion*, SCM Press, 1975.

Jennings, C., *Who Owns Ireland, Who Owns You?*, Attic Press, 1985.

Jessel, D., 'The Looking Glass Law', *The Guardian*, 10–11 February 1990.

Jimack, M., *Research into Hackney Jewry – A Summary of Current Information Relevant to the Planning and Provision of Jewish Social Services in Hackney*, Federation of Jewish Family Services, 1989.

Johnson, S. and J. Tamney, eds, *The Political Role of Religion in the USA*, Westview Press, 1986.

Kandiyoti, D., ed., *Women, Islam and the State*, Macmillan, 1991.

Kaufman, D., 'Women Who Return to Orthodox Judaism: A Feminist Analysis', *Journal of Marriage and the Family*, August 1985.

—— 'Patriarchal Women: A Case Study of Newly Orthodox Jewish Women', *Symbolic Interaction*, vol. 12, no. 2, 1989.

—— 'Paradoxical Politics: Gender Politics among Newly Orthodox Jewish Women in the USA', in V. Moghadam, ed., *Women and Identity Politics*, Clarendon Press (forthcoming).

Kelly, L., 'Preaching in the Black Tradition'; in J. Weidman, ed., *Women Ministers: How Women are Redefining Traditional Roles*, Harper & Row, 1981.

Khomeini, A., *Hallolmassael [Analysis of Problems], Article 2412* (Farsi).

Lee, J., 'Women and the Church Since the Famine', in M. McCurtain and D. O'Corrain, eds, *Women in Irish Society: The Historical Dimension*, Arlen House, 1978.

Lennon, M., M. McAdam and J. O'Brien, *Across the Water, Irish Women's Lives in Britain*, Virago, 1988.

Leon, A., *The Jewish Question*, Pathfinder Press, 1970.

Levi, A., *The Ultra-Orthodox*, Keter (Hebrew), 1989.

Levine, J., *Sisters: The Personal Story of an Irish Feminist*, Ward River Press, 1982.

Longley, E., *From Cathleen to Anorexia*, The Breakdown of Irelands, Lip Pamphlet, Attic Press, 1990.

Lubavitch Girls' Song Sheets (unpublished).

Lubavitch Women's Publication, *The Modern Jewish Woman: A Unique Perspective*, Lubavitch Educational Foundation for Jewish Marriage Enrichment, 1981.

Lustick, I.S., *For the Land and the Lord: Jewish Fundamentalism in Israel*, Council on Foreign Relations, 1988.

McCafferty, N., 'We're Not Half As Oppressed as You Think', *Everywoman*, no. 69, February 1991.

Mahdi, A., *Women, Religion, and the State: Legal Developments in Twentieth Century Iran*, Michigan State University, Working Paper 38, October 1983.

'Many Voices, One Chant: Black Feminist Perspectives, *Feminist Review*, no. 17, Autumn 1984.

Marsden, G., *Fundamentalism and American Culture*, Oxford University Press, 1980.

Meiselman, M., *Jewish Woman in Jewish Law*, Ktav Publications, 1978.

Mergui, R., and P. Simonnot, *Israel's Ayatollahs: Meir Kahane and the Far Right in Israel*, Al Saqi, 1987.

Miller, Y., *In Search of the Jewish Woman*, Feidheim, 1984.

Milotte, M., *Communism in Modern Ireland: The Pursuit of the Workers' Republic since 1916*, Gill & Macmillan, 1984.

Modood, T., 'British Asian Muslims and the Rushdie Affair', *Political Quarterly*, vol. 61, no. 2, April 1990.

Moghadam, V., 'Women, Work and Ideology in the Islamic Republic', *International Journal of Middle East Studies*, vol. 20, no. 2, May 1988.

—— 'The Neopatriarchal State in the Middle East: Development, Authoritarianism and Crisis', in H. Bresheeth and N. Yuval-Davis, eds, *The Gulf War and the New World Order*, Zed Books, 1991.

The Muslim Institute, *The Muslim Manifesto*, 1990.

Najmabadi, A., 'Hazards of Modernity and Morality: Women, State and Ideology in Contemporary Iran', D. Kandiyoti, ed., *Women, Islam and the State*, 1991.

Neustatter, A., *Hyenas in Petticoats: A Look at Twenty Years of Feminism*, Penguin, 1989.

Noonan Jr, J.T., *Contraception: A History of its Treatment by the Catholic Theologians and Canonists*, Harvard University Press, 1966.

O'Dowd, L., 'Church, State and Women: The Aftermath of Partition, in C. Curtin, P. Jackson and B. O'Connor, eds, *Gender in Irish Society*, Galway University Press, 1987.

O'Shea, M., 'Policing Irish Women in Britain', in C. Dunhill, ed., *The Boys in Blue: Women's Challenge to the Police*, Virago, 1989.

Packer, J., *'Fundamentalism' and the World of God*, Inter-Varsity Fellowship, 1958.

Paul, R., *Abortion and Liberty*, The Foundation for Rational Economics and Education, 1983.

Phillips, M., 'The Miracle of President Mary', *The Guardian*, 27 February 1991.

Plaskow, J., *Standing Again at Sinai*, Harper, 1991.

Pollack, A., 'Survey Shows 82% of Catholics Worship Weekly', *Irish Times*, 2 March 1991.

Poya, M., 'Iran 1979: Long Live Revolution! . . . Long Live Islam?', in C. Barker, ed., *Revolutionary Rehearsals*, Bookmarks, 1987a.

—— 'Iran: Background to the Gulf War', *Capital and Class*, no. 33, Winter 1987b.

—— 'Iran After the War and Iran After Khomeini', *Khamsin Bulletin*, nos 7 & 8, 1990.

—— 'The Role of Iran in the Gulf War', in H. Bresheeth and N. Yuval-Davis, eds, *The Gulf War and the New World Order*, Zed Books, 1991.

Prenderville, P., 'Divorce in Ireland: An Analysis of the Referendum to

Amend the Constitution, June, 1986', *Women's Studies International Forum*, vol. 11, no. 4, A. Smyth (ed.), Oxford, 1988.

Radford Ruether, R., *Religion and Sexism: Images of Women in the Jewish and Christian Traditions*, Simon & Schuster, 1974.

Ranelagh, J. O'Beirne, *A Short History of Ireland*, Cambridge University Press, 1983.

Rattansi, A., 'Changing the Subject? Racism, Culture and Education', in Rattansi and Reedar, eds, *Radicalism in Education*, Lawrence & Wishart, 1992.

Reagan, R., *Abortion and the Conscience of the Nation*, Thomas Nelson, 1984.

Reichley, J., *Religion in American Political Life*, The Brookings Institute, 1985.

'A Religious War? The Background, Facts, Analysis, Dangers and Significance for the Rise of the Religious Bloc in Israel', *Politics*, no. 24 (Hebrew).

Rex, J., *Race Relations in Sociological Theory*, Weidenfeld & Nicholson, 1970.

—— 'Multi-culturalism, Anti-Racism and Equality of Opportunity: The British Case', paper presented at a conference: Multiculturalism in Britain and Australia, Institute of Commonwealth Studies, May 1990a.

—— paper on Muslims in Birmingham presented at a conference: New Debates in Black Politics, Warwick University, May 1990b.

Richardson, R., *Religious Education 1991, Letter and Spirit*, Runnymede Trust Bulletin no. 249, October 1991.

Riddick, R., *The Right to Choose: Questions of Feminist Morality*, Lip pamphlet Attic Press, 1990.

Roberts, P. and D. Seddon, eds, *Fundamentalism in Africa: Religion and Politics*, special issue of *Review of African Political Economy*, no. 52, November 1991.

Rodinson, M., *Marxism and the Muslim World*, Zed Books, 1979a.

—— 'Islam Resurgent?', *Gazelle Review of Literature on the Middle East*, no. 6., Ithaca Press, 1979b.

Rolston, B., ed., *The Media and Northern Ireland: Covering the Troubles*, Macmillan, 1991.

Rose, G., 'Velayat-e Faghih and the Recovery of Islamic Identity in the Thought of Ayatollah Khomeini', in N.K. Keddie, ed., *Religion and Politics in Iran: Shi'ism from Quietism to Revolution*, Yale University Press, 1983.

Rose, R.S., 'An Outline of Fertility Control, Focusing on the Element of

Abortion, in the Republic of Ireland to 1976', unpublished Ph.D. thesis, University of Stockholm, 1976.

Rossiter, A., 'Granting Civil Rights to the Foetus in Ireland – A Victory to Christian Fundamentalists Worldwide', *Women Against Fundamentalism Journal*, no. 1, November 1990.

—— Abortion Information Case lost at European Court', *Women Against Fundamentalism Journal*, no. 3, 1992.

Rouhifar, Z., *In Exile: Iranian Recollections*, A Dual Language Publication, 1989.

Roy, O., 'Fundamentalism, Traditionalism and Islam', *Telos*, no. 65, Fall 1985.

Runnymede Trust, Educational Roundup, *Race and Immigration*, no. 250, November 1991, Runnymede Trust.

Rushdie, S., *The Satanic Verses*, Viking, 1988.

Russell, L., *Human Liberation in a Feminist Perspective: A Theology*, The West Minster Press, 1974.

Sahgal, G. and N. Yuval-Davis, 'Refusing Holy Orders', *Marxism Today*, March 1990.

Sanassarian, E., *The Women's Rights Movement in Iran, Mutiny, Appeasement, and Repression from 1900 to Khomeini*, Praeger, 1983.

Schools of Faith, Commission for Racial Equality pamphlet, 1990.

Schustler Fiorenza E., *In Memory of Her*, Beacon, 1986.

Schwartzbaum, A., *The Bamboo Cradle: A Jewish Father's Story*, Feldheim, 1988.

Shahak, I., 'Meir Kahana's Life, Death and Two Funerals', *Report*, no. 41, December 1990.

Smith, I., and W. Green, *An Ebony Cross: Being a Black Christian in Britain Today*, Marshall Pickering, 1989.

Social Trends, HMSO, 1989.

Southall Black Sisters, *Against the Grain*, Southall Black Sisters, 1990.

Spencer, D., 'How Bradford Held onto its Lead in Race', *Times Educational Supplement*, 7 October 1983.

Spicer, D., 'Church and State – A Case Study, the Irish Republic', *Church and State*, No. 37, Cork, Spring 1991.

Storkey, E., *What's Right with Feminism?* SPCK, 1985

Tabari, A., and N. Yeganeh, *In the Shadow of Islam: The Women's Movement in Iran*, Zed Books, 1982.

Tress, M., 'The Last Frontier: Women in Gush Emunim', in V. Moghadam, ed., *Women and Identity Politics*, Clarendon Press, (forthcoming).

Trivedi, P., 'To Deny Our Fullness: Asian Women in the Making of History', *Feminist Review*, no. 17, Autumn 1984.

Troyna, B., ed., *'Racial Inequality in Education*, Tavistock, 1987.

Tzadok, S., *The Characteristics of the Ultra-Orthodox Society*, Meir Publications (Hebrew), 1989.

Union of Jewish Students, *Kol Isha, Judaism and Feminism*, London, 1990.

Vaughan, R., *Transients, Settlers and Refugees: Asians in Britain*, Clarendon Press, 1988.

Wain, G., 'Black Women, Sexism and Racism: Black or Anti-Racist Feminism', *Feminist Review*, no. 37, Spring 1991.

Walker, D., *Appeal to the Coloured Citizens of the World*, 1829.

Waterman, S., and B. Kosmin, *British Jewry in the Eighties: A Statistical and Demographic Study*, Board of Deputies of British Jews, 1986.

Wilmor, G. S., *Black Religion and Black Radicalism*, Doubleday, 1973.

'Women, Religion and Dissent', *Feminist Review*, no. 37, Spring 1991.

Yazbeck, H., Y. Yazbeck and E. Banks Finley, *Women, Religion and Social Change*, State University of New York Press, 1985.

Yuval-Davis, N., 'The Bearers of the Collective: Women and Religious Legislation in Israel', *Feminist Review*, no. 4, 1980.

—— 'The Jewish Collectivity and National Reproduction in Israel', in *Khamsin: Women in the Middle East*, Zed Books, 1987a.

—— 'Marxism and Jewish Nationalism', *History Workshop Journal*, no. 24, Autumn 1987b.

—— 'Ethnic/Racial and Gender Divisions in Britain and Australia', in R. Nile, ed., *Multi-culturalism in Britain and Australia*, Institute of Commonwealth Studies, 1991.

Yuval-Davis, N. and F. Anthias, eds, *Women – Nation – State*, Macmillan, 1989.

Zabih, S., *The Communist Movement in Iran*, Cambridge University Press, 1966.

Zubaida, S., 'The Ideological Conditions for Khomeini's Doctrine of Government', *Economy and Society*, vol. 11, no. 2, 1982.

Notes on Contributors

Yasmin Ali teaches Social Sciences in the Department of Historical and Cultural Studies at Lancashire Polytechnic, where she is also Senior Lecturer with responsibility for Equal Opportunities in the faculty of Cultural, Legal and Social Studies. She has written a variety of papers and articles on race, culture and politics.

Elaine Foster is headteacher of Handsworth Wood Girls' School in Birmingham. She has written and lectured extensively on a range of educational issues. Her MA thesis is on 'Black Women in Black-led Churches in Britain'.

Saeeda Khanum is a freelance journalist and a regular contributor to *New Statesman and Society*. She has also worked as a researcher and interviewer for television programmes. Her work has given extensive coverage to various aspects of the lives of British Muslims. She was runner-up in the Periodical Publishers Association Awards, writer of the year (Consumer Magazines) 1992.

Sara Maitland is a novelist, and critic. Her most recent novel was *Three Times Table* (Chatto 1990; Virago 1991). She has written and lectured extensively in feminist theology and edited *The Rushdie File* (Fourth Estate 1990).

Maryam Poya is an Iranian, a researcher in Third World Studies, specializing in women and development. She teaches in London and has written many articles on the political economy of Iran.

Ann Rossiter is an Irish woman who has lived in London for the last thirty years, and an activist in Irish Feminism in Britain. She teaches Irish Studies at the College of North West London and has edited a forthcoming anthology to be published by The Women's Press, *Beyond the Pale: British Feminism and the Irish Question*.

Gita Sahgal is an independent filmmaker working in Britain and in India. She has made a number of current affairs programmes on gender issues for Channel 4 television, including *Struggle or Submission? Women under Islam*, on the impact of the Rushdie affair on Muslim women in Britain; and *The Provoked Wife*, on women who have killed their husbands after enduring years of domestic violence.

Nira Yuval-Davis is a Reader in Ethnic and Gender Studies at Thames Polytechnic. She has written extensively on theoretical and practical aspects of women, nationalism and racism in Israel and in Britain. She has recently co-edited *Women – Nation – State* (Macmillan 1989) and *The Gulf War and the New World Order* (Zed Books 1991), and has co-authored, with F. Anthias, *Racialized Boundaries: Ethnic, Gender, Colour and Class Divisions and the Anti-Racist Struggle* (Routledge 1992).

Index

....

OPENING THE GATES:
A Century of Arab Feminist Writing
Edited by Margot Badran and Miriam Cooke

**'Anyone interested in good writing should read this . . .
first-class stories . . . brilliant polemical writing'
– Doris Lessing, *Independent***

Arab women today live in more than twenty sovereign states,
as well as in occupation or exile; they come from an area that
stretches from Morocco to the Arabian Peninsula. Here, for
the first time, a collection of Arab women's writing is organised
within a feminist framework. It brings together many women's
voices; some are familiar – Etel Adnan, May Ziyada, Nawal
al-Saadawi, and Huda Shaarawi – many have never been read
in English before. In these wonderfully diverse documents –
personal letters, memoirs, speeches, fiction and poetry,
spanning over a century – women eschew their role as silent
helpmates. These documents in all their diversity and
sophistication not only challenge Arab patriarchy, but also
eloquently refute the myth of a monolithic western feminism.

THE HEART OF THE RACE:
Black Women's Lives in Britain
By Beverley Bryan, Stella Dadzie & Suzanne Scafe

'A balanced tribute to the undefeated creativity, resilience and resourcefulness of Black women in Britain today'
– Margaret Busby, *New Society*

Winner of the Martin Luther King Memorial Prize 1985

'Our aim has been to tell it as we know it, placing our story within its history at the heart of our race, and using our own voices and lives to document the day-to-day realities of Afro-Caribbean women in Britain over the past forty years.'

The Heart of the Race powerfully records what life is like for Black women in Britain: grandmothers drawn to the promise of the 'mother country' in the 1950s talk of a different reality; young girls describe how their aspirations at school are largely ignored; working women tell of their commitments to families, jobs, communities. With clarity and determination, these Afro-Caribbean women discuss their treatment by the Welfare State, their housing situations, their health, their self-images – and their confrontation with the racism they encounter all too often. Here too is Black women's celebration of their culture and their struggle to create a new social order in this country.

YOU CAN'T DROWN THE FIRE:
Latin American Women Writing in Exile
Edited by Alicia Partnoy

'The voice of exile ricochets off endless walls, never losing its resonance or shattering the walls . . . I cannot think of anyone who could have done a better job of gathering up these voices: for Alicia Partnoy is, herself, very much a part of this history'
– Margaret Randall

This important and moving anthology brings together contributions from thirty-five Latin American women writing in exile.

In essays, stories, poetry, letters and song, they bring us face to face with the horrifying experience of exile, torture and death. Yet these writings are never defeatist. Denouncing political repression, they testify resoundingly to the energy, courage and strength of Latin American women in exile in every corner of the world.

You Can't Drown the Fire brings home to us the individual differences, as well as the unifying political experiences of struggle voiced by women from Paraguay, Uruguay, Chile, Colombia, Guatemala, Bolivia, Argentina and El Salvador.

BREAKING THE BOUNDARIES:
Towards a feminist Green Socialism
By Mary Mellor

'Mary Mellor's attempt to offer us a vision is cheering in these gloomy times' *New Statesman & Society*

How can we stop the planet hurtling towards ecological destruction? The rich from consuming ever more as the poor become poorer, and women from having to bear the brunt of this crisis? Mary Mellor argues that we are faced with a stark choice between survivalism – short-term and privileging in its solutions – or socialism, a new and vibrant socialism based on feminist and green principles.

Among the many issues the author pursues with such urgent persuasion are: the retreat to nature – salvation or sell-out?; the consequences of the global market and exporting inequality to the Third World; who owns the wilderness?; development policies and their effects on women; who pays for pollution?; can capitalism really go green? She advocates that we must bring together elements of deep ecology, ecofeminism, spirituality, radical feminism and revolutionary socialism in a new and exciting synthesis to offer a political vision for the twenty-first century.